# The Offshore

# The Offshore World

*Sovereign Markets,
Virtual Places,
and Nomad Millionaires*

RONEN PALAN

CORNELL UNIVERSITY PRESS

ITHACA AND LONDON

First published 2003 by Cornell University Press
First printing, Cornell paperbacks, 2006

Printed in the United States of America

*Library of Congress Cataloging-in-Publication Data*

Palan, Ronen, 1957–
    The offshore world : sovereign markets, virtual places, and nomad millionaires / Ronen Palan.
        p. cm.
Includes bibliographical references and index.
    ISBN-13: 978-0-8014-4055-7 (cloth : alk. paper)
    ISBN-10: 0-8014-4055-6 (cloth : alk. paper)
    ISBN-13: 978-0-8014-7295-4 (pbk. : alk. paper)
    ISBN-10: 0-8014-7295-4 (pbk. : alk. paper)
    1. Investments, Foreign.  2. Investments, Foreign—Law and legislation.  I. Title.
    HG4538.P297 2003
    332'.042—dc21

                                        2002155043

Cornell University Press strives to use environmentally responsible suppliers and materials to the fullest extent possible in the publishing of its books. Such materials include vegetable-based, low-VOC inks and acid-free papers that are recycled, totally chlorine-free, or partly composed of nonwood fibers. For further information, visit our website at www.cornellpress.cornell.edu.

Cloth printing    10 9 8 7 6 5 4 3 2 1
Paperback printing    10 9 8 7 6 5 4 3 2 1

*For Olivia (1924–1976) and Dov Palan*

# Contents

List of Tables and Figures                                           ix
Preface to the Paperback Edition                                     xi
Acknowledgments                                                      xxi

Introduction                                                          1
1. The Offshore Economy in Its Contemporary Settings                17
2. State, Capital, and the Production of Offshore                    63
3. The Emergence of Embryonic Forms of Offshore                     83
4. The Growth of an Offshore Economy                                111
5. Offshore and the Internationalization of the State              130
6. Offshore and the Demise of the Nation-State                     147
7. Numerical Organizations, Nomadic Spaces, and                    162
   Modern Capitalism
   Conclusion                                                      181

Notes                                                              193
References                                                         203
Index                                                             221

# Tables and Figures

TABLES

1. International Financial Centers Ranked by Banks'      35
   External Assets: End of 2000
2. Scale of International Banking Activities in Selected     36
   Financial Centers, End of 2000
3. Tax Havens of the World      37
4. The World's Leading Capital Insurance Centers     44
5. Distribution of EPZs by Region, 1997     50
6. International Transport Workers List of Flag of     54
   Convenience Registries, 2000

FIGURES

1. Major Net Interbank Flows, 2000     84

# Preface to the Paperback Edition

The offshore world is a significant socio-economic development in the world economy, which consists, among other items, of the Euromarket, tax havens, export processing zones, flags of convenience, and certain developments in E-commerce. I have encountered this world not as a practitioner—an accountant, an economist, or a civil servant—seeking to understand the workings of this bizarre economy in order to offer professional advice to prospective clients or governments. Nor do I consider myself an activist, opposing what is clearly an instrument in the hands of the rich and powerful. This book was written from a different standpoint. I was always interested in the state, but less as a primary case of the "business of rule," as Gianfraco Poggi describes it, and more in terms of what Michel Foucault calls governmentality—as a mediating structure that renders imaginary constructions as "real" life experience.

To understand governmentality, and the complicated and intriguing ways by which the modern state is evolving, it is not sufficient to study the United States, Russia, China, or the advanced European states. The miniature island economies of the Caribbean and the Pacific and the anachronistic remains of feudal Europe, such as Luxembourg, Andorra, and Monaco, tell us something as important about the modern political economy and the continuing process of state formation. Globalization, I believe, is another chapter, intriguing, meandering, treacherous, no doubt, in the long historical journey of the formation of the modern state.

Politics is who gets what, when, and how, says the psychologist Harold Lasswell. Foucault responds: "I think I know who gets what, when and how; it is power I do not understand." I find Foucault's notion of power particularly intriguing, but, as some of my critics have pointed out, a Lasswellian theory of the politics of offshore—who gets what, when, and how—remains undeveloped in this book. This is not a matter of ignorance or oversight. I came to the conclusion, controversial as it may be, that vested interests and political intent frequently take advantage of situations they have not envisaged and often do not understand. The powerful gain their power less through control, more because they are in the best position to take advantage of opportunities whenever these arise. The idea of order and control emerges *after* the event. In the offshore world the existing state system, with its historical principles of taxation, sovereignty, wealth creation, and competitiveness, has created a plethora of opportunities, loopholes, and breaks that the powerful use to their advantage. I gradually concluded that, as one of the most bizarre and spectacular expressions of modern statehood, offshore is primarily a product of such dynamics rather than the product of intentional politics.

I wrote this book during a particularly interesting time in the life of the offshore economy, and there have been some important changes since the publication of the hardback edition in 2003. Appearances notwithstanding, attitudes toward the offshore economy and in particular toward the tax haven, at least until the late 1990s, could best be described as ambiguous. True, the fledgling offshore economy was never accepted with great enthusiasm by the advanced industrialized states. But the British dependencies in islands surrounding the United Kingdom and in the Caribbean and the Pacific were actively encouraged by the British state to develop their offshore economy as a way of reducing dependency on mainland. Similarly, the Dutch Antilles was developed by the Dutch state. The United States has encouraged, indirectly, the formation of the Liberian and the Marshall Islands flags of convenience. Things appear to have changed around the late 1990s. Reluctantly, I devoted a section of chapter five to the OECD and G-7 campaign against tax havens. I was reluctant to write about the new campaign not because I thought it was unimportant or irrelevant. I simply felt that it was far too early to reach conclusions about the nature and success of the campaign. At the end of 2005 things are much clearer.

The first sign of change was the publication of a 1998 OECD report titled *Harmful Tax Competition: An Emerging Global Issue*. The work for the report was carried out by the Forum on Harmful Tax Practices, a subsidiary body of the Committee on Fiscal Affairs of the OECD. Accepted by all OECD members except Switzerland and Luxembourg, it severely criticized what it described as "preferential tax regimes" within OECD member countries. The original report asked each member country to perform a self-review of its preferential tax regimes, to be followed by peer review of each reported regime. A second report, published in 2000, identified 47 preferential tax regimes in 9 categories as potentially harmful. A third OECD progress report was published in 2004, and more reports are on the way.

Meanwhile, in the wake of the Asian financial crisis of 1996 and 1997, a new body called the Financial Stability Forum (FSF) was established in Basel. The FSF brings together senior representatives of national financial authorities (e.g., central banks, supervisory authorities, and treasury departments), international financial institutions, international regulatory and supervisory groupings, committees of central bank experts, and the European Central Bank.

The FSF was set up to reform the international financial architecture. It was particularly interested in the regulatory standards in offshore financial centers (or tax havens). Its subcommittee on offshore affairs published an influential report in 2000 titled *Report of the Working Group on Offshore Centers*, which spelled out abuses perpetrated by tax havens and recommended a system of assessment for these havens. Since then it has produced yearly progress reports. The IMF has also published several reports on tax havens.

A separate body, the Financial Action Task Force on Money Laundering (FATF), was also established by the 1989 G-7 and worked throughout the 1990s without much publicity. FATF seeks to combat financial secrecy in offshore and onshore centers vulnerable to use by money launderers. It was given an additional mandate after 9/11 to investigate the financing of terrorism. FATF has adopted an aggressive "name and shame" tactic, publishing lists of noncompliant tax havens to encourage them to lift the veil of secrecy.

In another move, the European Union introduced two important directives: the Savings Tax Directive to crack down on evasion and the Code of Conduct on Business Taxation. These two directives are having considerable impact on the Channel Islands, the Isle of Man, and other U.K. and European dependencies. Principally aimed at individual savers, the Savings Tax Directive, which came into effect in 2005, is an agreement among the member states of the European Union to automatically exchange information about customers who earn savings income in one EU member state but reside in another. It also permits some member states to deduct tax at source from savings income, using what is called the withholding tax option.

The Code of Conduct on Business Taxation is not a legally binding instrument, but it does have political force. By adopting this code, the member states have undertaken to roll back existing tax measures that are considered harmful tax competition and to refrain from introducing any such measures in the future. Interestingly, the Code proposes clear criteria for identifying potentially harmful measures, among them:

1. an effective level of taxation that is significantly lower than the general level of taxation in the country concerned
2. tax benefits reserved for nonresidents
3. tax incentives for activities that are isolated from the domestic economy and therefore have no impact on the national tax base
4. granting of tax advantages even in the absence of any real economic activity
5. the basis of profit determination for companies in a multinational group departs from internationally accepted rules, in particular those approved by the OECD
6. lack of transparency

Tax havens are not unfamiliar with criticisms and the occasional threat. But concerted efforts by so many related international bodies, combined with rather aggressive bilateral pressure emanating from the United States and the European Union (some tentative signs indicate a similar debate starting in China as well), suggest that something important is going on. The immediate reaction of the havens to the new policies was to be expected: enter into negotiations with the international bodies, adopt delaying tactics, make only minor concessions wherever possible, and try to work behind the scene to change the elite's attitude. It is becoming clear, however, that traditional delaying tactics are no longer working, and tax havens are having to resort to plan B: innovate new, highly complicated laws and regulations that appear to comply with demands but in reality perpetrate offshore abuses or shift their efforts to as-yet-unregulated areas of offshore, such as gambling and e-commerce. But how long will they be able to get away with it? Do they have a plan C? Or will the offshore world wither away? What are the prospects for the offshore world?

First, it should be noted that there is no sign of a comprehensive criticism of the offshore world. The debate surrounding the Tobin tax, for instance, which proposed an international, if rather light, tax on speculative foreign exchange operations—and, therefore, could be considered an attempt to re-regulate offshore finance—still reverberates in Europe but appears to have subsided elsewhere. And while there is growing international concern about the phenomenal rise of derivatives, I see little sign of international efforts at regulation. A study conducted for the

French parliament has tried, correctly in my view, to identify traditional centers such as London with tax haven abuses. Still, London's as
well as the more limited U.S. and Japanese offshore types of financial facilities are definitely not targeted by current policies, which are aimed
exclusively at tax haven phenomena and not at the offshore world as
such. Offshore is not at risk right now.

Second, as I point out, while multilateral and bilateral campaigns are
aimed at delegitimizing certain practices associated with tax havens,
the net effect is paradoxically to legitimize, perhaps for the first time,
the tax haven phenomenon. Prior to the campaigns, tax havens were
considered marginal, a tolerated form of abuse perpetrated by a motley
crew of Lilliputian quasi-states too small and unimportant to bother
with. Academics may have debated why advanced industrialized states
tolerate this abuse but, frankly, the debates tended to be speculative.
The sad truth is that there was too little discussion of tax havens in policy circles. The implicit but unmistakable message of the new campaigns, by contrast, is that tax havens are important and legitimate provided they abandon particular practices. As a result, small jurisdictions
such as the Cayman Islands and Bermuda find themselves, for the first
time in their history, invited to participate in discussions as full partners in various multilateral bodies, where they participate in weighty
debates about the merits of an international tax regime, global financial
stability, global terrorism, and so on. They are considered legitimate
partners in these negotiations, and inevitably their interests are reflected to some degree in the outcome. One consequence is that havens
no longer simply view one another as rivals but are beginning to develop a sense of common interest, which strengthens their bargaining
position. Furthermore, as the number of forums increases, and there are
nearly twenty of them now, including regional gatherings, the cost of
negotiation increases. Many havens are recruiting foreign companies,
including the large accounting firms, and foreign experts to help them.
A new layer of irony: negotiators are forging new and powerful international political alliances between tax havens, large international accounting firms, international law firms, and international banks and
libertarian think tanks. The Washington-based Center for Freedom and
Prosperity, for instance, credits itself, in its official publication, for
"working with many of our friends to educate and influence lawmakers
and policy makers in Washington on why tax competition is beneficial
for the U.S. and other free-market countries. We have been quite successful in educating Washington lawmakers and policy makers." The

Center is now shifting its attention to combating the European Savings Directive. Meanwhile, a number of NGOs, in association with new organizations such as the Tax Justice Network, are countering such think tanks by pursuing a highly effective campaign against tax haven abuses.

Legitimacy has its costs. The price for implementing new regulations, including anti-money laundering laws, is likely to increase the cost of doing business offshore and by the same token reduce its attractiveness. Hiring economists, accountants, and legal experts to implement the different regulations is an expensive business and may take a considerable financial toll on the smaller havens, potentially wiping out the attractiveness of the offshore sector. Antigua and Barbuda, for instance, have withdrawn from the offshore game precisely on these grounds. There are, indeed, voices in some of the less successful and smaller havens in the Caribbean and the Pacific calling for the abandonment of offshore business in order to avoid the spiraling cost of diplomacy!

The debate has shifted, therefore, and is no longer about the viability or morality of the tax haven phenomenon. Rather, it is about achieving common standards through negotiations to ensure that tax havens play by the rules of the advanced industrial countries that by and large represent—let us have no illusions—business interests. From the perspective of the tax havens themselves, they are offered, whether they like it or not, a Faustian bargain that offers them legitimacy at the price of some degree of regulation. Their aim, generally speaking, is to achieve the highest degree of legitimacy with as little regulation as possible—which in their case means as little change or concession as possible. The advanced industrialized countries, whose representatives tend to have close links with business (or perhaps, as many believe, it is the other way around: diplomacy works for business interests!), have a primary concern with accumulation, to ensure political and economic stability, and only a secondary concern with social issues such as just taxation, income distribution, and so on. Bearing this in mind makes developments during the past two to three years appear more comprehensible.

Although these are early days, it appears to me that the debate has finally settled on two issues. First is the issue of transparency. The Financial Task Force has been particularly successful in pushing its hardline views about secrecy and transparency (not least because of 9/11 and terrorist financing). As a result, those who are close to the tax haven phenomenon have concluded that there is now solid political will to remove, once and for all, the veil of secrecy offered by tax havens. The Financial Task Force routinely publishes its findings, and tax havens are adopting measures to ensure they are removed from the FATF list. In addition, bilateral pressure, particularly from the United States, is yielding results. A persistent stream of money laundering and embezzlement scandals make strict bank secrecy of the sort that Switzerland and Austria used to offer difficult to justify. As a result of all these efforts, there appears to be more transparency than ever before, and in cases of money laundering, criminality, or blatant tax evasion the authorities, if they act persistently and with determination, can obtain information that was unavailable to them a few years ago.

One ironic effect of the decline in secrecy, as I predicted in 2003, is a rapid rise in the number of offshore entities. The years 2003, 2004, and 2005 have witnessed an increase of offshore entities in the major havens averaging 15 percent and more, according to annual figures published by tax havens. Secrecy and anonymity may not be as tight as they used to be, but the new rules of transparency are cumbersome, time-consuming, and work on a case-by-case basis. The result is a huge incentive for companies and individuals to open multiple businesses in various havens in the hope that if an investigation occurs, it will drag on endlessly. In addition, with the introduction of European directives, there are different rules for EU (including EU-related havens such as British and Dutch dependencies) and non-EU havens. Once again companies and individuals have an incentive to set up shop in both emerging legal regimes.

The second interesting topic of debate during the past five to six years is in the realm of tax competition. The original OECD report of 1998 saw no problem in denouncing what it described as harmful tax competition. Many states, led by havens such as Switzerland, Luxembourg, and the Caribbean havens, argued that a tax regime is a sovereign prerogative, and the OECD campaign amounted to a new form of imperialism whereby powerful states dictate terms to weaker states. This argument gained a powerful ally once the first Bush administration came to power and broke ranks with the OECD by coming out in favor of tax competition. Its reasons: to protect the sovereignty of small states (yet, at a bilateral level, American negotiators put unprecedented pressure on the Caribbean havens to negotiate away these sovereign prerogatives!) and the Bush administration's belief that tax competition between states should be encouraged because it stops governments from imposing unnecessarily high and punitive taxes. As a result, the debate about harmful tax competition and abuse has undergone an interesting development. The trend at the moment, as seen in the case of the European Savings Directive, is to argue that tax competition is no longer an abuse per se but that it is unacceptable for a state to offer advantages to foreigners, whether individuals or companies, over and above what it offers its own population. If a state wishes, for instance, to impose no corporate taxation whatsoever, that decision is fine as long as it does not distinguish between domestic and foreign corporations or activities. In practice, the havens would have to find other sources of government income—an interesting idea, because it overcomes the argument about imperialism and sovereign rights. One of the first countries to respond to the new initiative was Ireland, which has introduced a "10 percent manufacturing rate of tax" that applies quite widely in and out of manufacturing and is applied equally to the financial sector. At the time of writing, the Channel Islands are experimenting with all sorts of probably unacceptable schemes that appear to comply with the European Directive but, in reality, do not.

The international legal regime that evolved from the mid-to-late nineteenth century, which, as I describe in chapter three, gave rise almost by default to the offshore economy, was motivated by the theory that to encourage trade and foreign investment foreigners should be given the same legal and political protections as citizens. One of the paradoxes of the offshore world is that foreigners are given an advantage over local residents. The theory at the heart of the offshore world is under attack.

So where are we now? There is little doubt that tax havens are taking the new initiatives very seriously. Antigua has closed its offshore facilities, but there are new players, among them Botswana, the Comoros Islands, several Russian republics, and, most recently, New Zealand. The majority of tax havens are reluctantly complying with the new directives, although the most recent research suggests that they are still flourishing and the various campaigns have not had the desired effect. Nevertheless, in Switzerland, Luxembourg, and Jersey, we are witnessing the beginning of a debate about the character of a post-offshore world. At the same time, largely due to the rise of China and India and the return of Hong Kong to Chinese hands, Singapore is emerging as a serious challenger to Switzerland as the most important tax haven. Indeed, Asia is undoubtedly the next area of growth for offshore.

So offshore is undergoing changes, but so far the offshore economy is still growing, and growing rapidly. The offshore world is not an isolated phenomenon. It has gone through a number of phases already, and they in turn reflect the general trajectories of a globalizing capitalist economy. The offshore economy now under attack from the various multilateral agencies is a product of the 1970s—the dynamics that are associated with the collapse of Fordism and the rise of neoliberalism. As the world economy enters a new phase, shifting from nationally based regulatory schema to a globally regulated economy, so the offshore world is re-regulated and yet becomes an embedded dimension of contemporary statehood. To the extent that the offshore world is beginning to be regulated, so the on-shore world is legitimizing a more liberal regulatory regime of the sort that we associate with offshore. In that sense the offshore economy plays a vitally important role in contemporary politics.

In drafting this preface I have relied on countless conversations with many friends and associates at the Tax Justice Network, including John Christensen, Sol Picciotto, Jason Sharman, and Ian Goldman. Richard Murphy, Christian Chavagneux, and Mallary Gelb made specific and extremely helpful comments, for which I am ever grateful.

*Herzliya*, December, 2005

# Acknowledgments

Every book is a collective effort, and this one is no exception. My ideas about offshore were shaped over a long period of time in debates and discussions with many friends and colleagues—too numerous, I am afraid, to mention by name. They will know who they are, and I thank them for their help and support. I have learned a tremendous amount from my students here at the University of Sussex, as well as at the Hebrew University of Jerusalem and York University, Toronto, where I served as Visiting Professor. Teaching a course on offshore has proved to be a wonderful experience, an opportunity to let our imaginations loose (some would say, too loose!). My students gave me the confidence to think beyond the conventions, and for that I am forever grateful.

The late Susan Strange was an enthusiastic supporter of this project. To her last days, Susan insisted on reading earlier drafts, commenting on and debating my ideas. Christian Chavagneux and Robert O'Brien sent me material, newspaper clippings, and relevant Web sites, and alerted me to the latest developments in the offshore economy. Gary Burn taught me the intricacies of the Euromarket, and Kees Van Der Pijl read the entire manuscript with a critical eye and made many a crucial comment. Angus Cameron had the dubious pleasure of reading the entire manuscript not once, but twice, and commented on every aspect of the project. Susan Barnett, Karen Laun, and Gavin Lewis did an excellent job in ensuring the book ran smoothly through the production process. Last but not least, I would like to thank Roger Haydon of Cornell University Press, who believed in me and in this book. Uniquely among book editors, Roger read the entire manuscript with great care and made many excellent suggestions. The book is much improved as a result.

Chapter 3 is a revised and expanded version of "Tax Havens and the Commercialization of Sovereignty," *International Organization* 56, no. 1 (2002).

# Introduction

In 1939, with the might of the Nazi armies massing on its border, the Soviet Union was faced with a formidable dilemma. Following a particularly vicious debate, the so-called Lysenko affair, the Soviet ideologues had decreed that system thinking, the mainstay of modern engineering and computing sciences, contravened the principles of Marxist dialectics and was in fact a bourgeois science.[1] How then could they develop modern weaponry? Luckily, the Soviet penal system, the dreaded gulag, had been filling up with scientists, thousands of them, accused of spying for one or other capitalist country. Labeling them traitors to the socialist cause, and tucking them safely behind prison walls, the state was no longer interested in maintaining their ideological purity. They were, therefore, given free access to the latest scientific literature from the West and the freedom to express themselves. A few trusted scientists were even allowed to travel between camps. This resulted in the emergence of a few relatively comfortable punishment camps, serving, in effect, as the research and development centers of the Soviet Union's military-industrial complex (Kerber 1996).

There are many fascinating aspects to this disturbingly absurd tale—so profoundly characteristic, one senses, of the twentieth century—and many lessons to be learned from it for our topic: the emergence of an offshore economy in the twilight years of the twentieth century. Of particular relevance is the manner in which the Soviet state deployed techniques of spatial constraint to resolve some of the contradictions produced by its ideology. Is it not ironic that spatial constraint is increasingly practiced, albeit for different strategic and competitive reasons and with very different results, by a growing number of capitalist states in order to handle the conflicting pressures generated by globalization? The past three decades have witnessed a spectacular proliferation of uniquely modern types of spatio-juridical enclosures in the spheres of manufacturing, services, finance, and increasingly retail, as states establish specialized enclaves characterized by "designer rate tax and regulatory regimes"[2] aimed at harvesting rent from the world economy. These designer rate regimes, collectively known as "offshore," come about as states divide their sovereign domains into two juridical realms: "onshore," where they apply fully their regulations and taxation, and myriad offshore enclaves, where they relax or withdraw some of those regulations.

"Offshore" evokes images of the high seas and exotic locations. But often this is not the case: offshore economic activities do not take place on some barge floating in the middle of an ocean. On the contrary, offshore financial transactions, for instance, take place very much onshore: in the vast majority of cases, they are conceived and handled in the great financial centers of London, New York, and Tokyo. Similarly, offshore manufacturing is carried out in territorial enclaves within national states that are otherwise jealous of their powers and sovereignty. The offshore economy may appear external to the system of states, but it is a product as well as an integral part of it. In fact, the offshore economy is not off shore at all. The term has stuck for good reasons, as we will see, but it can be misleading.

Thus "offshore" refers not to the geographical location of economic activities, but to the juridical status of a vast and expanding array of specialized realms. These realms are of various shapes, sizes and designations, and their concrete manifestations vary from one country to another and from one sector to another. The abstract character of modern finance has given rise to zero or near-zero regulation in offshore cyberspaces (often called the Euromarket) facilitating an enormous growth in financial transactions. Since the early 1970s, offshore financial markets have been joined by a plethora of real territorial enclaves, called special economic zones or export processing zones, over 850 at a recent count, providing employment to over 27 million workers worldwide (ILO 1998).[3] To this we may add the rising number of flag of convenience states (including landlocked countries such as Luxembourg), and the fledgling Internet-driven facilities such as offshore pornography (Niue, Guyana) and offshore gambling (Costa Rica, Guernsey). All of this has recently been capped by potentially the largest offshore sector, electronic commerce. To this, we should add the reemergence of nonstate commercial law, the *lex mercatoria*, which may serve in the future as the legal foundation of these new offshore spaces.[4]

In recalling the Soviet gulag I do not wish to suggest that offshore is to be compared directly to the reprehensible penal system of the Soviet state. Offshore offers access to cheap labor and low taxation, and, in so doing, "liberates" capital from social responsibility and a good portion of the taxation it would otherwise owe national governments. It offers capital a stick to wave at recalcitrant states that have failed to deregulate their economies sufficiently. But these crucial differences should not mask the areas of commonality between offshore and the Soviet gulag. Both are techniques of spatial constraint employed by states to achieve determinate goals. Both are social innovations that were adopted for a variety of reasons but which effectively, if not intentionally, are used to resolve some of the contradictions thrown up by complex systems. The Soviet Union wished to exploit the knowledge and imagination of the very people it forbade to dream, and it found a solution to its conflicting demands by incarcerating them and calling them traitors. In the case of offshore, the creation of extraterritorial and virtual spaces helps mitigate conflicts between forces of market integration and the concomitant decentralization of the state within a global economy.

The offshore economy is the product of this bifurcation of the sovereign realm, and it is proving an ingenious device to reconcile two apparently incompatible trends. Instead of confronting the state directly, the more mobile and yet traditionally heavily regulated sectors of the economy, such as shipping, finance, pornography, gambling, and—with the advent of the Internet—commerce, are relocating to relatively unregulated realms that present themselves as external to the state. As these more mobile sectors of the economy transfer offshore, states have learned to refocus their own rules and carry on discharging their traditional duties in the territories remaining under their jurisdiction as if nothing had happened. I am not for a moment suggesting that offshore has not, and will not, affect the state. Clearly it does—and that indeed is a primary subject of this book. I am proposing, however, that in this fiction of offshore, states have found a politically acceptable, albeit awkward, way of reconciling the growing contradictions between their territorial and nationalist ideology so critical for the maintenance of capitalist (global) order, and their support for capitalist accumulation on a global scale.

The world of offshore is deceptively simple, and only under close scrutiny are layers upon layers of intriguing complexities revealed. As Richard Johns observes (1983,2), offshore does not fit the rules of textbook economics. Nor can it easily be explained by conventional political science. Indeed, from a strictly economic point of view, offshore appears to be a great anomaly—a world of pretense and empty boasts. It simply makes no sense for the Cayman Islands to be the fifth largest financial center in the world. It does not make sense that tiny Luxembourg boasts more banks than Switzerland, a country that itself has more banks than dentists. There is no particular reason that war-torn Liberia should have become the biggest shipping nation in the world; or that the genteel island of Guernsey should be the world's premier captive insurance center.[5] The citizens of the Dutch Antilles are not so chatty as to spend an average of three months per year per person on international phone calls, and why should Bermuda and the Virgin Islands, of all places, provide such a large share of Hong Kong's inflated foreign direct investment?[6]

Ironically, the closer we get to the textbook view of an "efficient" market—a market almost entirely free of state regulation—the more contrived that market appears. For in this strange world of offshore, companies and wealthy individuals pay a premium to appear to reside somewhere other than where they are actually located, or even to disappear altogether. Millions of dollars are spent on lawyers, accountants, licenses, and so on, for the purpose of acquiring, in most cases, virtual residence in virtual spaces. Of course, everyone knows that the Cayman Islands are not truly the fifth largest financial center in the world, that Liberia is not the world's largest shipping country, and that neither Bermuda nor the Virgin Islands is a large foreign direct investor: it is all a fiction. Side by side with the state system, therefore, emerges a virtual world of make-believe, driven by a commodified form of sovereignty. This virtual world nevertheless comprises key nodal points of the global economy outside the reach of what we normally take to be the "real" world of states and their "real" economies.

But as a growing number of individuals and firms find themselves confronted on a daily basis with the reality of this apparently virtual world—as they discover the market for sovereignty and as they learn to exchange virtual citizenship in one state for virtual citizenship in another (without ever moving)—questions arise. What gave rise to the offshore economy? What are the implications of the emergence of such nonterritorial, virtual spaces for state and society? How can these identities and social attachments survive the blatant (mis-)use of sovereignty as a commercial tool? What is real and what is fiction? And what is lacking in the apparently secure and coherent state system that has led it to produce such bizarre and contradictory virtual spaces?

The offshore world has been attracting much attention lately. As investigations into the ill-gotten gains of bloodthirsty dictators, from Idi

Amin Dada of Uganda to Ferdinand Marcos of the Philippines and General Abacha of Nigeria, are followed by criminal investigations into corporate abuse by companies such as Enron or Tyco, tax havens are never far from the headlines.[7] Following the terrible events of 11 September 2001, at least half a dozen tax havens felt the need to announce publicly and without prompting that they had never served as conduits for Al-Qaida's money. Was this perhaps an admission of guilt? As the "war on terrorism" joins the "war on drugs" and the "war on poverty," the public profile of offshore finance and tax havens has risen to new heights. But tax havens are only part of the story. Issues such as harmful tax competition and ecological and social abuses may not be as prominent as drugs and terror, but they are of growing concern, and they too thrive in tax havens, in export processing zones (EPZs), and on board vessels flying flags of convenience. The East Asian crisis of the late 1990s, meanwhile, rekindled anxiety about the volatility of the financial system, or what Susan Strange called "casino capitalism," operating, as she was only too keenly aware, largely by courtesy of the offshore financial markets (Strange 1986, 1998).

Recent attention given to the offshore world by the media and policymakers must be considered a positive development. Welcome as the current debates are, however, they unfortunately remain focused too narrowly on issues of money laundering, criminality, and tax abuses, leaving some of the more important and relevant questions unanswered. Too much attention is paid to actors' motives and rationalities for using offshore, too little to the structural and institutional conditions that gave rise to offshore in the first place. It is an irony that the growing interest in offshore, and the urgency and immediacy of the problems that it poses, has served only to focus attention on short-term effects and on the pressing need for remedial policies, to the detriment of a serious causal and socio-economic study of the phenomenon.

Conventional accounts explain the rise of tax havens (and by extension other offshore sectors) with reference to the tremendous increase in state regulation and taxation during the 1960s and 1970s. The heavier the regulation and taxation, so the argument goes, the keener some people are to avoid them. "It is no coincidence that banking, insurance and ship registration are three of the main pillars of offshore business; they are among the most heavily regulated industries in developed countries"(*Euromoney* 1989, 6). An influential report on offshore financial centers (OFCs—tax havens to you and me) reiterates this commonly held view: "the main contributing factor identified for the historical growth of offshore banking and Offshore Financial Centers," it states, "was the imposition of increased regulation . . . in the financial sectors of industrialized countries during the 1960s and the 1970s" (Financial Stability Forum 2000, 6). Faced by a growing demand for permissive regulations, these accounts claim, a number of microstates began to offer zero or near-zero regulation in order to attract businesses to their territories.

These theories are not entirely wrong. No doubt much of the recent expansion of offshore is driven by the all too common desire to avoid taxation, regulation, scrutiny, and other forms of public interference. Indeed, as we will see, rising taxation and regulation in the 1960s played an important role in encouraging the diffusion of the offshore economy, but, as I shall show, they did not actually produce offshore in the first place. True, the motives of the countless firms and individuals who joyfully participate in the offshore economy need little explanation. But the desire to reduce the burden of taxation and state regulation cannot serve as an adequate explanation for the emergence of such vast, legally sanctioned, relatively unregulated and untaxed spaces. The reasons that some states have chosen to relax regulation in order to attract business to their territories may not be too difficult to divine, but understanding their motives gives no inkling of the reasons that they were able to use their sovereignty in such a way in the first place. Can we simply assume that the offshore world was always there waiting, as it were, for the surge of regulation and taxation to emerge into the daylight? Was it always possible to use sovereignty as a commercial asset? Or is there a history yet to be told, which is ignored in current debates? If so, what were the conditions that gave rise to offshore?

My interest in the offshore world arose out of conflicting sentiments of fascination and frustration. I am fascinated by one of the more spectacular and intriguing developments in modern capitalism: the emergence of virtual spaces, supported and sustained by the state system, and yet apparently so adaptable to the needs of capitalist accumulation. It appears to me that the offshore economy has put paid to the convention that the state is withering away under the pressure of globalization. The state, and the state system collectively, have managed to produce, whether intentionally or not is a matter of dispute, a set of unique juridical enclaves operating in a number of economic sectors and perfectly suited to the needs of global capitalism. Furthermore, the state system seems to have done so against the explicit policy wishes of the hegemonic power, the United States—although closer scrutiny will show that the United States has played a far more ambiguous role in the emergence and spread of the offshore economy than might at first appear. Is the offshore economy a product of the state system? Or is it a product of capitalism? Or is it perhaps the work of individual renegade capitalists, abusing the state and the state system to their own advantage? But then, identifying the culprits may not answer all our questions. Can we simply assume whoever was implicated in the establishment of offshore still controls it?

But my interest in offshore arose equally out of a sense of frustration—in particular with the treatment of offshore as merely a peripheral development on the margins of the world economy. The sheer size of the offshore economy demands serious examination. Not only has the number of EPZs enormously expanded in the past thirty years; in addition, an estimated 80 percent of international financial transactions (by value) is conducted through the offshore financial markets! The foreign exchange market, through which an estimated $2 trillion pass daily, is almost entirely offshore. More than half of international lending passes through financial centers, over seventy of which may be described as tax havens. An estimated 20 percent of the total private wealth in the world is "invested" in tax havens. A large portion of the $44 trillion worth of private banking business is transacted through offshore financial centers, and about 22 percent of banks' external assets are located in tax havens.

But even these staggering statistics give a false impression of the actual, and more important, the potential impact of the offshore economy. To begin with we need to bear in mind the offshore economy's uncanny ability to expand into new realms. The concept of duty-free shops, for example, served as blueprint for some of the early export processing zones; the concept of flag of convenience spawned imitations in offshore aircraft leasing, passport sale, corporate relocation, and Internet domain names. Meanwhile tax havens are branching into whole new sectors including gambling, e-commerce, and pornography. Considering the rate of offshore's expansion and its potential for further growth, it comes as no surprise that Walter and Dorothy Diamond, the grandparents of offshore studies, believe that the twenty-first century will be the "Century of Offshore Investment" (1998, 1).[8] Whether the offshore economy is about to become the defining characteristic of the twenty-first century is moot, but there is little doubt that offshore has the potential to expand much further.

The expansion of the offshore world or rather, the expansion of the practice of sovereign bifurcation, by which states intentionally divide their sovereign space into heavily and lightly regulated realms, suggests, and this is my second point, that something fundamental is afoot. Not only has the splitting of the sovereign realm become a competitive strategy of a growing number of states (Palan and Abbott 1996), but it is also symptomatic of a process that is leading to a radical redrawing of states' boundaries and an important transformation in both the nature of sovereignty and the relationship between state and capitalism.

It would be a mistake, therefore, to confine our investigation to matters pertaining to state policy. The strange world of offshore raises a whole set of empirical and theoretical questions that have a bearing upon crucial aspects of contemporary change. In effect, the evolution of offshore mirrors faithfully the development of capitalism over the past century and a half. But the offshore world was never a mere passive participant in the flow of history, shadowing the general trend in modern society; rather, offshore has participated actively in shaping the character of contemporary capitalism. As it has evolved through distinct phases from the late nineteenth century to today, however, its role and function have undergone some important changes.

The more central and pertinent questions regarding the offshore world relate, therefore, not necessarily to the surge in regulation and taxation or to the activities of criminals and money launderers, but to the changing configuration of state and sovereignty in the modern world. Can we truly detach the huge expansion of the offshore economy in the twilight years of the twentieth century from the general trends in economy and society that go under the label of "globalization"? Are we satisfied with the treatment of the bifurcation of the sovereign space as a mere by-product of human greed? Conversely, can we take seriously those globalization theories that are ignorant of offshore? For what, after all, is global finance, a central concept in the globalization debate, without the offshore financial market and the tax havens?

My aims in this book are conventional enough: to provide an explanation of the rise of the offshore economy and to analyze its contemporary impact. In method and scope, however, the book is unconventional. The typical approach is to isolate the subject at hand from a complex and confusing mass of extraneous information, to delineate its boundaries, and to work within those boundaries in order to understand the essential characteristics and processes at work. This has been the model followed by the bulk of existing literature on offshore. But in isolating offshore from the general trends in capitalism, conventional accounts explain only the rise of tax havens, the paradigmatic case of offshore; and they do so in terms of the tremendous increase in state regulation and taxation during the postwar period and particularly since the late 1960s.

My approach is different and, not surprisingly, my conclusions are different as well. While I define offshore as juridical spaces characterized by a relative lack of regulation and taxation, I do not isolate offshore from broader trends in economy and society. On the contrary, my aim is to analyze the emergence and development of offshore within the context of a changing capitalist world economy. I will seek to show that far from being an opportunistic development at the margins of the world economy, the rise of offshore is an inherent tendency of an internationalizing economy operating within a particularistic political system. But offshore is not simply an effect of the capitalist system as it grew in size. It has also served "to dislocate the international state system and induce its substantial reconstruction," reinforcing trends towards the internationalization of capital (Picciotto 1999, 43).

The book also differs from conventional accounts in more subtle ways. The theoretical justification for this study hinges on the proposition that what may have appeared as disparate and unrelated sets of events and processes, spanning time and place and ranging across sectoral boundaries, can be treated under the umbrella term "offshore." But the mere act of "naming" (Hobbes [1651] 1951, chap. 4) these events as "offshore" can easily lead to a further unwarranted assumption: that the unity of the subject matter implies a unity of its history—in other words, that there is one continuous, uninterrupted history of the offshore economy. This, in turn, may lead to yet another such assumption: that the future impact of offshore will be simply more of the same. But is this the case? There is no reason to assume that the origins of offshore necessarily explain its growth, or that the diffusion of offshore explains its contemporary impact. Indeed, there is no particular reason to assume that the past and present tell us much about the future impact of offshore. These are, to my mind, open questions that need to be resolved through analysis and interpretation. In my analysis, the history of offshore is not in fact continuous but discontinuous, characterized by breaks and mutations: the offshore economy plays different roles, and interacts in a variety of ways with its environment throughout its existence. This implies that there was never a single, or even a predominant cause for the rise of offshore.

This conclusion determines the structure of this book. Although it is organized chronologically, from chapter 3 which examines the origins of offshore to chapters 6 and 7 which reflect on its future impact, the structure should not imply a necessary progression in the narrative: The book is a history of discrete moments, not a continuous story.

It is now becoming more generally accepted that the core capitalist economies underwent a profound transformation toward the end of the nineteenth century (Chandler 1990; Duménil and Lévy 2001). The change took place most likely in response to a crisis that began in the early 1870s, combined with the settlement of the Civil War in the United States and the opening of the entire North American West to agricultural exploitation and commerce. The result was the emergence of a new type of capitalist enterprise: the large corporation backed and controlled by mobile finance. Run by salaried managerial and clerical personnel, these corporations eventually came to be organized along the lines of "scientific" management (Taylorism) and "rational" production methods (Fordism). The new corporations soon began to spill beyond national boundaries and extend their operations overseas.

Less appreciated is the fact that the nineteenth century also saw the final phase of consolidation of an international system based on discrete territorial units each boasting its own national economy and national culture (Braudel 1979). The internationalization of capital driven by financiers and the new type of finance and an increasingly insulated and rigidly defined state system, were contradictory trends, and had great potential for conflict. But the ruling classes of the major states were keen to avoid such a conflict. Take, for instance, the imposition of business taxation, a new development that came about at the end of the nineteenth century, first in the United Kingdom, then in France in 1909, in the United States in 1913, and in Germany in 1920 (Braithwaite and Drahos 2000, 93). This innovation threatened to double-tax companies that were operating in more than one country. To avoid penalizing these firms, states established mechanisms of cooperation, while leaving some of the more complex technical matters of determination of business taxation and sovereign control to the arbitration of second-tier policymaking personnel such as lawyers and accountants. I show in chapter 3 that the different solutions proposed by these various institutions and individuals amounted to a medley of principles and agreements, some of which inadvertently laid the foundations for the offshore economy. My analysis shows that in order to maintain the discrete national territories required by nationalist ideology, and yet preserve a commitment to transnational capitalism, states had—though they did not knowingly intend—to create offshore. To put it in more provocative terms, in order to create onshore, the state system generated the legal fiction of offshore. Offshore was not, therefore, caused by rising taxation and regulation, but rather emerged at the very point of their original imposition. Offshore enabled onshore, or the modern nationally based state, to emerge in the first instance, after which it took on a new salience as the state began to exercise its powers of regulation and control.

The question arises, of course, why these two contradictory trends, the internationalization of capital and the formation of the discrete nation-state, should have occurred almost simultaneously. I discuss these matters in chapters 3 and 6. I do not believe these developments were a historical accident. On the contrary, I believe that the two trends can both be traced back to the core dynamics of nineteenth-century capitalism. It was the rise of capitalism in the early nineteenth century that gave an impetus to the consolidation of these national entities. It was not the case, however, as some have argued, that national entities were directly and functionally related to capitalism, serving the goals and aims of some coherent transnational ruling class. Rather, the consolidation of nation-states and national cultures became a viable and desirable strategy in the context of the emergence of ideas, including scientific and cultural ideas, whose specific characteristics are ultimately traceable to the dominant political economy of the time. The formation of national economies was therefore not a conspiracy or a project driven by some determined and visionary capitalist class.[9] But equally, it was not the outcome, as the constructivists suggest, of new ideas, divorced from the social and economic conditions of the time.[10]

The logic of the argument dictates that chapter 4 should follow with an analysis of the relationship between capitalism and the discrete state system. I have, however, deviated from this logic: chapter four narrates the next three phases of the evolution of the offshore world, during the twentieth century. The reason is that the full implications of the origins of offshore are revealed only much later, toward the end of the twentieth century. For it is only when the offshore economy achieves maturity that the true significance of this contradictory coupling at the heart of its formation becomes clear. Only now does the offshore economy undermine the very ideals of the discrete nation-state upon which it relied. I return, therefore, to the analysis of international capitalism and the nation-state in chapter 6.

The study of the historical relationship between offshore and the discrete state system sets this book apart. It also supports my principal contention, namely, that the offshore world is not a peripheral development but is structurally related to, and indeed enables, the globalizing tendencies of the modern economy.[11] And yet the basic principles that would later be exploited to develop the offshore economy were not evident at the outset in the late nineteenth century. True, there were a few isolated incidents which have resonance in later developments, such as Delaware's and New Jersey's competitive corporation laws which have similarities to both tax havens and EPZs, but the intentional policy of sovereign bifurcation took place much later. The earliest incidences of such purposeful policies can in fact be traced back only to the early 1920s. Why is that? The reasons have largely to do with the defeat of Germany. As we will see in chapter 4, the system of reparations imposed on defeated Germany stimulated the rise of Switzerland and Liechtenstein as tax havens. (Liechtenstein had just broken its legal ties with Austria and ended up with much the same tax code as the Swiss.) Similarly, the emergence of the Panamanian flag of convenience was originally linked, if only indirectly, to the Reparations problem.

Corporate capitalism entered a profound crisis in 1929, a crisis that was resolved only after World War II with the emergence of new social compact—what is called the "Fordist social compromise" or "embedded liberalism" (Ruggie 1982). The period of Fordism brought about qualitative and quantitative rises in taxation and state regulation. During this period—after 1957 to be exact—there emerged a new breed of offshore financial market, the Euromarket. Understandably, the golden years of the postwar economic boom (1945–1970), characterized by strict financial regulation throughout the world and rising personal and business taxation, also saw a steady rise in the use of offshore facilities, particularly of flags of convenience which reached their apogee in the 1960s. Yet, less obviously, a veritable explosion of offshore took place later, during so-called "crisis of Fordism" in the 1970s and 1980s. This period saw important changes in the nature of capitalism, most notably the rise of neoliberalism, which included at its core the liberalization of markets and in particular financial markets. It was only now, when national restrictions and regulations on economic activity were being rapidly reduced, that the offshore economy came into its own. Thus, rising taxation and regulation could not have been the principal cause of the huge expansion of the offshore economy in the 1970s—for the simple reason that the increase in taxation and regulation preceded the most rapid proliferation of offshore by a good few years. A number of authors have suggested that the rise of the Euromarket, tax havens, and EPZs had to do with more fundamental changes in the nature of capitalist economies. In particular, they emphasize the new phase in the internationalization of American business (Arrighi 1994; Duménil and Lévy 2001). The Euromarket and the tax havens provided, they argue, financial support for the new wave of relocation and investment overseas, and EPZs pulled investment into the Third World by providing the material infrastructure for the internationalization of manufacturing. Similarly, the Internet is nowadays providing the material infrastructure for the internationalization of retail and services.

The new phase of internationalization is a prelude for a more comprehensive reorganization of global capitalism. At this stage, we can see how the offshore economy is playing also an important ideological role in the construction of what Stephen Gills calls "global constitutionalism." In his words: "What is being attempted is the creation of a political economy and social order where public policy is premised upon the dominance of the investor and reinforcing the protection of his or her property rights. The mobile investor becomes the sovereign political subject" (Gill 1998, 25).

Why is the "freedom" of the investor—operating primarily through offshore, as this book will show—so closely associated with a new global constitutionalism? Every society adopts an organizing myth, constituting itself in the name of some absent presence: God, or the nation, or the working classes (Debray 1981). These unifying categories are simultaneously present, in that they concretely shape societal goals and values, and yet absent, in that they invoke a speculative reality and hence require an interpreter who can tell the rest of society what God, the nation, or the working classes demand of it. The abstracted consumer/investor plays precisely such a role in modern discourse, as the unifying abstraction of the new organizing myth: everything is legitimized in the name of this supposedly aggrieved consumer/investor. New structures of penalties and rewards are installed, often violently, in the name of these abstract social categories which are intentionally ambiguous, depicting a faceless mass of individuated subjects. For "investors," "savers," or "consumers" are abstract identities. However prevalent these terms may be in current political discourse, they do not approximate concrete political constituencies. There is not, nor can there be, a social class of investors—although neoliberal ideologists openly seek to universalize the concept by presenting everyone as at least a potential investor (for example, through pension funds). It is important, therefore, that the political project of global constitutionalism is advanced in the name of identities that by their very nature cannot mobilize politically; the program recognizes, of course, their inability to mobilize and hence presents "responsible" governments with the task of speaking in the name of this supposedly disenfranchised silent majority. Global constitutionalism is advanced as the new human rights of the global investor, and offshore, not surprisingly, is often treated in terms of basic human rights: the right of small states to determine their own laws; the right of individuals to place their savings where they wish; the right of corporations to avoid punitive taxation and regulation.

And yet it is difficult to dissociate the apparently rising power of the "sovereign investor" from the broader shift in society away from the goals of full employment and universal welfare, and toward consumers' rights and business-friendly regimes, from national political economies centered on citizenship to a global political economy centered on open-market ideology. This shift is violent: its effects on the majority of the population in the world are violent, and it is all too often advanced by violent means. But it is presented in technocratic, neutral language—the language of market efficiency, equilibrium, and so on. Neoliberal discourse therefore privileges the "domestic" consumer whose "freedoms" are increasingly measured in terms of rights to consume goods and services wherever and whenever they desire. It is a discourse that is self-fulfilling, bringing about the very changes it seeks to achieve in the name of these aggrieved abstract constituencies. These freedoms are commensurate with Gill's "investor" who seeks protection from nationally (i.e., socially and sometimes democratically) sanctioned interventions that may inhibit his or her "freedoms." The Diamonds imply, as we saw above, that such "protection" is best found in the realm of offshore; hence their belief in the coming century of offshore investment.

Now, political programs and ideologies do not operate in a vacuum; they interpret, shape, and harness a realm of possibilities. The presentation of offshore (as indeed it is popularly understood) as external to the state helps define praxis by holding out prospects of "practical possibilities" open to states and businesses. Thus, offshore provides the perfect legitimization of the goals of neoliberalism in terms of pragmatic social aims, defined as "what can we reasonably expect under current circumstances," conveniently forgetting that the realm of possibility is a socially constructed one.

In that sense offshore has a very clear and disturbing role in the organization of the absent promise of globalization and the resulting requirement that state and society bow to necessity and adapt to globalization. From an ideological standpoint, it is crucial, therefore, that offshore establish not only juridical boundaries, but also imaginary boundaries between the discourse of flows and that of stability; between its own unhindered, mobile, and dynamic space and the territorially immobile nation-state (Cameron and Palan 1999). Offshore is the praxis that celebrates the futility of state response to capital, for it is "inherent in its [capital's] nature constantly to drive beyond its own barrier" (Marx [1858] 1973, 270). We can see now why offshore is centrally related to neoliberal globalization and the project of global constitutionalism.

At this moment, the very condition that brought about the world of offshore, a system of discrete national entities, seems to be under threat—not least from the expansion of the offshore world. The threat is not only material, in the sense that offshore erodes the tax base of modern states, but just as much ideological and cultural: offshore erodes, I contend, the ideological foundations of the nation-state. Offshore is certainly not the sole cause for the decline of the nation-state (which, I should stress, is different from the state—offshore in fact gives the state a new lease on life) but it must be seen as an important contributing factor.

Beyond the erosion of nationalist ideologies and the nation-state, something more fundamental is taking place. The nature of space itself is changing, or rather the relationship between power, space, and territory is undergoing important transformations. I end this book with a speculative argument, suggesting that offshore has become the vehicle for a transformation from territorial *striated* spaces to the *nomadic* spaces of modern "numerical" capitalism. Capitalism is a nomadic social organization, and nomadic spaces are oddly nonterritorial. They present themselves as "smooth" territories as Deleuze and Guattari (1987) describe them, in which spaces and distances take on a new meaning. Offshore has a lot of similarity with such nomadic spaces, and this suggests that offshore may be at the very heart of the transformation of modern politics. Indeed, I believe we can already see in the contemporary configuration of offshore the contours of a new type of political formation. Is it the beginning of "postglobalization"?

# CHAPTER ONE

# The Offshore Economy in Its Contemporary Settings

Conjuring images of pristine sandy beaches adorned by lone palm trees, the offshore economy has been attracting attention recently. Offshore captivates our imagination with its contradictory promises: it is the last frontier, the last remaining truly exotic feature of the age of global capital. This is the domain of the "PTs," the "permanent tourists," a nomadic tribe of tax exiles floating between foreign lands, never truly reaching home, never needing or wishing to moor in the heavily regulated and taxed "dry land" (Maurer 1998). From the shores of Barbados to the Channel Islands and the Seychelles, offshore has set deep roots in former pirate hideouts; and like the pirates of old, it is romanticized and feared in equal measure. Not surprisingly, offshore has become a metaphor for a way of life, for the great escape. Business has not been slow to appreciate the power of this dream. Banks advertise offshore accounts in the back pages of financial journals; lawyers and accountants dangle the promise of substantial reductions in taxation by going offshore; countries publicize their tax advantages in travel magazines.

But offshore has also been attracting unwanted attention lately—mainly on account of its role in facilitating every kind of illegitimate activity. Already by the early 1990s, the combined value of the international drug business was estimated at $300 billion a year, making it one of the largest economic sectors in the world (Gilmore 1992). This criminal underworld takes advantage of the veil of secrecy surrounding tax havens and the offshore world to launder its ill-gotten gains into apparently legitimate money. In addition to drugs, arms trafficking and other international criminal activities have all been linked to the offshore world. The finances of virtually every insurrection, civil war, terrorist attack, and greedy dictator appear to be conducted offshore.

But however important the criminal side of the offshore economy may be, it pales into insignificance when compared to offshore's true impact on state and society. This book is grounded in a proposition that is admittedly neither universally accepted nor widely debated—namely, that a considerable portion of the world economy already has migrated, or is in the process of migrating to these unique juridical spaces. What then is the offshore world? Where are its boundaries? Who set it up? This chapter offers a broad overview of the offshore economy. I begin with an examination of the legal and analytical aspects of the term.

### THE MEANING OF "OFFSHORE"

Key in "offshore" in your library's database and you are likely to come up with texts about the oil industry and offshore drilling. Your library's database may also contain references to "offshore investments." For instance, a publication of the Organization for Economic Cooperation and Development (OECD) describes the foreign direct investments of national telecommunications carriers as "offshore investments" (OECD 1995). This latter meaning chimes well with another, frequently heard, expression, "going offshore," which means investing abroad or alternatively is used sometimes as a euphemism for the legal evasion of domestic restrictions. The International Monetary Fund (IMF) and the World Bank classify an extensive range of material under the label of "offshore assembly lines,"—usually (though, frustratingly, not always) in reference to manufacturing and assembly lines situated in export processing zones (EPZs) and special economic zones.

The financial literature employs the concept of offshore in a more restricted sense to describe unregulated international financial markets (the Euromarket). But this meaning has been a source of controversy. An influential study commissioned by the Australian government in the early 1980s takes the view that the Euromarket is only one, albeit important, dimension of a broader category called the "offshore financial market" (Hewson 1982) For Roberts, in contrast, offshore markets are simply "markets for currencies, loans, bonds and a host of other financial instruments which exist beyond the reach of regulation by the originating national economy" (1994, 93). More recently, the category of "onshore-offshore banking" has entered the vocabulary of international finance in reference to the establishment of "international banking facilities" (IBFs) in, among other places, New York, Chicago, Tokyo, and Bangkok.

The IMF and the Bank for International Settlements (BIS) have added to the confusion by characterizing tax havens as "offshore financial centers." These are defined as "jurisdictions in which transactions with non-residents far outweigh transactions related to the domestic economy" (Dixon 2001). The BIS duly established the Offshore Supervisors Group consisting of the representatives of the following countries: Aruba, Bahamas, Bahrain, Barbados, Bermuda, Cayman Islands, Cyprus, Gibraltar, Guernsey, Hong Kong, Isle of Man, Jersey, Lebanon, Malta, Mauritius, Netherlands Antilles, Panama, Singapore, and Vanuatu (BIS 1996). Although this list includes some of the better-known and more notorious tax havens, and many of those that conform to the exotic image that the term conjures up, it does not include the world's largest offshore center—the City of London. Despite accounting for a significant proportion of the total trade passing through the offshore economy, London is not considered by the BIS as an offshore financial center at all.[1]

A number of authors have applied the concept of the tax haven to other spheres of activity such as flags of convenience (Oppenheimer 1985) and export processing zones. The list of offshore and tax haven activities has recently grown to include such items as Internet pornography routed through jurisdictions such as Guyana, Tuvalu, and Niue (*Economist* 1997; Hussein 1997), on-line gambling by way of Costa Rica and Gibraltar, and the rapid rise of offshore e-commerce (McLure 1997).[2]

Given such a wide range of definitions, it comes as no surprise to learn that many scholars raise doubts whether the term "offshore" can be used with any precision. In many ways the doubters are correct, for there are obvious differences between, say, offshore finance (which operates in juridical spaces that are fundamentally fictive) and EPZs (which involve the manufacturing of real goods in real places). I believe, however, that the term is worth keeping. For the apparently bewildering array of economic transactions that constitute the offshore economy shares one important attribute: they all take place in specially designed juridical enclaves distinguished from their onshore counterparts by the removal of some or all state regulation. Offshore, therefore, refers not to a geographical location but rather to a set of juridical realms marked by more or less withdrawal of regulation and taxation on the part of a growing number of states. Often the bifurcation of the sovereign space of the state that this implies is performed in order to attract international business. The idea is that in the age of mobile capital, domestic laws affect not only those residing within a given territory, but also those outside. In that sense, offshore laws and regulations belong to the category of what Alfred Conrad calls "strictly-for-export" laws

(1973, 633)—laws enacted by the domestic authorities of states, but aimed exclusively at persons and institutions located beyond their borders.[3] Some of these offshore enclaves are territorial in nature, such as EPZs, while others are virtual juridical enclaves that have no physical boundaries, such as the Euromarket, flags of convenience, and IBFs. Often offshore tax and regulatory regimes apply to specific sectors throughout an entire territory. Tax havens, for example, often apply extremely liberal tax regimes and a minimal degree of regulation to some sectors (particularly international finance and more recently e-commerce) throughout their territory. At the same time, these states regulate and control other sectors such as tourism and construction, just like other states. They may appear, therefore, to be paradigmatic liberal nation-states, maximizing the national income in pursuit of the common goals of the nation, but they are not. In fact, they differ fundamentally from the conventional nation-state in that they divide their sovereign territories into distinct offshore and onshore spaces. In this sense, offshore has to be distinguished from other trends in the world economy such as privatization and deregulation. These usually apply to entire sovereign territorial spaces, albeit targeted at specific industrial and service sectors, and reflect a conventional liberal philosophy of enhancing "national" corporate economic efficiency. Offshore, by contrast divides the sovereign corporate space of the nation into (at least) two virtual territories characterized by different degrees of regulation and taxation, specifically to attract mobile international business. The boundaries between offshore and onshore, however, are constantly changing as states try to lure businesses back onshore by removing or easing domestic regulation and taxation.

It is only to be expected that the great number of offshore jurisdictions and the ingenuity they display defy any attempt at a simple and straightforward definition. We find, for example, many cases on the margins: special laws and regulations enacted to attract certain businesses and sometimes even wealthy individuals. Nevertheless, the combination of juridical bifurcation and regimes designed to attract international investors by offering lower regulation and taxation can be considered a universal characteristic of offshore.

This description of our subject matter alerts us to the intimate relationship between state, sovereignty, and the offshore world. On the one hand, the offshore economy is driven by the desire of individuals and firms to escape regulation, taxation, and public scrutiny. Paradoxically, however, the offshore world was created in the first place, and has been supported and maintained ever since, by the very state system it is supposed to evade. It is, therefore, the relationship between state and sovereignty which is at the heart of the offshore phenomenon. Here, again we need to be cautious with our terminology. As we will see, some of the more successful tax havens, such as the British Virgin Islands or the Channel Islands, are not fully sovereign, but are dependencies of sovereign states—in these cases, the United Kingdom. But these jurisdictions' offshore strategies rely on a crucial factor, namely, that they have the right to make law within their territories—a crucial attribute of sovereignty that can also be accorded to dependencies. This allows them to participate in the offshore phenomenon, and it is this aspect of sovereignty that is being commercialized. But offshore cannot be understood simply in terms of the interaction between state and sovereignty. Rather we need to see this relationship in the light of a third dimension, namely, capitalism.

## THE ORIGINS OF THE TERM "OFFSHORE": THE EXAMPLE OF RADIO LUXEMBOURG

Andrew Sayer observes that "new concepts can only be developed from pre-existing ones. We generally try to explain the unfamiliar by reference to the familiar. It is therefore not surprising that closer examination of our vocabulary shows it to be rich in metaphor" (1982, 63). The contemporary association of the metaphor of offshore with certain types of economic activities evolved precisely in this manner and, indeed, the term "offshore" was in use for a long time prior to its recent appropriation by political economists and bankers. A collection of poetry published in the late nineteenth century, for example, was entitled *Offshore*. It celebrated Britain's status as an offshore island, near to the European continent and yet sufficiently separated from it to have a distinct identity (Fitzgerald 1979). It was, however, only in the early 1970s, that the idea of proximity combined with separateness was employed to describe certain sectors of the world economy.

The financial services industry trade journal *The Banker* claims to have coined the term "offshore" as a description of the Euromarket in 1971.[4] *The Banker* does not explain, however, why it adopted the metaphor in the first place. The explanation may be gleaned from elsewhere. In *The International Money Game* (1976), Robert Aliber devotes a chapter to a comparison between Radio Luxembourg and the Euromarket; both, he says, are offshore stations. Although Aliber makes no claims about the origins of offshore, the similarities between the pirate radio stations that appeared during the 1960s and the Euromarket must have struck contemporaries.

Like other sectors of the offshore economy, broadcasting was traditionally heavily regulated; but just like finance, it had the inherent capacity to transcend national boundaries. During the 1930s a number of English-language stations based in France took advantage of the difficulty of blocking radio transmissions and began to broadcast popular programs aimed at a British audience. Radio Luxembourg, which began broadcasting in 1959, took up where the French radio stations left off. It was a commercial broadcasting station based in Luxembourg, with what was then considered a massively powerful 1.2 megawatt transmitter. Radio Luxembourg's principal audience lay in Britain and France, neither of which then licensed commercial radio stations.

The success of Radio Luxembourg attracted imitations, some enchanted by the prospect of moneymaking, others driven by political motives. These imitators, the "pirate" or "offshore" radio stations of the 1960s, took the next logical step. As the *Offshore Echo* magazine observes (2002), these stations occupied the " 'no mans land' of international waters, outside countries' boundaries." The most famous among them was Radio Caroline which made its first broadcast on Easter Saturday 1964 from the MV *Caroline* anchored in the Thames River estuary. She was soon joined by a host of other offshore stations located on ships and abandoned wartime antiaircraft forts.

Radio Luxembourg and other radio pirate stations served as vivid examples of the sort of arrangements that lie at the heart of the offshore economy. Strictly speaking, the stations were legal; they simply took advantage of principles enshrined in international law. It was entirely within the rights of Luxembourg, as a sovereign state, to frame its broadcasting laws as it wished. Notwithstanding the small size of its territory, it was entirely within its sovereign rights in allowing a huge radio transmitter to be erected. No doubt, the Luxembourg broadcasting authorities were perfectly aware of the true intentions of the station, not least because the capacity of the transmitter far exceeded the requirements of a domestic broadcaster. The great success of Radio Luxembourg generated jobs and income for the people of Luxembourg, something few governments could be persuaded to forgo.

Whereas Radio Luxembourg sheltered behind the sovereignty of a territorial state—essentially rendering Luxembourg a broadcasting tax haven—the other offshore radio stations took advantage of the same set of legal principles to locate in international waters. In that sense they served, as we will see below, as the broadcasting equivalent of the Euromarket. In both cases unique juridical spaces were created with the aim of subverting or even eliminating state regulation.

The popularity of the offshore radio stations probably helped the dissemination of the concept of offshore more generally. In its modern usage, however—not on dry land, near the coast—it may have originated as an oblique reference to a set of legal precedents and principles that inform the treatment of coastal waters, namely, the law of the sea.

The relationship between offshore and the law of the sea is, however, open to a number of interpretations depending on the legal assumptions underpinning it. In Roman law, the sea and the right to exploit its resources, for example by fishing, belonged to all humanity. By extension, offshore might be interpreted as any area that belongs to all humanity. It may be argued that this ancient legal principle was employed at a later date by emergent nation-states to legitimize the creation of territorial sovereignty. How is that? The very concept of territorial sovereignty (which is, as we will see, a relatively recent development in human history) implies the division of the surface of the earth not only among states, but also between sovereign and nonsovereign territories. Some territories are under the exclusive rule of one sovereign state, but other territories, such as the oceans or space, are under no such control. In other words, to establish territorial boundaries, the state system had to establish legal boundaries not only between one state territory and another, but also between national and international spaces (Kish 1973). Offshore may be understood metaphorically as extraterritorial, international space, a universal "common," possessing much the same status that the oceans have in the conventions that make up the law of the sea. In the same way, offshore places certain activities "outside" the territorial boundaries of any one state but within the confines of the principles of sovereignty which define, as in the case of the sea, such common areas.

Intriguingly, however, offshore also alludes to a different aspect of the law of the sea; its provisions regarding coastal waters. The earliest legal provisions for coastal waters involved the distribution of favors by rulers, such as exclusive rights to shallow fishing grounds and salt deposits in tidal marshes, exemption from port or harbor dues, and unhindered transit through straits (Prescott 1975, 24). Concomitantly, the law of the sea dealt with strategic problems. Since naval operations take place in waters purportedly outside state boundaries, the danger of foreign ships approaching the shore and bombarding at will had to be averted. Monarchs felt obliged to make claims to areas beyond the physical boundaries of the state and in doing so they established the principle that decrees that a state's legal boundaries do not necessarily strictly correspond to its land boundaries.

In the European historical context, the emergence of a particularistic political order coincided with the strengthening of such claims. Historically, two conflicting trends are in evidence. During the Middle Ages, many seas had been more or less appropriated by states. The most notable examples were the republic of Venice, which assumed sovereignty over the whole of the Adriatic Sea, and the republic of Genoa, which advanced similar claims over the Ligurian Sea. The Scandinavian countries extended their dominion over the Baltic, and the English crown claimed sovereignty over the "English Sea" (the Channel and part of the North Sea). The most extravagant claims were promulgated by the pope who divided, rather optimistically, the whole expanse of the great oceans between Spain and Portugal in the late fifteenth century (Fulton 1911). Such extensive claims were, in fact, abandoned by the seventeenth century, and replaced by more modest and pragmatic claims to sovereignty over adjacent territorial waters. As we will see, this shift can be seen as part of a more general trend that saw the establishment of clearly demarcated nation-states. The earliest published claim to a specific width of the coastline was made in the fourteenth century when the Paduan jurist Bartolous made the recommendation that one hundred miles was the correct distance (Prescott 1975, 24). For the next four centuries, a great number of unilateral declarations were made about the extent of the territorial waters, but there was no international agreement or norm until the early nineteenth century. In any case, coinciding with these developments, the law of the sea increasingly acknowledged certain limitations on sovereign claims over territorial waters and recognized that "there were jurisdictions of various kinds and for various purposes"(Fulton 1911, 3).

The law of sea established, therefore, three principles that have subsequently played an important role in setting up the offshore economy. First was the idea that certain regions of the planet are "universal commons" belonging to all humanity. Second—a principle which will become progressively more significant as we explore the virtual character of offshore spaces—was the idea of what may be described as discontinuity between legal and physical boundaries. While sovereignty in the past four centuries has become increasingly territorial in nature, the law of the sea recognized that sovereign rights need not correspond precisely to the physical contours of the land. Crucially, that meant that sovereign claims were no longer bound strictly by topography but could draw on theoretical arguments about effective sovereignty and special economic rights (McDougal and Burke 1962, 597). This principle opened the door for a definition of boundaries of states along fictional or imaginary lines, such as the upper limit of airspace, which on occasion could be entirely divorced from geographical or topographical limitations.

At the same time, a third principle evolved throughout the centuries, recognizing the possibility of relative rather than absolute sovereign claims over certain territories. For example, the law recognized a limited sovereignty of states over their coastal waters. Based on this third principle offshore may be deemed, from a legal point of view, to be an area adjacent to sovereign territory that is subject to relative rather than absolute sovereignty. In this way, the term "offshore" captures rather well this extraordinary combination of juridico-political phenomena within lightly regulated sovereign enclaves.

These three principles proved particularly useful in guiding modern law with regard to developments in communication and transportation technologies. As we will see in chapter 4, once the principle of imaginary shores was established, it was extended not only horizontally but also vertically, so that the juridical boundaries of the state were extended upward to an agreed point in the sky. This upper limit to state sovereignty—the "Von Kármán line"—was set at 50.550 miles (Cohen 1981, 18). At the same time, the right of innocent passage of airplanes and other flying objects was extended to the new atmospheric "shores" or "airspace," establishing in effect a kind of a three-dimensional sovereign cage. The idea could be extended further and serve as the basis of juridical "shores" the boundaries of which are not topographical or geographical, but merely specify objects or processes that are considered to be within territorial sovereignty. Thus discontinuity between physical and juridical boundaries could serve as the basis for a de facto increase in the size of the spatial domain of the state, as national laws invaded other states' territories. But also, surprisingly, the discontinuity permitted states to voluntarily decrease the size of their holdings, slicing off portions of their sovereign domains and defining them as "offshore." Thus, states could simply decree, either explicitly or implicitly, that certain types of transactions or objects be considered offshore.

The concept of offshore alerts us, therefore, to something jurists knew all along, that the presumption of strict territorial sovereign boundaries may be a necessary fiction, but cannot be sustained in reality. We tend to assume that the state contains all that happens within its geographical boundaries, but that is strictly speaking incorrect. The state is a juridical-political entity, whose realm of activities and control are defined in and through the vocabulary of the law. The law, in turn, draws on different systems of thought that have evolved over a long period of time. Offshore demonstrates to us that in a subtle way, the juridical domain of the state corresponds only very roughly to its geographical territory, and that the social and legal character of the state certainly takes precedence over commonsense representation of its territorial domain. Thus, contrary to common perception, "shores" in legal parlance do not necessarily define the outer boundaries of sovereignty, but rather define areas or territories in which claims of sovereignty are more complex.

The ambiguities of the different principles of the law of the sea are contained in offshore—rendering it a complex and dynamic phenomenon. The ambiguities are also exploited to advance certain political and economic interests. In any case, these complex juridical processes ensure a central role for lawyers in the construction and sustenance of the offshore economy. At the same time we should not lose sight of the important social and political interests served by offshore, masquerading under the guise of esoteric legal parlance and juridical niceties.

### OFFSHORE FINANCE

We can now turn to the contemporary offshore world. Although a late arrival, the most significant portion of the contemporary offshore economy is undoubtedly the offshore financial market(s). I have already mentioned that financial experts lament the lack of exact definition of offshore finance (Financial Stability Forum 2000; Hewson 1982, 406). Some use the term as though synonymous with "Euromarket." For others the Euromarket is merely the "quintessential" manifestation of a broader type that they call offshore finance (Roberts 1994, 3). For others again, offshore finance is associated primarily with the offshore financial centers, or tax havens.[5] The International Monetary Fund prefers to define offshore finance as "the provision of financial services by banks and other agents to non residents" (IMF 2000, 2).

Notwithstanding, the generally accepted view is that the offshore financial markets consist primarily of the various segments of the Euromarket. Among these, the Eurodollar market is essentially a market for lending and borrowing the world's most important convertible (hard) currencies. It is a "wholesale" or interbank market used primarily by commercial banks. The exact origins of the Euromarket remain in dispute (Burn 1999 and 2000; Schenk 1998). Difficulties in dating the origins of the Euromarket are due, in part, to a failure to distinguish between the market for dollars that emerged in Europe in the late 1940s, and the almost entirely unregulated market for foreign currencies, initially trading in American dollars, that emerged in 1957.[6]

It is still not clear whether the Euromarket was the product of intentional policy decision or of a series of fortuitous developments. But whatever the precise cause for its emergence, there is little doubt that the British government played a key role in its establishment. London's position as the heart of the offshore financial market can be traced back to attempts by successive British governments to reestablish London as the center of global financial activities after World War II. Under the 1939 Currency (Defense) Act which established exchange controls at the beginning of World War II, British banks had been prevented from dealing in foreign currencies. However, under the 1947 Exchange Control Act, some banks were given permission to deal in foreign currency. In December 1951, the foreign exchange market opened in London. However, while all other currencies were traded freely, sterling remained controlled and could be sold and bought only by designated banks.

The Foreign exchange market handled primarily nonresident dollars. Milan and Paris vied with London as a home for these early dollar deposits. But as Burn argues, "it was only when UK local authorities were prevented from raising money through the Public Loans Board in 1955, and began to look for another source of funding that an alternative, more profitable, use for these expatriate dollars was found outside of the US banking system; subsequent, of course, to them being exchanged for sterling and moving into Britain's domestic money market"(2000, 134). Yet for the Eurodollar market to become a true offshore market, dollars had to be deposited and re-lent outside the jurisdiction of—not only the U.S. banking system, but all national banking systems. This innovation took place, according to Burn, in September 1957.

The immediate impetus for the innovation seems to have been the sterling crisis of 1957. This crisis had originally been caused by the U.S. administration, which sold large quantities of sterling in order to put pressure on Britain to withdraw from its occupation of the Suez Canal.

The British government responded by increasing the bank rate from 5 to 7 percent, and simultaneously reducing demand for sterling by restricting its use in non–sterling area trade, and reducing the maximum period for other sterling credits. "This latter measure," writes Burn "had the direct effect of cutting off the source of funding by which British merchant and overseas banks conducted a considerable amount of business." The small, undercapitalized merchant banks were unable to call directly on the cheap deposit base of the clearing banks. They were forced to look for a new source of finance, which they found in nonresident dollars collecting in the Eurodollar market.

The Eurodollar in effect allowed the merchant banks to continue with their business. Yet, "with these dollars deposits not needing, necessarily, to be swapped into sterling (or any other currency) before being traded and, hence, not coming under exchange control regulations, what marked the start of the City's role as an entrepôt center, also heralded the beginning of the offshore Euro-dollar market proper" (Burn 2000). The new method of financing by the merchant banks produced a subtle but important reinterpretation of the purview of British sovereignty. It placed dollar transactions—and all other third-party currency transactions for that matter—outside the exchange rate regulations, reserve regulations, or any other regulations of the British state. But since these transactions took place within the territorial boundaries of the United Kingdom, they were also sheltered from the regulation of any other state. They were de facto under the regulation of no state![7] The British government allowed, and perhaps even encouraged the merchant banks to turn to American dollars, for otherwise they would have gone out of business. This is the basis of one prevalent interpretation that holds the British government responsible for the rise of the Euromarket (Helleiner 1994). Although there is some evidence that certain key officials and bankers were aware of the possibility of such a loophole, Gary Burn's research found no direct evidence for such encouragement.

We need to appreciate, however, that the term "British government" has to be approached with great care. As Gary Burn has shown, mention of the Euromarket in both British and U.S. official documents cannot be traced prior to the early 1960s. Indeed, it appears that the Bank of England and the U.S. Federal Reserve banks both kept their respective governments out of the loop. However, in Britain at least, there was a lively interchange of personnel at all levels between the commercial banks and the Bank of England, formally an agent of the state. Hence representatives of these smaller banks played a key role in setting the agenda of the Bank of England. So whether or not the British government intentionally established the Euromarket depends to a large extent on one's definition of the government. There is no doubt, however, that subsequently the British government knowingly supported the growth of the Euromarket in the City of London. In fact, it became a cornerstone of British economic policy.

Burn argues that, on the one hand, "the nascent Eurodollar market inherited a large part of its institutional structure and techniques from the City's Victorian system for financing international trade. The Euromarket emerged effectively out of a regulatory vacuum in the City" (2000, 234). In fact, as we will see in the case of the tax havens, the emergence of the Euromarket in London rests to some extent on a quirk of history. Unlike continental law which prescribes what is allowed, English common law prescribes only what is forbidden. As it happens, the Bank Control Act of 1947 did not prohibit authorized dealers from dealing in foreign currency deposits between nonresidents, and in addition "the nature of the Bank's supervisory role as one constrained by the absence in English law of any definitive legislation either to define organizations as banks, or to define and sanction the Bank's role as a supervisory authority over the banking system [resulted in the inability] of the Bank to impose supervision on banks to meet the Bank of England's own wish"(Burn 1999, 236).

To ensure the legality of their third-party transactions, the British banks, soon joined by branches of American and other foreign banks in London, kept two sets of books: one for "onshore" financial transactions in which at least one party to the transaction was British; and the other for the Euromarket or "offshore" transactions where both parties were non-British. Thus, as Hanzawa (1991) notes, despite its size and importance, the Euromarket might be considered as essentially no more than a bookkeeping device! It is the financial equivalent of the offshore radio stations—deemed to be located in no-man's-land, yet protected by the very principles of sovereignty (Aliber 1976).

For a decade or so, this arrangement remained a small interbank operation used primarily by a few commercial banks, and occasionally by central banks like the Bank of Italy and the Bundesbank (Fry 1970; Grant 1967; Higonnet 1985; Kane 1983). In 1963, however, the interbank currency market was supplemented by the Eurobond market, dealing in bonds underwritten by international banking syndicates and not subject to any country's securities laws (Park 1982). By this time the

British government was firmly behind the new market. Many have argued that misconceived U.S. policies also unwittingly gave stimulus to an enormous expansion of the Eurocurrency and Eurobond markets.

Confronted by the periodical panics over real or imagined declines of U.S. economic power, the Kennedy administration sought to slow down the migration of its currency abroad, some of which fueled the Euromarket. Worries about a deteriorating balance of payments led to what David Calleo describes as "the temporizing policy known as adhockery, a series of expedients designed to bolster the dollar during what was imagined to be only a temporary period of weakness" (1982, 20). Among these "adhockery" policies two measures stood out. First was the United States Revenue Act of 1962, which contained a series of amendments designed to curtail the use of tax havens by American companies. The paradoxical result, note the Diamonds, was to encourage the use of tax havens throughout the world (Diamond and Diamond 1998, 1). Normally profits become taxable only when they return as dividends to the home country. Companies have learned, therefore, to place their profits in tax havens, which in turn enables working capital to be used in its cheapest form. Tax havens are used as central points for handling paperwork and preparing and processing trade documents. The amendments to the 1962 Revenue Act sought to restrict the use of tax havens by limiting the deferral form of current U.S. taxation to earnings of less than 30 percent of profit. The Tax Reduction Act of 1975 then reduced this further to 10 percent. This simply discouraged American companies from repatriating profits to the United States, thereby greatly furthering the spectacular rise of various new offshore financial centers.

The other significant "adhockery" policy came in the form of a series of amendments to U.S. financial laws designed to keep capital at home and reduce the pressure on the dollar. In July 1963, Congress enacted the so-called Interest Equalization Tax on the acquisition of foreign securities. The law provided for the imposition of a tax upon the purchase by a U.S. resident from a foreign resident of common stock issued by a foreign corporation, or of a debt obligation with a remaining life in excess of one year. The idea was to discourage U.S. residents from investing in foreign bonds and shares (Dufey and Giddy 1987). Failing this, the Federal Reserve then instituted the Voluntary Foreign Credit Restraint Program to curb borrowing by foreign firms and governments in U.S. markets. At the same time the Foreign Direct Investment Program was declared, which limited the amount of capital U.S. firms could ship abroad (Kapstein 1994, 35). The effect was if anything the opposite to that intended, as U.S. firms simply refused to repatriate their earnings.[8] The excess liquidity fueled the growth of the Euromarket.

Although it was strictly speaking a virtual or fictional market, the Euromarket grew by leaps and bounds. The Euromarket's main advantages were the almost complete lack of regulation. There were no interest rate ceilings, reserve requirements, and exchange controls, nor any withholding of interest income to meet tax or disclosure requirements. Furthermore, financial intermediaries were not subject to the regulation that might have inhibited expansion in their domestic markets.[9] Due to these competitive advantages, banks and other financial intermediaries were able to offer better rates in the offshore financial markets. As a result, from small beginnings, the Euromarket grew exponentially to dominate international financial transactions.

Today the offshore financial market comprises several markets: Eurocurrency deposits, Eurocurrency bank loans, Euronotes, Eurobonds, Eurosecurities, and the foreign exchange market "as a particular 'infrastructure' for all cross-border transactions"(Filipovic 1997, 21).[10] The exact size of the combined Eurocurrency markets is hard to measure. Morgan has estimated that the gross size of the Eurocurrency market in 1998 stood at $4,561 billion; the net size was put at $2,587 billion. Morgan also reported that Eurodollars made up 67 percent of gross Eurocurrency liabilities, putting the gross size of the Eurodollar market at $3,056 billion (The Turin Group 2002). An estimated 80 percent of international banking transactions are made in Eurocurrencies (Rose 1995), and by June 1997, 88 percent of international loans were Euroloans (Lewis 1999, 91).

Not surprisingly, the success of the Euromarket bred imitators. Since the early 1970s, the Euromarket has spread throughout the world and the U.S. dollar has been supplemented by all the major international hard currencies. Hence the term "offshore financial market" is deemed more appropriate than "Euromarket" (Rose 1995). Of the various Euromarket segments, the best known is the foreign exchange market, which is most closely associated in the popular mind with the turbulence of the global financial markets. The amount of money passing through this market is astounding. It fluctuates in times of turbulence, with peaks of, for example, $4 trillion in 1994 and $1.5 trillion in April 1998. But throughout the decade it has never been under $1 trillion a day. To this can be added an average daily turnover of $1.4 trillion in the derivatives market (BIS 2002).

The offshore financial market is not entirely unregulated. It is sub-

ject to so-called self-regulation based on "market principles," the effec-
tiveness of which is much disputed, by the banks and other financial
actors that use the market. The best known among a series of self-
regulating agreements was the Capital Adequacy Agreement or Basel
Accord of 1988, which seems to have had a measure of success in pushing up capital requirements. In addition, for the sake of convenience,
clearing goes through New York, giving the U.S. government some
leverage over the market.

The Euromarket is a quintessentially offshore arrangement, enabled
and constrained by the principles of sovereignty. Like the radio stations,
the Euromarket achieves its offshore status because the state on whose
territory it was originally located, the United Kingdom, accepted, or
even produced, an interpretation of its own laws that permitted the fiction that certain types of financial transactions did not take place
within that territory. The principle of territorial sovereignty and the
right of national self-determination ensured that the laws and policies
of the British government had to be accepted by other states. Of course,
if it so wished, the British government could have abandoned this
arrangement. It could have done so in 1957 by extending its policies and
rules to any transactions that took place physically within its territory;
it could have done so in the early 1960s, when the Labour government
got wind of the new market; it could have joined forces with the United
States in the late 1970s in trying to re-regulate the market, and it can
still do so today! However, as time has passed and the Euromarket has
grown in size and complexity, attempts to re-regulate it have become
increasingly dangerous as they risk disrupting the entire international
financial system. The arrangement may have originated in a loophole,
but it is legally sanctioned, and it is ultimately, maintained for political
reasons—because somebody benefits from it. This is something we
should not forget.

An unregulated Euromarket has been, of course, a source of some
concern. Financial experts were initially worried that the money-
creating capacity of the Euromarket could contribute to global infla-
tionary pressures. Although, this concern has faded, the more serious
problem is the volatility of a largely unregulated global financial market of such magnitude, and its concomitant capacity to subvert policy
aims of even the largest states.[11]

## THE SPONTANEOUS OFFSHORE CENTERS: LONDON AND HONG KONG

In spite of being located in a juridical no-man's-land, the offshore financial market (or markets) operates through various financial centers, all of which are subject to the sovereign control of states (Sassen 1991). Many states, however, have gone out of their way to provide legal and political support for the offshore market in their territories. They have produced, broadly speaking, three types of arrangements: the so-called spontaneous offshore sites, such as London and Hong Kong; international banking facilities (or onshore-offshore centers) such as New York and Tokyo; and tax havens. It goes without saying that this typology is not exact and each of its components must be considered an ideal type, since every offshore financial center and tax haven offers its own unique bundle of regulations.

The best-known and the most important among the offshore financial centers is the City of London. It has been dubbed "spontaneous" because its offshore facilities emerged, allegedly, without official direction or even notice. This is a dubious proposition, as we have seen, but the label has stuck. In any case, from 1957 there ensued in Britain a period of progressive relaxation of exchange controls, culminating in the 1979 Banking Act, the first legislation of the Thatcher government, which abolished exchange controls. Since then London has been considered effectively as an offshore financial market.

As a crown colony until its return to Chinese sovereignty, Hong Kong shared the legal and financial regimes of the United Kingdom, and hence with the emergence of London's offshore center, it too developed as an offshore financial center. Hong Kong is generally considered a tax haven because it offers the facility of zero taxation to certain classes of foreign companies. Interestingly, China has chosen so far to maintain the status of Hong Kong as a tax haven.

## INTERNATIONAL BANKING FACILITIES:
### NEW YORK, TOKYO, SINGAPORE, AND THAILAND

An international banking facility is a more stringent type of offshore center, where, in contrast to the spontaneous offshore centers, companies must apply for a license to trade. IBFs have been set up intentionally in order to compete with the spontaneous offshore centers and the tax havens (Lewis 1999). The first IBF (although it was not so called) was the Asian currency units (ACUs) set up in Singapore in 1968. As the widening Indo-China war increased foreign exchange expenditure in the

Asia-Pacific region in the mid-1960s, a tightening of credit occurred in 1967 and 1968 that contributed to rising interest rates in the Eurodollar market. As a result, it became attractive for many banks to tap exiting dollar balances in the region. Singapore responded by setting up facilities that gave incentives for branches of international banks to relocate there. Its first license was granted to a branch of the Bank of America to set up a special international department to handle transactions for nonresidents. As with all other Euromarket operations, the ACUs created separate sets of accounts in which all transactions with nonresidents were recorded. Although the ACUs are not subject to exchange controls, the banks are required to submit to the exchange control authority detailed monthly reports of their transactions (Hodjera 1978).

The better-known IBFs are situated in the United States. The first New York IBF came about as the result of prolonged and complicated battles between the U.S. Treasury, the Swiss government, and a number of Caribbean tax havens. The United States had tried hard to re-regulate the Euromarket in 1979 (Kapstein 1994). Failing that, and with the active encouragement of the New York banking community, particularly Citibank and Chase (Naylor 1987), the U.S. Treasury came to the conclusion that rather than fight the onset of offshore centers, the United States stood to gain more by encouraging its own offshore centers (Hines and Rice 1994). A swift volte-face took place, culminating in the establishment on 3 December 1981 of a New York offshore market, the New York International Banking Facilities (IBF). A decade later more than 540 IBFs have been established across the United States to take advantage of these cost and tax benefits. New York has the largest number (over 250), California has 100, and Florida 80 IBFs. But due to their high degree of regulation compared with other offshore centers, interest in IBFs has waned lately (Lewis 1999).

The New York IBF spawned, in turn, the creation of the Tokyo IBF, otherwise known as the Japanese Offshore Market (JOM). In 1982 the Hosomi plan was put forward in imitation of the New York IBF to spur domestic liberalization. The Tokyo IBF allowed foreign banks into the city, deflecting some of the criticism made by those banks (Hanzawa 1991). Similar facilities are in place in Dublin, Malta, Thailand, and a number of other centers.

In this way, the spontaneous offshore centers and the IBFs have contributed to the creation of an integrated juridical if nonterritorial space defined by differential degree of regulations and taxation which is called the offshore financial market.

*Table 1*
International Financial Centers Ranked by Banks' External Assets, End of
2000 (US$ billions)

| | |
|---|---|
| *United Kingdom* | 2,095 |
| *Japan* (including the Japanese offshore market)[a] | 1,199 |
| Germany | 975 |
| *United States* (including international banking facilities)[b] | 951 |
| **Cayman Islands** | 782 |
| *Switzerland* | 740 |
| France | 640 |
| *Luxembourg* | 510 |
| *Hong Kong* | 450 |
| *Singapore* (including Asian currency market) | 424 |
| Netherlands | 290 |
| Belgium | 285 |
| **Bahamas** | 276 |

*Source:* BIS 2000.
Financial centers with considerable offshore activity are italic; OFCs are bold.
[a]In 1997, around half of the total figure was placed in the Japanese offshore market (Lewis 1999).
[b]In 1997, nearly one third of the total figure was placed in the IBFs (Lewis 1999).

Because of the confusing terminology noted above, official statistics often identify only tax havens as offshore financial centers. The U.S. and U.K. treasuries, however, increasingly use the concept of the "gross domestic product (GDP) multiple," the ratio of GDP to international banking activities, to demonstrate the scale of offshore operations (see table 2). The GDP multiple shows clearly those financial centers, including London, that are employed primarily as entrepôt offshore centers, facilitating financial flows around the world.

*Table 2*
Scale of International Banking Activities in Selected Financial Centers,
end of 2000

|  | GDP | BIS banks' location claims | |
|---|---|---|---|
|  | (US$ billions) | US$ billions | Multiple of GDP |
| Cayman Islands | 0.9 | 482 | 518 |
| British Virgin Islands | 0.3 | 25 | 86 |
| Crown Dependencies | 4.6 | 234 | 51 |
| Bahamas | 5.6 | 172 | 31 |
| Bermuda | 2.4 | 32 | 13 |
| Luxembourg | 19.3 | 245 | 13 |
| Singapore | 85 | 221 | 2.6 |
| Hong Kong | 159 | 193 | 1.2 |
| United Kingdom | 1,442 | 1,508 | 1.05 |
| United States | 9,152 | 2,096 | 0.2 |

*Source:* Dixon 2001, based on BIS, World Bank, CIA, and Bank of England
data.

TAX HAVENS

Tax havens are the paradigmatic examples of offshore. As we will see in
chapter 3, modern tax havens preceded the emergence of the Euromarket by a century or so, and have grown to serve a great many functions
and roles, including money laundering and tax evasion. Some, however,
have evolved into veritable financial centers.

Tax havens present their own definitional problems. The complexity
of modern national tax systems has rendered practically every offshore
center a potential tax haven for foreign residents (Ginsburg 1991). The
Gordon Report to the U.S. Treasury states that "there is no single, clear,
objective test which permits the identification of a country as a tax
haven" (1981, 21). Nonetheless, certain types of financial centers have

*Table 3*
Tax Havens of the World

| Africa | Asia and Pacific | Europe | Middle East | Western Hemisphere |
|---|---|---|---|---|
| Djibouti | Cook Islands | Andorra | Bahrain | Anguilla |
| Liberia | Brunei | Austria[a] | Israel | Antigua |
| Mauritius | Guam | Campione[b] | Jordan | Aruba |
| Seychelles | Hong Kong | Cyprus | Lebanon | Bahamas |
| Tangier | Japan[c] | Dublin, Ireland | Oman | Barbados |
| | Labuan Malaysia | Gibraltar | United Arab Republic | Belize |
| | Macao | Greece | | Bermuda |
| | Marianas | Guernsey | | British Virgin Islands |
| | Marshall Islands | Hungary | | Cayman Islands |
| | Micronesia | Isle of Man | | Costa Rica |
| | Nauru | Jersey | | Dominica |
| | Niue | Liechtenstein | | Grenada |
| | Philippines | London, U.K. | | Montserrat |
| | Singapore[d] | Luxembourg | | Netherlands Antilles |
| | Tahiti | Madeira | | Panama |
| | Thailand[e] | Malta | | Puerto Rico |
| | Vanatu | Monaco | | St. Kitts and Nevis |

| Africa | Asia and Pacific | Europe | Middle East | Western Hemisphere |
| --- | --- | --- | --- | --- |
| | Western Samoa[g] | Netherlands | | St. Lucia |
| | | San Marino | | St. Vincent and Grenadines |
| | | Switzerland[f] | | Turks and Caicos Islands |
| | | | | United States[h] |
| | | | | Uruguay[i] |

*Sources:* Compilation based on IMF 2000 and Diamond and Diamond 1998. IMF 2000 used the following sources: joint BIS-IMF-OECD-World Bank Statistics on External Debt; Offshore Group of Banking Supervision; Financial Stability Forum's Working Group on Offshore Financial Centers.

[a]Austria is not considered a tax haven, but has strict bank secrecy laws and numbered bank accounts (Diamond and Diamond 1998).

[b]Campione is an island measuring only one square mile in Lake Lugano (Italy). The Italian tax authorities do not enforces taxes on the worldwide income of foreigners establishing residence there. Residency is established by renting, buying, or acquiring a time-share in a property (Diamond and Diamond 1998).

[c]Japanese offshore market.

[d]Asian currency units.

[e]Bangkok international banking facilities.

[f]Additional European centers whose status is in dispute include:

Trieste (Italy) free trade zone. Under a 1990 law foreign companies can borrow and lend to nonresidents.

Chechen Republic (Russia) is treated by Moscow as having a tax-free status, similar to the one existing in Ingushetia.

This is an international business center under a law signed by Yeltsin in 1996. Its current status is unclear.

Norderfriedrichskoog. A hamlet with only fifty residents, located on the north German coast, which registers offshore companies. A German duke relieved inhabitants from taxes as a reward for building sea walls three hundred years ago. The village started welcoming foreigner in 1996. Although it has tried to stem the flow, there are now seventy companies.

Svalbard, a Norwegian archipelago (Diamond and Diamond 1998).

gDiamond and Diamond (1998) classify the following Pacific islands as failed tax havens: Karitane, New Caledonia, Pitcairn Island, and Tonga.

hIncludes: (1) International banking facilities (IBFs). (2) The U.S. Virgin Islands, which are not considered tax havens but have attracted foreign investors since 1987 because of opportunities to establish tax-exempt companies. (3) State of Montana: the first to offer offshore banking services to foreigners, under the Montana Foreign Capital Act, passed by the state legislature in 1997. It has become a rival to the Cayman Islands and Switzerland (Diamond and Diamond 1998).

iDiamond and Diamond (1998) list St. Barthélemy as a special tax haven.

distinguished themselves, if that is not a contradiction in terms, as tax havens. The Bank for International Settlements classifies tax havens as "offshore banking centers" or regional financial centers that did not grow organically (BIS 1996). The bank, however, does not clarify the distinction between organic and nonorganic growth of financial centers. Some authors prefer to define tax havens quite simply as countries that promote themselves as such—although such a definition would exclude such venerable tax havens as Switzerland and Luxembourg (Ginsburg 1991, 1).[12] I prefer Adam Starchild's view, according to which tax havens are "countries that have enacted tax legislation especially designed to attract the formation of branches and subsidiaries of parent companies based in heavily-taxed industrial nations" (Starchild 1993, 1; Banoff and Burton 1994). In a similar vein, Richard Johns defines tax havens as states having deliberate policies that aim "to attract thereto international trade-oriented activities by minimization of taxes and the reduction or elimination of other restrictions on business operations" (1983, 20).[13]

Under the criteria established in the 1998 OECD Report, a tax haven is a jurisdiction that imposes no or nominal direct taxes on financial or other mobile services income and also meets one of three additional criteria: its regimes lack transparency; it does not engage in effective information exchange; and its regimes facilitate the establishment of entities with no substantial activities (U.S. Treasury 2001).

Tax havens share a number of characteristics. First and foremost, they boast minimal or no personal or corporate taxation. The reason for this may be historical: some of the European microstates such as Monaco and Andorra have maintained their nineteenth-century low tax regimes throughout the twentieth century, rendering them attractive to foreign capital. Alternatively, it may be intentional, as with most of the small states of the Caribbean, which have adopted low tax regimes as a developmental strategy. We need to bear in mind, however, that there is a great variety among tax havens. Only a few of them have no income tax or corporate tax whatsoever. These jurisdictions tend to derive their income from selling corporate license fees. Most tax havens display a more complex tax regime: they may be characterized either by low taxation, by taxation levied only on internal taxable events, or by low or nonexistent taxation on profits from foreign sources. In addition, some countries have enacted tax privileges for certain types of companies or operations.

Low taxation is only one distinguishing characteristic of tax havens. In addition we normally find the following provisions:

- Effective bank secrecy. Quite often bank or state officials are barred by law from disclosing the origins, character, and names of holders of funds. That is the case in Switzerland, Austria, and Luxembourg among others.
- Professional or commercial secrecy obligations preventing lawyers, accountants, or company employees from revealing confidential information about clients, including violations of other countries' laws.
- Company and trust laws with very loose disclosure requirements, for example rules allowing shares to be issued to a bearer, so that the true owner is concealed.
- Few, and preferably no restrictions or regulations concerning financial transactions.
- Ease of establishment of new companies. Companies may be required to hire local residents to serve as dummy directors for an appropriate fee, but the true identity of the owners may be protected by legislation. Companies are normally required to pay a yearly license fee, ranging from about UK£150 to £1000.
- The territory must possess political and economic stability—hence, preferred jurisdictions are dependencies of large, prosperous, and stable states
- The tax haven should be either supported by a large international financial market, or equipped with sophisticated information-exchange facilities and/or be within easy reach of a major financial center. Gibraltar, for instance, has invested heavily in communications infrastructure;
- The territory's name should not be tainted by scandals, money laundering, or drug money.

- Lastly, it is desirable that such havens have agreements with major countries to avoid double taxation.

Under the title of "a paradise for many reasons," an advertisement in the *Financial Times* placed by the Bahamas Investment Authority sums up nicely the nature of tax havens: "there are no personal, corporate, income, capital gains, estate, gift or inheritance taxes. Easy access to major world markets, political stability, security and economic oppor tunities . . . all a reality of business in the Commonwealth of the Bahamas" (21 December 2001). There are about seventy or so countries and jurisdictions in the world that possesses these characteristics.[14] They tend to be small jurisdictions serving the larger international trading blocks.

## OFFSHORE AND TAX AVOIDANCE

The main attractions of tax havens lie no doubt in the reduction in taxation and regulation they offer. This is achieved in a variety of ways. To understand the impact of this low-tax policy, in combination with other provisions such as bank secrecy, we need to dwell briefly on the nature of business and personal taxation. Currently, there are two favored jurisdictional standards for assertion of business income liability. The first is the source standard, whereby countries assert tax jurisdiction over income earned within their territories. The source standard does not distinguish between resident and nonresident income. The residence standard, on the other hand, taxes on the principle of residence rather than source income. Due to difficulties in establishing source income, residency has become the standard principle of worldwide taxation of corporations. The residency principle has proved to be a great boon to tax havens, since companies and banks find it beneficial to shift as much of their operations as possible to low- or zero-tax regimes. As tax havens are often minute island economies, the sort of companies and individuals that can take advantage of their laws are precisely those whose business lies in large onshore markets. As a result, a whole set of innovative entities has emerged to take advantage of tax havens. There are different techniques for tax avoidance,[15] among which the better known include the following.

*Offshore Banking Licenses*

Multinational corporations set up offshore banks to handle foreign exchange operations or to facilitate financing of international joint ventures. Low-cost bank licensing fees, combined with zero or near-zero regulation and taxation render such transactions far more profitable. In addition, offshore financial subsidiaries provide fund administration services such as fully integrated global custody, fund accounting, and transfer agent services.

Tax havens provide these financial institutions with a number of advantages:

1. Due to the residency tax principle, the banks can then either avoid or at least defer taxation they might incur in their home countries.
2. Financial institutions find it easier to organize complex financial operations involving numerous banks and other financial institutions (syndication) in low- or zero-taxation and regulation jurisdictions.
3. The Euromarket is restricted to third-party transactions, but companies and banks can overcome these restrictions by using their offshore subsidiaries, thereby making the Euromarket effectively open to all.
4. National regulation often limits the purview of financial institutions. For example, the United States has long tried to maintain strict boundaries between different financial markets, with the result that U.S. banks were prohibited from opening up branches in more than one state of the union. In addition, banks could not sell mortgages, or insurance policies, and so on. But U.S. banks have discovered that they could do all these things offshore.
5. Last but not least, offshore banks help administer and reroute wealthy individuals' accounts (private banking). It should be born in mind, however, that wealthy individuals are transferring wealth to offshore centers for other reasons, such as avoiding inheritance tax and punitive divorce proceedings. This last point is significant. The Diamonds believe that the single most important factor leading to the rise of offshore entities in the past decade has been the growing litigation, inheritance tax, and divorce settlements in advanced industrial countries (Diamond and Diamond 1998).

Not so long ago, private banking, most of which is conducted offshore, was the preserve of the superrich, and not many banks would have considered managing a portfolio of less than $1 million—indeed, many insisted on at least $5 million. But offshore accounts can now be opened on the mainland with deposits as low as $500, and if investors fear reprisal from tax authorities, they can subscribe to a system of offshore credit and debit card accounts to avoid being traced. The offshore economy is rapidly becoming part of daily life.

The great beauty of it all is that all these complex operations need not actually take place in tax havens, although a number of tax havens have been successful in attracting a certain amount of "real" financial activity.[16] It is enough if these operations are legally located in tax havens. Thus, among the Caymans Islands' 465 banks, most are mere brass plates (Cana 2000). The important point is that the cost of administrating financial transactions is transferred to zero- or near-zero-tax regimes, taking advantage of transfer pricing. The offshore entities are subject to no capital tax, no withholding tax on dividends or interest, no tax on transfers, no corporation tax, no capital gains tax, no exchange controls, light supervision, and less stringent reporting requirements, and less stringent trading restrictions.

### Captive Insurance Companies

Captive insurance companies are subsidiaries located in OFCs to reinsure certain risks underwritten by their parent companies and reduce overall reserve and capital requirements. Alternatively, an onshore reinsurance company may incorporate a subsidiary in an OFC to reinsure catastrophic risks. The attractions of an OFC in these circumstances include favorable income, withholding, and capital tax regimes, and low or weakly enforced actuarial reserve requirements and capital standards. Over four thousand captive insurance companies have been established in tax havens (Diamond and Diamond 1998, 59).

### Offshore Corporations or International Business Corporations (IBCs)

These are limited liability corporations registered in tax havens. They are used typically either to own and operate businesses, issue shares or bonds, or raise capital in other ways. They may be set up with one or more nominated directors from the OFC host country. This has not only become a lucrative business for the citizens of small tax havens such as Gibraltar or the Cayman Islands, but may also serve "to conceal the identity of the true company directors"(Diamond and Diamond 1998, 14). Many countries now demand full disclosure from resident companies of their offshore financial activities. Whether companies provide the correct information or not to their tax authorities is

*Table 4*
The World's Leading Capital Insurance Centers, 2001

|                        | Number of Companies |
| ---------------------- | ------------------- |
| Bermuda                | 1,405               |
| Caymans                | 535                 |
| Vermont                | 527                 |
| Guernsey               | 300                 |
| British Virgin Islands | 129[a]              |

*Source:* Internet search. 2001.
[a]1997.

anyone's guess. There is no doubt that tax havens serve to conceal the true identity of owners. In some tax havens, bearer share certificates may be used. Others require registered share certificates, but no public registry of shareholders is maintained. In some countries, such as Luxembourg, there are provisions for current and saving accounts that are officially not on the books. But even if companies provide full information about their offshore finances, they can still significantly reduce their tax burdens.

### Special Purpose Vehicles

One of the most rapidly growing features of OFCs is the establishment of special purpose vehicles (SPVs) by onshore corporations to take advantage of the favorable tax environment. The issuance of asset-backed securities is the most frequently cited activity of SPVs. The Bank for International Settlements monitored the spectacular rise of these vehicles during the 1990s and came to the conclusion that "many U.S.-based institutions aimed at exploiting discrepancies in regulatory and tax treatments"(BIS 1997, 127). In other words, the rise of nonbank financial entities is linked directly to the offshore economy.

### Segregated Account Companies

Tax havens can be used in other ways. In fact, the possibilities are endless. Bermuda, for example, allows international companies to set up segregated account companies. These are corporate entities that keep records, distribute shares and dividends, and may be wound up subject to the appointment of an official receiver, all separately from the main company. A segregated account company enables a creditor or a shareholder's investment to be insulated from creditors of the main company. Over one hundred such companies have been established in the past ten years. In addition, a loophole in the U.S. federal tax law allows companies to move their headquarters to Bermuda. "It's a new type of Bermuda triangle where revenues disappear," reported the *New York Times* (7 March 2000).

### Use of Tax Havens by Individuals

It is more than likely that each and every multinational bank and corporation, including virtually all the household names, maintains at least one, if not many tax haven subsidiaries.[17] But not all offshore entities are subsidiaries of real companies. Many serve as fronts for individuals, enabling them to transfer their assets offshore. For example, a wealthy individual can buy a company X "off the shelf" in a tax haven. The identity of the individual may be concealed by means of bearer shares, and he or she may use Swiss, Luxembourg, Austrian, or Channel Islands numbered accounts to do the deal. Most likely the individual will use a private banker to organize the operation. If this person is very careful, then he or she will use assets from company X to set up company Y in another tax haven, with the secrecy provisions of both havens concealing the true identity of both entities. Company Y can then "sell" certain consulting or financial services to the individual who set up company X, and in this way that person can shift money to a tax haven. Indeed, he or she may claim a tax deduction from their home country for the cost of services provided by company Y! If the tax authorities are particularly vigilant and achieve the almost unheard-of success in finding out the owner of company Y, that will only lead them to company X, located in another tax haven. Penetrating the mask of secrecy takes years, by which time the wealthy individual will have shifted the assets elsewhere.

#### SIZE AND IMPACT

What is the size of the tax haven phenomenon? And how does it affect the taxing and regulating powers of the state? Due to the opacity of tax havens, with their bank secrecy laws and other measures to preserve the anonymity of those who do business there, no one truly knows the size of the phenomenon or its precise impact on taxation. Recently, the

U.S. Internal Revenue Service estimated that between 1 and 2 million Americans use offshore credit and debit accounts. The IRS reached its conclusion from records that it had compelled MasterCard to provide about 230,000 bank accounts in three tax haven countries. Prominent lawyers and economists immediately rejected the IRS's estimate (Johnston 2002).

Another way of estimating the size of the tax haven phenomenon is by studying the volume of cross border assets (i.e. assets traveling through tax havens and through tax haven financial subsidiaries). This was estimated by the IMF by the end of 1997 at $4.8 trillion, and reached $5.1 trillion by 1999. The latter figure represented 52.7 percent of the total cross-border bank claims in the world (Errico and Musalem 1999, 10; Financial Stability Forum 2000; Diamond and Diamond 1998). This ratio is confirmed by other studies (Cassard 1994; Oxfam 2000). The IMF puts the figure by the end of 1999 at $4.6 trillion or about 50 percent of cross-border assets. Of this, $0.9 trillion was in the Caribbean, $1 trillion in Asia, and most of the remaining $2.7 trillion was accounted for by London, U.S. IBFs, and Tokyo's JOM (IMF 2000). In any case, these figures gave rise to the popular, though somewhat misleading, notion that "half of the global stock of money goes through tax havens."(Ginsburg 1991). The figure for international loans and cross-border assets is confirmed by another striking statistic. Tax havens account for only 1.2 percent of world population and 3 percent of world GDP, but by 1994, they accounted for 26 percent of assets and 31 percent of profits of American multinationals (Hines and Rice 1994; Oxfam 2000).

Yet another way of estimating the size of the tax haven phenomenon is through "private banking,"—a nice way of describing the practice of banks' handling wealthy individuals' accounts by and large in tax havens. Switzerland is the heavyweight in this business, and it uses its bank secrecy code to great effect. Swiss banks manage an estimated 35 to 40 percent of all foreign-managed assets, or Swfr 2,000 billion to 2,500 billion (*Euromoney* 1996). According to another estimate, the sector manages some $2.1 trillion in assets, and business is growing at up to 15 percent a year (Stewart 1996).

It is more difficult to estimate the number of offshore entities, such as banks, financial institutions, companies, and special purpose vehicles, located in tax havens. A number of tax havens have begun to publish annual accounts of the aggregate number of such entities in their territories. In 1999, the Cayman Islands, for example, claimed to have posted a 51 percent increase in the number of offshore entities registered in its territory, to a staggering figure of 57,900 (*Cana* 2000). In 2001 Mauritius had over 14,000 offshore entities registered in its territory.[18] In 1999 Bahrain announced an increase of approximately 10 percent in operating assets of its offshore banking units.[19] In 2001, the Bahamas had 106,000 IBCs in its territory, and 16,000 were being added every year. In the same year, the British Virgin Islands posted a 19 percent increase in the number of its IBCs, up to 368,000 (*British Virgin Islands Sun* 2001).

What do these figures tell us? First, that there are probably between two to three million offshore entities located in the seventy or so tax havens in the world. In addition, despite the well-publicized assault on offshore jurisdictions conducted by the OECD, tax havens are posting an unprecedented rise in the number of offshore entities located in their territories. An average increase of 10 to 15 percent a year is probably a low estimate. Each of these entities costs a small fortune to set up. In addition to setup fees, there are lawyers' and accountants' fees, yearly license fees, the rental of brass plate location, if nothing grander, and the remuneration of local dummy directors.

The overall effect of a phenomenon of such a magnitude is difficult to measure. There are immediate issues of tax avoidance and evasion and, of course, money laundering, but also deeper questions concerning the changing nature of state and sovereignty in the modern age. As this book is mainly concerned with the latter, I will do no more than report on current knowledge of the former. There is little doubt that individuals and enterprises rely on banking secrecy and opaque corporate structures to avoid declaring assets and income to the relevant tax authorities. The scale of the phenomenon is simply unknown. According to an OECD report that tries to estimate the effects of harmful tax competition, in the past three decades taxes on income and profit have declined slightly in OECD countries, a decline that has been matched by an increase in consumption taxes and social security contributions (Palan 1998b). The report focuses on geographically mobile activities, such as financial and other service activities. It specifically targets "the distorting effects of harmful tax practices in the form of tax havens and harmful preferential tax regimes around the world" (Clark and de Kam 1998). The report, however, does not try to attach any figure to the impact of tax havens. A study published by Oxfam reports "conservative estimates" that tax havens have contributed to revenue losses for developing countries of at least $50 billion a year (Oxfam 2000). That figure appears to me on the low side.

*Money Laundering*

The offshore world provides a safe haven for the proceeds of political corruption, illicit arms dealing, illegal diamond trafficking, and the global drug trade. Havens facilitate the plunder of public funds by corrupt elites in poor countries, which can represent a major barrier to economic and social development. It has been estimated that around $55 billion was looted from Nigerian public funds during the Abacha dictatorship.

Switzerland, Luxembourg, and the Channel Islands have made strenuous attempts to distance themselves from the less reputable aspects of tax havens. They apply stricter regulatory standards than many other tax havens (Stewart 1996). In 1989 Luxembourg strengthened its laws concerning drug trafficking and money laundering and included the possibility of prison terms and confiscation of property. In March 1990 the Swiss Government passed a bill outlawing the laundering of funds from criminal activities and requiring bankers to check the identity of account holders (Garlin 1990). But this may be largely in response to outside pressure as tax havens seek to fill market niches and accommodate the specific needs of their larger neighbors. No-tax countries, which tend to be newcomers to the tax haven game like Aruba, Antigua, or Seychelles, earn income primarily through the issuing of license fees and seek to attract as many banks and corporations as possible. Such countries, however, lack a sophisticated financial infrastructure. They have tended, therefore, to attract less desirable elements.

Gibraltar is another case of a niche player that gains specific advantage from the Maastricht treaty. Like any other European bank, after 1992 banks registered in Gibraltar were able to set up branch offices throughout Europe. A Gibraltar-based bank operating in France or Spain owes French or Spanish tax authorities whatever taxes are payable on its earnings in that country, but where bank profits are earned is not easy to define. As Duggan (1991) notes: "A few deft cross-border currency trades or leasing transactions can make earnings at a branch in Paris disappear there and resurface elsewhere. If the elsewhere is Gibraltar, corporate taxes could be 0%" (Duggan 1991). The Channel Islands, on the other hand, which act as conduits for the City of London, seek to attract a small number of banks and building societies with large funds. Guernsey, for instance, is keen to draw "managed" banks to its shores. These banks have no physical presence and the island's authorities see this as a way of raising banking output without unduly increasing the pressure on limited staff resources and space (Stuart 1990). Jersey has recently enacted a law designed to attract accounting firms. The law provides firms that operate as partnerships with corporate-style caps on liability while letting them avoid the higher taxes, and the disclosure requirements to which ordinary limited companies are subject (*Economist* 1996).

Contrary to conventional wisdom, the leading industrial countries' attitude to tax havens has been ambiguous. Richard Johns argues that "the transformation of some of these centers [into offshore financial centers] resulted from the tacit or complicit permissive attitude of other, mainly onshore, countries" (Johns 1983, 15). The U.S. Treasury, traditionally hostile to tax havens, has been the most persistent in seeking to raise the veil of secrecy surrounding financial activities there (Fehrenbach 1966: Hudson 1998). But there is evidence of a shift in policy beginning around the early 1980s. Many leading tax havens, such as the Cayman Islands, British Virgin Islands, and Channel Islands, are dependencies of the British state. Indeed, in 1990 the U.K. government commissioned the accounting firm Coopers & Lybrand, to carry out a review of offshore regulation in several British territories with a view to enhancing their international competitiveness. As the *Economist* (1996) notes: "The British government tolerates the offshore financial industry on the assumption that it brings more money into Britain by channeling more expatriate and foreign wealth into London than is taken out by people working tax dodges."

### OFFSHORE FINANCIAL MARKET—AN INTEGRATED MARKET

There is nowadays a truly integrated global offshore financial market. London, New York, and Tokyo serve as primary centers for worldwide clients and act as international financial intermediaries for their market regions. Booking centers such as Nassau or the Cayman Islands are used by international banks as the location for "shell branches" to book both Eurocurrency deposits and international loans. Funding centers such as Singapore or Panama play the role of inward financial intermediaries, channeling offshore funds from outside their markets to local uses. Collection centers like Bahrain engage primarily in outward financial intermediation. Such a hierarchy is testimony to the degree of specialization and interdependence among offshore centers. Supported by their respective states and boasting slightly different packages of legislation, these centers are the platforms upon which an integrated offshore financial

*Table 5*
Distribution of EPZs by Region and Key Countries, 1997

|                          | Number of zones |
|--------------------------|----------------:|
| North America            | 320 |
| United States            | 213 |
| Mexico                   | 107 |
| Central America          | 41 |
| Honduras                 | 15 |
| Costa Rica               | 9 |
| Caribbean                | 51 |
| Dominican Republic       | 35 |
| South America            | 41 |
| Colombia                 | 11 |
| Brazil                   | 8 |
| Europe                   | 81 |
| Bulgaria                 | 8 |
| Slovenia                 | 8 |
| Middle East              | 39 |
| Turkey                   | 11 |
| Jordan                   | 7 |
| Asia                     | 225 |
| China                    | 124 |
| Philippines              | 35 |
| Indonesia                | 26 |
| Africa                   | 47 |
| Kenya                    | 14 |
| Egypt                    | 6 |
| Pacific                  | 2 |
| Australia                | 1 |
| Fiji                     | 1 |
| Total                    | 845 |

*Sources:* World Economic Processing Zones Association (WEPZA) and International Labor Organization (ILO)

system has evolved. In that sense the state system itself is providing the material and legal infrastructure of offshore (Palan and Abbott 1996).

EXPORT PROCESSING ZONES

Export processing zones are duty-free zones dedicated to manufacturing for export.[20] Most EPZs have rather relaxed labor and environmental laws. Normally no customs duties are charged for importing raw materials, components, machinery, equipment, and supplies used to produce manufactured goods, provided these are then exported. EPZs tend to be relatively small and scattered areas within a country, the purpose of which is to attract export-oriented industries, by offering them favorable investment and trade conditions as compared with the remainder of the host country. In particular, the EPZs provide for duty-free importation of goods to be used in the production of exports. Within the zones normally all the physical infrastructure and services necessary for manufacturing are provided: roads, power supplies, transport facilities and low-rent buildings. In a number of cases restrictions on foreign ownership that apply in the country as a whole are waived for foreign firms locating in the zones. Export processing zones may be seen, therefore, as the manufacturing equivalent of tax havens.

In some countries, EPZs are indistinguishable from modern business complexes, but in many others they take the form of ring-fenced enclaves of industrial monoculture. But as an ILO study observes, "no matter what form EPZs take, the free trade, foreign-investment and export-driven ethos of the modern economy has transformed them into vehicles of globalization"(ILO 1998).

Export processing zones evolved from two sources. One line can be traced back, through the Shannon Airport EPZ, established in 1959,[21] to the basic duty-free principle. Another source is the free trade zones established in the United States by the Roosevelt administration, as we will see in chapter 4, which served as the model for Puerto Rico's EPZ. There were only a handful of EPZs in developing countries in the 1960s, including India, Taiwan, and Puerto Rico. The first maquiladora in Mexico was established in 1965 (ILO 1998).[22] As with tax havens, the numbers of EPZs began to grow rapidly in the 1970s; in fact, nearly all the EPZs in the world were established after 1971. By 1986 there were 116 of them worldwide. It is estimated that globally some 1.3 million workers were employed in 116 EPZs in 1988. Today the World Export Processing Zones Association international directory lists over 845 zones.[23] Asia has over 60 percent of those employed in EPZs, with the majority concentrated in Singapore and Hong Kong.

The annual value of merchandise handled by EPZs is in excess of $110 billion. The ILO estimates the total number of people working in export zones at 27 million worldwide, 90 percent of whom are female (ILO 1998). Excluding China, however, the number of people working in EPZs falls to 4.5 million (Cling and Letilly 2001).

FLAGS OF CONVENIENCE

The International Transport Workers Federation defines flag of convenience (Foc) countries as those "which offer their maritime flag registration to owners from another country." Foc registers, traditionally, offer "easy" registration, low or no taxes, and no practical restrictions on the nationality of crews. The shipping industry is, in theory, one of the more regulated sectors of the world economy, and by transferring a ship from a genuine national register to a flag of convenience, an owner runs away from taxation, safety regulations, and trade union organization (ITF). Not surprisingly, a number of countries lacking what Johns (1983) describes as an "internal profit making capacity" offer cheap and hassle-free registration of ships.

The U.S. government and U.S. companies played a prominent role in the emergence and growth of flags of convenience. In the 1920s, under the guidance of the U.S. custom and excise administration, the United Fruit Company created the Honduran registry to ensure the cheap and reliable transport of its bananas. At the same time, Prohibition led to the birth of a Panamanian registry. The owners of two U.S.-flag passenger ships who wanted to serve liquor on board were permitted by the U.S. government to switch to the Panamanian flag so they could do so (Morris 1996). The main impetus for the Panama registry's growth came initially from Standard Oil, whose Esso Shipping Company had twenty-five ships, originally German-registered, transferred first to the flag of the Free City of Danzig in 1935 and then to the Panamanian flag. Standard Oil's motives were in part the fear of war (Knudsen 1973). Liberia's flag of convenience was encouraged by the United States after World War II, to provide Liberia with a much-needed economic boost and the United States with a fleet of neutral ships to draw upon in the event of Soviet aggression (Morris 1996). This was accomplished through the services of Stettinius Associates of New York, which founded the

Liberia Company to develop Liberian mineral resources, and "arranged the formalities for granting Liberian registration on terms still more liberal than those of Panama" (Knudsen 1973, 47). The United States has developed the Marshall Islands flag of convenience for similar purposes (Van Fossen 1992). More recently, the Sealift Doctrine, approved by the Joint Chiefs of Staff under the Bush administration in 1989, considers merchant ships as available for military purposes so long as they are owned by U.S. citizens and flagged in one of five "effective(ly) U.S.-controlled" registries: the Marshall Islands, Honduras, Panama, Liberia, and the Bahamas (Tirschwell 1995).

With more then than fourteen thousand ships and 85 million in total gross tonnage registered, Panama boasts the biggest merchant fleet in the world. Panama's diplomatic consulates worldwide accept registry applications. To ensure that Panama remains competitive, new legislation has eliminated the annual service fees that consulates charged, and registration fees may be paid in installments. A close second, Liberia's maritime ascendancy came, as mentioned above, during the Cold War. In recent years a number of traditional tax havens, including the Bahamas, Antigua, and the Cayman Islands, have pushed aggressively into the market. So have two Pacific islands, the Marshall Islands and Vanuatu, and even landlocked Luxembourg! It is estimated that over two-thirds of world merchant shipping is registered in such havens (Morris 1996).

Shipping registry is increasingly run as an international business. The Liberian registry—as well as that of the Marshall Islands—is run out of Reston, Virginia, by International Registries Inc. Panama's fleet safety operation is based in Manhattan, not in Panama City. The business is a lucrative one. Panama collected 5 percent of its federal revenues from ship registration fees and annual taxes in 1995, and another $50 million or so from maritime lawyers, agents, and inspectors (Morris 1996). Indeed, Panamanian consulates that bring additional business are rewarded handsomely.

*Table 6*
International Transport Workers List of Flag of Convenience Registries, 2000

| | |
|---|---|
| Antigua and Barbuda | Gibraltar |
| Aruba | Honduras |
| Bahamas | Lebanon |
| Barbados | Liberia |
| Belize | Luxembourg |
| Bermuda | Malta |
| Bolivia | Marshall Islands |
| Burma | Mauritius |
| Cambodia | Netherlands Antilles |
| Canary Islands | Panama |
| Cayman Islands | Sri Lanka |
| Cook Islands | St. Vincent |
| Cyprus | Tuvalu |
| Equatorial Guinea | |
| Vanuatu | |

*Source:* http://www.itf.org.uk/seafarers/foc/report_2000/index.html. This list is drawn up by a joint committee of International Transport Workers Federation seafarers' and dockers' unions which runs the ITF Campaign against Focs (the Fair Practices Committee). Countries are added to the list according to various criteria, the most important being that a majority of vessels in a register are foreign-owned or foreign-controlled.

## ELECTRONIC COMMERCE AND THE INTERNET

The Internet provides great new opportunities for the expansion of the offshore economy. As Charles McLure notes, e-commerce "has burst on the fiscal scene almost as suddenly and as brilliantly as the Hale-Bopp comet [and] is on a collision course with state tax systems" (1997, 731–32).[24] During the late 1990s, on-line commerce was doubling in value every hundred days. By the end of 1999, on-line retail business made up 8 percent of the total retail industry in the United States (*Globe and Mail* 1999). U.S. companies traded $700 billion electronically, most of it company-to-company, compared to $330 billion for the rest of the world. At the same time, the laws governing electronic commerce remain unclear: "No one is sure whose rules govern. . . . the question of jurisdiction remains unresolved, both internationally and within the United States. . . . What consumer laws, contract laws, privacy laws and other laws apply to e-commerce transactions?" (Waldmeir 1999).

Not surprisingly, tax havens are taking advantage of the situation and are busy extending their financial laws to lure e-commerce to their territories. "E-commerce is truly the wave of the future, and Bermuda has every intention of riding this wave to the fullest," explains Bermuda Minister of Telecommunications and E-Commerce Renee Webb. "We are also the only jurisdiction with legislation that preserves a flexible operating environment while promoting the regulatory regime and transactional clarity that businesses need"(*Royal Gazette* 2000). Bermuda set up a code of conduct (Standard for Electronic Transactions) which came into effect on 3 July 2000, and was an extension of the island's 1999 Electronic Transactions Act. As is to be expected from a tax haven, the code offers, besides predictability, also "security and confidence to e-business providers and customers in Bermuda"(*Royal Gazette* 2000). In other words, the principle of anonymity and secrecy is extended to e-commerce sectors, with a view to creating e-commerce havens. Vanuatu, a small Pacific atoll, is doing the same (Chesher 2000), and so has the Bahamas (Caribbean News Agency 2000). Panama, is following a different route and has replicated its successful Colón Free Zone in the form of the International Technopark of Panama within its City of Knowledge technology program. But truly, the possibilities for adapting tax havens as bases for on-line retail services are endless. We are already witnessing the reemergence of the pirate radio principle, as one company, HavenCo, set itself up on an abandoned World War II antiaircraft fortress located six miles from the British coast, used previously as a pirate radio station (*New York Times* 2000). HavenCo will provide telecommunications, gambling, and software services.

The Internet and e-commerce help expand the offshore economy in

a number of ways. First and foremost, the Internet is proving a great fa-
cilitator for the transfer of resources. A growing number of offshore
banks are offering customers on-line access to their accounts, providing
greater secrecy and anonymity. Everyone can now open a bank account
in offshore jurisdictions by post or telephone, or through the Internet.
All the major British banks and building societies, from the Bank of
Scotland, to the Abbey National and the Halifax, proudly advertise their
offshore accounts in the press. Savers need not pay the obligatory tax on
deposit appreciation. Of course, taxpayers are required by law to declare
these accounts, and are supposed to pay their taxes once the money is
repatriated onshore, but whether they do so is anyone's guess. In any ·
case, these institutions are also offering offshore credit card services so
that customers need never repatriate their money. So big is the business
that Merrill Lynch, the U.S. investment bank, and HSBC Holdings, the
U.K. banking group, are spending $1 billion to establish an on-line fi-
nancial institution aimed at non-U.S. clients with at least $100,000 to
invest. Many jurisdictions are now allowing on-line company incorporation, exposing what offshore experts knew all along, that the idea of
scrutiny is a sham. The Caribbean Development Bank reports that 219
offshore companies registered in Anguilla during the second half of
1999, fifty-eight more than were reported for the same period in 1998.
The bank said that the increase was facilitated by Anguilla's on-line incorporation procedure (*Daily Herald* 2000).

The impact of these measures on tax revenues is obvious. Larry Summers, U.S. Treasury secretary in the Clinton administration, speaking
in Washington to the Inter-American Center of Tax Administrators,
warned that offshore e-commerce and encryption technology allowed
businesses to use the Internet to escape the tax net. It was easy, he said,
"for e-commerce companies to operate from jurisdictions that were unwilling to share taxpayer information, selling their goods worldwide
without any scrutiny from international tax agencies" (Summers 2000).
In this way the Internet offers a new degree of security, anonymity, and
ease of access to the offshore economy.

But the effects of the Internet go deeper. Current sales taxes systems
were designed for a world in which local traders sold manufactured
products. It is far more difficult to impose taxes on intangibles such as
services. The information society, notes Anne Branscomb, "has produced a rich marketplace of new informational products" (1994, 5).
Branscomb demonstrates the enormous value of previously nontraded

items such as names and addresses, telephone numbers, medical histories, images, and electronic messages. Information that until recently could not be easily stored or transported, such as lectures, theater performances and concerts, sporting events, visits to the doctor, or tourism (McLure 1997, 735), can now be sold over the Internet. Similarly, computer software, images, and movies can be sent from anywhere in the world avoiding value-added and other consumption taxes. Tax havens such as Panama, Costa Rica, Bermuda, and Bahamas see themselves as future centers for such activities.

The potential and impetus for the development of offshore merchandising arises, in addition, from an extension of the laws regarding mail-order sales. The U.S. Supreme Court has ruled that states where purchasers are located cannot force out-of-state vendors to collect sales tax (McLure 1997, 733).[25] The U.S. courts have recently extended the ruling to 2006 (*Wall Street Journal* 2000). There are extensive discussions about the application of sales tax to electronic vendors, but the U.S. Congress's Advisory Commission on Internet Taxation has reached an impasse. At the time of writing, the commission had agreed to support the current ban on Internet taxation for five more years, not to tax Internet access or digitized goods such as music and software, and to repeal the 3 percent excise tax on telecommunications. The United States also responded critically to EU initiatives to tax on-line businesses (*Financial Times* 2000b). On-line out-of-state business is, therefore, untaxed. A recent report by Forrester Research found that states were losing about $500 million in taxes on on-line sales (TheStandard.com 2000).

## TELECOMMUNICATIONS, ON-LINE SEX, AND OFFSHORE CASINOS

The Internet and e-commerce also generate entirely new offshore sectors. Technological advances and international deregulation in the telecommunications industry offer new opportunities for offshore developments. The globalization of the telecommunications business has developed from two complementary movements. On the one hand, public telecommunications operators (PTOs) have stretched their service provision to foreign countries. On the other hand, efforts are being made by many PTOs to invite international corporate network users to locate their hubs in the PTOs' home countries. As PTOs expect to make high profits from the lease of large-capacity circuits and increased international traffic, countries construct cables and set low transmission rates to attract higher volume. This competitive usage is leading to a liberalization of rules and regulations, with the predictable result that some countries are aggressively promoting themselves as hassle-free telecommunications centers (OECD 1995, 29).

One of the more interesting recent converts to offshore is on-line sex. "Telephone sex may be good for development." Who says? The International Telecommunication Union, the staid club of PTOs (*Economist* 1997). It is reckoned that 1.5 percent of all international traffic is telephone sex, with a global turnover of around $2 billion a year. The key to the business is the international settlement system which ensures that the country in which an international call originates and the one in which it terminates share the revenue from the call. This settlement system means that the PTO of a small developing country can benefit hugely if it can generate a large amount of incoming traffic. While a great many countries censor on-line sex, a number of small countries, including Guyana in Latin America and the small islands of Niue and Tuvalu in the Pacific, have leased their codes and numbers in bulk to specialized sex firms. On-line sex does not usually originate in these countries but is merely rerouted through switching mechanisms located, in the case of the Pacific atolls, in New Zealand. The origin of the phone calls remains unknown, but because of the settlement system they are logged as if emanating from these countries and the small countries share in the revenues from these incoming calls. With their small populations, islands like Niue have short, four-digit numbers that are attractive to businesses all over the world. The numbers are merely leased and rerouted to the bigger trading and financial centers. As the *Economist* sarcastically comments: "Dial the international access code of 683, and another four numbers will connect you to your heart's desire" (1997).

These procedures can produce a significant amount of revenues for a small country. Both Tuvalu and Niue are reputed to derive approximately 20 percent of government revenues from such deals (Hussein 1997). In fact, Niue, a New Zealand protectorate, has more telephone lines than inhabitants. After Guyana's PTO was taken over by ANT, an American company, in 1991, the volume of incoming calls increased from 23.8 million minutes to 139.7 million in 1995. As a result, the country's yearly revenue from telecommunications services is now around $130 million, or the equivalent of 40 percent of the country's 1993 GDP. Of course, not all this money stays in Guyana, but it is a significant contribution to the country's deteriorating finances. Similarly, in 1994 the Dutch Antilles was receiving the equivalent of 2,600 minutes of incoming calls for every telephone subscriber in the country and generating at least $1,000 per head from settlement payments (*Economist* 1997).

One of the latest offshore developments is on-line gambling, which is expected to generate revenues of up to $75 billion by the year 2010. Companies simply set themselves up in tax havens and offer their services over the net. The United States has managed to convict American gambling companies located in tax havens under the Wire Act, but British companies continue to offer their services to American customers, claiming that the U.S. government can only go after U.S. companies. "We are operating under a British license in a jurisdiction where the law says the transaction takes place where the web servers are located and where the risk management and payment transaction takes place, which in this case is Alderney [one of the Channel Islands]," says Mark Blandford, founder of Sportingbet.com. (*Financial Post* 2000).

One notes the prevalence among the latecomers in the tax haven game of businesses providing on-line sex. To make up for their lateness and their distance from the traditional financial centers, these countries are obliged to extend the principles of offshore to new areas. As another instance of the extension this principle, the government of the Marshall Islands has hired sales agents to sell its passports. Because of its special relationship to the United States, Marshall Islands citizenship is a ticket to entry into that country. Since the mid-1980s, passport prices have ranged from $30,000 to $250,000. By 1996 passport sales reached close to 1000, providing upwards of $15 million in revenues to the Marshall Islands government (Johnson 1994).

### COMMERCIALIZED SOVEREIGNTY

As we have seen, one of the intriguing aspects of the offshore economy is its predication on practices that appear to be in sharp contradiction to the very institution that gave rise to it in the first place, namely, sovereignty. For offshore comes about because governments are prepared to use an attribute of sovereignty—the right to make the law—for pecuniary gain. They draw rent surpluses, as Fabri and Baldacchino note, from the income that otherwise would accrue to larger states (1999, 48). I call this phenomenon the commercialization of state sovereignty. By this I mean that offshore jurisdictions are offering sovereign protection or a right of abode, whether real or fictional, and using this as a source of revenue.

Sovereign protection and the right of abode are not the same throughout the world. Some states can, or are perceived to, offer more reliable
protection than others. That is why democratic states such as Switzerland and Luxembourg, or dependencies of large and powerful states,
such as the Cayman Islands, Gibraltar, the Channel Islands, and the
Dutch Antilles, are rated among the more successful tax havens. At the
other extreme lie some failed tax havens, most them atolls in the Pacific, including ambiguous sovereignties such as the "Dominion of
Melchizedek." Melchizedek is a self-proclaimed sovereign state controlled by a Christian sect.[26] *Melech* in Hebrew means king; *zedek*
means "justice"; the name therefore means "the kingdom of justice" or
"land of the Messiah" as Melechzedek is one of the names given to the
Messiah in the Bible.[27]

The vast potential for commercialization of state sovereignty has
long been recognized, particularly with reference to offshore locations.
The International Transport Workers Federation's vigorous campaign
against flags of convenience, for instance, has generated a great number
of publications deriding the inappropriate use of sovereignty. Rodney
Carlisle entitled his study of the Panamanian and Liberian flags of convenience *Sovereignty for Sale* (1961). In 1933, in a dissenting opinion in
*Liggett Co. v. Lee*, Justice Brandeis mentioned how "companies were
early formed to provide charters for corporations in states where the
cost was lowest and the laws least restrictive. The states joined in ad-
vertising their wares. The race was one not of diligence but of laxity"
(Conrad 1973, 631). Alfred Conrad notes that indeed "there is nothing
very unusual about a race between states [but] what is unusual about
the race of laxity in corporation codes is that its effect will be felt
among those almost entirely outside the state." He calls this the
"strictly-for-export aspect of corporation code" (1973, 633).[28] Among international tax experts the expression "treaty shopping"—refering to
companies relocating subsidiaries to countries which have signed a preferred list of international treaties—has come into wide usage.[29] Tax
havens have taken the idea of commercialization of sovereignty to new
heights: here governments charge "rent" or license fees in return for
granting firms a right of incorporation. In so doing, governments of
(often) small jurisdictions in effect represent themselves as the financial
equivalent of parking lot proprietors: the owner of a parking lot who
could not care less about the business of the customer and merely
charges for the period vehicles are parked in the lot. Likewise, corporations pay for the privilege of "parking"—that is, appearing to reside, in

tax havens. Tax havens have learned to use their legislative powers as bait to attract business into their jurisdictions—mostly in the form of virtual companies, but also of virtual residents.[30]

Robert Aliber describes a deal struck between the Swiss government and Elizabeth Taylor, "a mobile factor of production" as he calls her. "Miss Taylor and the Swiss have struck a bargain. The Swiss sell Miss Taylor tax-avoidance services. The right to live in a low-tax jurisdiction. Miss Taylor buys this service because she likes the higher after tax income; better to live where taxes are low than where they are high. The Swiss profit from the transaction, for Miss Taylor's tax payments greatly exceed her demand on local public services" (1976, 182).

Both the Swiss government and Elizabeth Taylor are pursuing rational strategies in the sense that both are gaining something from the bargain. Such rational arrangements between states and private individuals are perfectly legal and yet they are deeply disturbing, not least because the two parties to the exchange, one of them a sovereign government, handle highly charged normative issues, such as citizenship and nationality, in purely utilitarian ways. The willful misuse of ideas and practices that go to the very heart of the legitimacy of the modern state as a national state is the most disturbing aspect of the tax haven phenomenon.

This misuse is founded on the willingness on the part of certain governments to treat something that goes to the very heart of modern sovereignty—citizenship—as a marketable product. But as sovereignty is packaged and commodified, it is turned into a service commodity whose price can be reckoned with some accuracy: it is published on the Internet, and in the back pages of the *Economist*, the *Financial Times*, and the *European*. Only that sovereign protection is purchased this time not against some imagined enemy, the other, but against the sovereign itself. This is the paradox of offshore. While companies and tax haven states appear to undermine sovereignty by commodifying it, at the same time by paying for the right of abode, they are reaffirming sovereignty.

The question, then, is why are these companies prepared to encumber themselves with the not inconsiderable costs of maintaining fictional subsidiaries in tax havens? The simple answer is that they do so in order to reduce their tax bills and obtain freedom from regulation. This is undoubtedly the case, but such an answer only begs a further question: What precisely are these companies paying for, and conversely, what do these jurisdictions offer them in return? In other words, what is it about the nature of the world that renders such trans-actions rational and profitable? Evidently, license fees are paid for the privilege of incorporation in a tax haven. The payments are made for the right of abode: for legal rights of residence in a particular regulatory do-main. The right of abode is an absolute necessity for the conduct of business in the modern world. Residential requirements prescribe, however, that only members of recognized states gain legal recognition and (some) protection, it does not specify what sort of relationship there should be between states and their subjects: indeed, it is the privilege of sovereignty that such matters are left to each individual state. In an in-creasingly competitive environment, this provision has proved to be a loophole to the extent that it offered states the opportunity to play a competitive game in attracting business by effectively lowering the cost of the right of abode. Conversely, it has offered firms an opportunity to exercise choice regarding their preferred place of residence, and hence their preferred "bundles of regulation." A new market is evolving in which states supply juridical residence and firms and individuals pro-vide the demand for this. In other words, sovereignty is up for sale.

This chapter demonstrates two things. First, offshore facilities are not located offshore, but very much onshore; they are a development that has taken place in its entirety within the bounds of sovereignty. Indeed, we have seen how certain principles enshrined in the law of the sea serve as the basis for the offshore economy. Sovereignty can be thought of as enabling: it is a constitutive requirement of the offshore economy. Consequently, as the next chapter will show, far from signaling the end of the state, offshore must be seen within the context of the continuing process of state formation. Second, the staggering growth statistics, and the vast range of offshore markets that are already in place, suggest that the offshore economy is far larger and more diversified than is normally assumed.

# CHAPTER TWO

# State, Capital, and the Production of Offshore

As Wilber (1982) notes, each and every aspect of social life is like a holo-gram, containing within it the entire world. There are no natural boundaries or limits attached to any particular social scientific issue or subject matter. The holographic principle appears particularly apt when it comes to the offshore world. What are the relevant questions to be asked with regard to offshore? To some, the key issues are money laun-dering, criminality, and harmful tax competition. To others, however, the focus on criminality is misplaced. Offshore, they argue, is a struc-tural development, an expression and a symptom of what happens when states overregulate and overtax their societies. For others again, the latter theories may contain a kernel of truth; yet they miss the point. Offshore is first and foremost a *political* program, serving the in-terests of the rich and the powerful. But, of course, the practice of reg-ulatory differentiation, by which states intentionally divide their sov-ereign territory into offshore and onshore spaces, is spreading. Seen in this light, offshore can be understood as a technology of the state—one that is proving to be highly mobile and transferable. This suggests, in turn, that the key issues are those concerning the changing nature of state and sovereignty in the modern world.

Such an understanding casts the nature and implications of the rise of the offshore economy in a new light. Sandrine Tesner, for instance, observes that "In a global system where the nation-state no longer has a monopoly on the realm of politics, metanationals exist not across but above borders. They do not operate against the sovereign state, nor do they seek to de-legitimize it. Rather they function in a space of their own, separate and above that of the nation-state—a metaspace" (2000, 26). The offshore economy is not the exclusive metaspace Tesner is talking about, but an important condition of a new spatiality corre-sponding, as we will see in chapter 7, to some deeper changes in the nature of capitalism. In this sense, offshore is not only about taxation and regulation but also about globalization and the changing nature of contemporary capitalism, as well as involving issues of power and agency.

This chapter therefore offers an introductory survey of current thinking on offshore with a view to clarifying the way I am going to handle these latter issues throughout the book.

## ECONOMIC LOGIC AND HISTORICAL INTERPRETATION

In his seminal study of the post–World War II social consensus in the United States, Michel Aglietta argues that certain historical developments in state and society cannot be explained as "the product of an exclusively economic logic" (1979, 72). Aglietta does not reject economic logic or instrumental rationality, but insists that the analysis of historical events cannot be reduced to a single logic of action. Stressing the conjunctural origins of what he calls the "Fordist mode of regulation," he makes much of the specific political, institutional, and cultural conditions of the time to explain the economic success of the United States.

I will be adopting a similar point of view, with all necessary caveats arising from the fact that I apply these broad principles on a wider scale of time and place. Like many of the key aspects of the New Deal policies and Fordism more broadly, the origins of the offshore economy were not predetermined, but neither were they a mere accident of history. Contrary to Aglietta, however, who advanced a novel interpretation of capitalist societies in general, I restrict myself to the study of only one dimension in a broader set of transformations within modern capitalism. Inevitably, this means that the offshore economy is somewhat arbitrarily isolated from the broader picture. This can be justified on two grounds. First, the offshore economy in and of itself has not been sufficiently understood, and yet its sheer size and complexity warrant a dedicated study. Second, unlike Fordism, which was already at the point of the collapse when Aglietta wrote his book, the offshore economy is only now beginning to show its true face. As Aglietta acknowledges, "history is initiatory. But it is only possible to construct a theory of what is already initiated—which puts a decisive limit to the social sciences" (1979, 68). A study of what has only been initiated is fraught with difficulties. However, at this point a comprehensive account of the changing nature of capitalism in conjunction with the offshore economy is too speculative and my aim in this book is accordingly more modest.

Having said that, no theory of the offshore economy can be considered complete unless it is able to offer a plausible explanation of the goals and policies of three different sets of actors:

1. Offshore jurisdictions.
2. Advance industrialized countries.
3. Users and consumers of the offshore economy.

As we will see below, a number of theories combining all three have evolved. We may broadly distinguish, however, between two sets of theoretical perspectives: those drawing on *static* theories of change, and those drawing on *dynamic* theories of change. Static theories of change are our point of departure. Such theories provide plausible linkages between actors' rationality and the environmental conditions in the world economy. They operate, however, within a static grid, assuming that both actors' rationality and the basic structural conditions in the world economy are fixed and given. Change in the system is therefore external; it comes about as a result of changing environmental circumstances—in the case of offshore, rising taxation and so on.

Dynamic or holistic theories, in contrast, are predicated on the assumption that the institutional and structural environmental conditions that gave rise to offshore are historical constructions and are changing over time. Furthermore, the relationship between agency and structure is not immediate but mediated so that structural conditions shape a realm of possibilities. Hence an analysis of the structural conditions that gave rise to offshore should both contain a concept of evolving structures, and also supplement it with a detailed historical explanation of the reasons that certain courses of action were chosen over others. The assumption, in other words, is that structural analysis can tell us why offshore became a possibility, but not why it became a reality—the latter requires an agency-centered analysis.

A survey of the literature on offshore is further complicated because save for a few specialized works (Johns 1983; Johns and Le Marchant 1993; Hampton 1996; Hampton and Abbott 1999; Picciotto 1992), offshore has been largely ignored. The bulk of the literature on tax havens and offshore finance (as well as other aspects of the offshore economy) imputes rational, advantage-maximizing behavior to individuals, firms, and states (Blum 1984; Grundy 1987; Doggart 1997). But for reasons which are entirely legitimate, this literature is not so much concerned with theoretical matters as with policy issues of money laundering, criminality, and financial stability. In fact, although tax havens, and the offshore financial market have attracted considerable interest since the 1970s (Atman 1969; Aliber 1976), the two phenomena are not normally treated together, let alone linked to EPZs or flags of convenience.

Notwithstanding this, a consensus has emerged in recent debates. The consensus does not speak of the offshore economy in its entirety, but rather centers more narrowly on offshore finance and, particularly, tax havens. Tax havens are viewed as a development strategy that is particularly suitable for smaller states. The literature acknowledges that the motive of these states is to draw rent surpluses from the income that otherwise would accrue to larger states. Some view this as an abuse of the rules and codes of sovereignty. Others view it as a perfectly legitimate strategy. They acknowledge that it can lead to abuses such as tax evasion and money laundering, but believe that these abuses can be corrected if stricter international standards are agreed and acted upon. The consensus seems to be, however, that tax havens flourish in response to rising regulation and taxation in the advanced industrial countries. Offshore is viewed as an expression of a broader principle, demonstrating what happens when states introduce unpalatable and unsustainable regulatory policies (U.S. Treasury 2001).

## A STRUCTURAL THEORY OF OFFSHORE

In contrast to the views expressed in a number of recently published policy reports, the more theoretically oriented literature recognized long ago the role played by structural and institutional factors in the construction of the offshore economy. The degree of regulation or taxation in advanced industrialized countries, argues Richard Johns, provides at best a partial explanation for the emergence of the offshore economy. For a fuller explanation, we should look instead to the structural impurity of an economy operating in the context of competing sovereignties. The reasons are straightforward: "In the 'real' as opposed to the 'textbook' world of international exchange industrial specialization at the state level is both 'artificially' created and constrained by the existence of domestic and foreign national barriers to trade and other restrictions" (Johns 1983, 7). Since economic specialization is artificially created, small and poor states are no different from their larger brethren and have a legitimate right to use whatever means are at their disposal to attract business to their territories. One of the preferred tactics adopted by small states and less developed countries to attract business consists of the reduction of regulation and taxation for business through the vehicle of specialized financial laws or export processing enclaves. Offshore occurs, in other words "because governments—national, state, or local—often regulate the same transactions or activity in different ways" (Aliber 1976, 114).

This is a structural theory because it identifies the causes of offshore in the very structure of the state system. The theory suggests that small and poor states would tend to adopt tax haven strategies for a combination of reasons. Lacking an internal profit-making capacity, they cannot attract large manufacturing, commercial, or financial businesses into their territories and need therefore to offer incentives to capital. They also have less stake in the capitalist system and have proportionally less to lose from the deleterious systemic effects of the offshore economy. They are in effect free riders, who are able to more than compensate for declining revenues that result from low taxation by harvesting rent from other countries, balancing out the reduction in taxation by tapping into larger markets (Fabri and Baldacchino 1999, 141).

There is, therefore, nothing particularly mysterious about tax havens. The reason the subject has been ignored for so long has simply to do with a collective myopia in the advanced industrialized countries, where power is equated with size and strength. Johns offers, in addition, a straightforward explanation for the interest of business in offshore. Business is naturally attracted to these jurisdictions because of the freedom from regulation and reduction in taxation they offer. Indeed, business, too, has a legitimate reason to use offshore facilities because, as Lord Clyde suggested in an important court ruling, "no man in this country [the U.K.] is under the smallest obligation, moral or other, so to arrange his legal relations to his business or to his property as to enable the Revenue to put the largest possible shovel into his stores" (Johns 1983, 47) Thus, tax avoidance, as differentiated from tax evasion, is simply prudent financial management. Business uses of offshore are, therefore, legal and morally right.

Johns acknowledges the fact of system abuse and the tendency toward a "race to the bottom." In his words, "given that some countries adopt a permissive regulatory environment and others a stringent one, gaps and differentials arise in national systems of regulation. These differences can lead to perverse competition in regulatory laxity and a gravitation by some institutions to the least regulated financial centers" (1983, 6). Although minimal regulation is not always to the long-term development benefit of offshore centers (Johns 1983, 6) and there is no evidence that the least regulated financial centers such as Anguilla or Nauru are attracting much investment, concern with international regulatory competition and the problems associated with a race to the bottom are certainly justified.

The implication of Johns's theory is that offshore is not illegal and can only be eliminated if government-induced frictions and factor immobility are eliminated as well. As these frictions are an inherent outcome of the diverging policies of sovereign states, they can only be removed if the sovereignty of these states is removed as well, or alternatively if all states agree to harmonize and standardize their laws and regulation—which amounts to the same thing. Advanced industrial countries, whose companies and wealthy individuals are the principal consumers of offshore, are therefore caught in a dilemma: they can try to eliminate the offshore phenomenon entirely, but they can only do so at heavy cost to the general principles of sovereignty and the right of self-determination.

## REGULATORY COMPETITION AND PUBLIC CHOICE THEORY

Johns demonstrates convincingly that the tendency toward regulatory competition is inherent in a system of competing sovereignties. But policy, of course, is about making decisions in difficult conditions, some of which may appear structural and unchanging. We need, therefore, to probe deeper into the mechanisms of state policy and ask why the advanced industrialized countries have permitted offshore to continue and flourish without much resistance. Two very different theories have evolved to explain the puzzle. The first draws on public choice theory.

In his testimony before the U.S. Senate's permanent subcommittee investigating harmful tax practices, the former U.S. Treasury Secretary Paul O'Neill points to some key issues of principle: "I was troubled by the notion that any country, or group of countries, should interfere in any other country's decisions about how to structure its own tax system. I felt that it was not in the interest of the United States to stifle tax competition that forces governments—like businesses—to create efficiencies. I also was concerned about the potentially unfair treatment of some non-OECD countries" (U.S. Treasury 2001). O'Neill expresses the dilemma of sovereignty and power which was discussed above. While he claims to care a lot about the sovereign rights of smaller states, he simultaneously undermines their sovereignty by using U.S., power to extract special bilateral concessions from them (U.S. Treasury 2001). Furthermore, O'Neill appears to be less troubled by other aspects of the offshore economy, notably the fact that its impact, as far as we can tell, is not socially neutral. Notwithstanding these contradictions, to understand his objections to the international harmonization of business tax laws we need to delve briefly into public choice theory and the so-called "Tiebout efficiency postulate."

Writing in the specific context of competitive deregulation among municipalities in the United States, Charles Tiebout (1956) developed, in his own words, an "extreme" theory according to which municipalities provide individuals and firms with a bundle of public services and tax regulations. Individuals and firms are likely to choose municipalities that offer desirable bundles of regulations by moving into them, and to reject those that offer less desirable bundles of regulations by moving out of them. Municipalities are therefore in competition over what Tiebout called "consumers-citizens." He postulated that regulatory competition among municipalities would result in optimal regulations balancing out the provision of public services with the need for taxation.

Public choice literature suggests, therefore, that regulatory competition can moderate the tendency to overregulate and tax, and hence can provide the mechanism for an optimization of regulatory regimes (Hufbauer 1992; Garrett 1998; Rodrik 1997). Indeed, the Tiebout efficiency argument is explicitly harnessed for use against the principle of international business tax harmonization and the apportionment principle.[1] This theory forms the core argument in favor of continuing regulatory competition in the international system.

The technical issues raised by the apportioning formula and Tiebout efficiency theory notwithstanding, it is important to note that proponents of the theory, as evidenced in Paul O'Neill's apparent dedication to the principles of sovereignty and the right of self-determination of smaller states, are effectively arguing for the superiority of market discipline over the sovereign rights of states. Under the guise of a highly technical issue, a clear political program is advanced aiming at letting market forces adjudicate among state regulation and taxation regimes. Equally, the theory contains a tacit admission that sovereignty, or the right to make law, can be used as a commercial asset, for clearly the theory sees states as "selling" regulatory packages to eager consumers. Whereas for Johns, regulatory competition is an effect of a clearly defined existing international structure, here we encounter a lively debate

in policymaking and academic circles about the nature of this structure. This suggests in turn that the international structure can be subject to change. Just as the international structure may create certain
outcomes, social and political as well as economic, so also it is itself the
outcome of political forces.

### OFFSHORE AS A DIMENSION OF NEOLIBERAL GLOBALIZATION

Considering that international institutional arrangements necessarily
change over time (Braithwaite and Drahos 2000), the international
structure that encourages regulatory competition must be seen as politically contested, held in place by a balance of forces. This, at least, is
the premise upon which alternative explanations of the policies of advanced industrialized countries are based. These theories emanate from
the critics of neoliberal globalization who view public choice theories
and the like as mere ideological instruments for the advancement of a
neoliberal hegemonic project. They view the international institutional
and legal configuration as the product of transnational class strategies
(Gill 1995, 1998; Van Der Pijl 1998). The offshore economy, they claim,
works for the benefit of certain social groups and to the detriment of
others. The modern state has evolved mechanisms that were meant to
alleviate some of the excesses of capitalist exploitation and environmental degradation, generating as it were countervailing structures of
penalties and rewards. By siphoning off capital from the onshore realm,
and by avoiding the taxing and regulating arms of the state, the offshore
world is proving the prime site for the removal of such protection. This
can be seen most clearly in the case of EPZs and flags of convenience,
whose competitive advantage vis-à-vis their onshore equivalents is
measured by the degree to which taxation and labor and environmental
regulations are removed. The ostensible legality of offshore, the use of
the sovereign right to make law, is therefore nothing but a political program aimed at outflanking and redrawing the complex power compromises engendered in the (welfare) state—which, however skewed, were
still compromises (Poulantzas 1973).

   But, then, how has this political program of neoliberal globalization
come to be intermingled with the offshore world? To the best of my
knowledge, a direct link between the neoliberal globalization theories
and the offshore economy has not been established. But we can extrap-
olate from the literature an interpretation according to which the rise
of the offshore economy is linked to a shift in the balance of forces in
domestic politics (Cerny 2000).

POLITICAL POWER AND THE OFFSHORE ECONOMY

One set of theories presents the offshore economy as the aggregate out-come of conscious policy decisions—decisions that were subsequently camouflaged and mystified by general theories like those of Johns. There are a fair number of detailed studies showing how interested in-dividuals and companies played important roles in establishing offshore jurisdictions to advance their personal or corporate interests. Tom Nay-lor (1987) for instance, provides an in-depth, detailed, and persuasive tale of the criminality, drug trafficking, and money laundering that make up, or so it seems, the offshore world. Naylor traces some of the early legislation of the Caribbean tax havens to the work of the Mafia and its associates, specifically the Meir Lansky gang, and their lawyers (see also Robinson 1995). Individuals have played important roles in other cases as well. Sir George Bolton, a deputy chairman of the Bank of England, who left the bank in 1957 to take the chairmanship of the Bank of London & America, is regarded, as having been the foremost pi-oneer of the Eurodollar market (Burn 2000; Fry 1970). As we will see in chapter 4, similar stories also surface with regard to flags of conve-nience.

These are fascinating tales; they bring the offshore world alive. But what more do they tell us? We know that the offshore world is a by-product of sovereignty, and hence, that in each and every case somebody must have played a role in enacting the required specific legislation. But as Burn (2000) demonstrates with regard to the Euromarket, while Sir George Bolton was important, an explanation for the emergence of the Euromarket must take account, first and foremost, of the broad insti-tutional, political, and historical situation of the time, of which Bolton simply took advantage. Burn's analysis is applicable to other cases as well. But why have offshore jurisdictions mushroomed exactly in recent decades? Why have they served different functions at different times? Agency-based theories of the kind proposed by Naylor cannot provide a satisfactory explanation.

Class-based theories, in contrast, offer more plausible explanations. Mark Hampton (1996) shows how diverging domestic class and institu-tional interests explain the different types of offshore centers. The con-tinuing power of the British financial elite produced a predisposition in the U.K. toward financial liberalization (see also Burn 1999, 2000). The relative weakness of the U.S. financial establishment and its subordi-nation to productive capital explains the traditional hostility of U.S. administrations to the offshore world (see also Burn 2000). But the U.S. banking sector was able to exploit its political weakness and transform it into strength by transferring (or threatening to transfer) operations to London and to Caribbean tax havens. As we will see in chapter 5, by the early 1980s the U.S. banking community, led by the New York banks, was successful in changing U.S. policy with regard to the offshore economy. Hampton demonstrates, in other words, how the offshore economy has played a dual role in domestic politics: at times it appears as an expression of the domestic balance of forces; at other times it appears as an external factor changing that balance. This dual internal/external role will form an important theme in subsequent chapters of this book. Similarly, Don Marshall (1996) identifies the rise of the Caribbean offshore states with their autochthonous class structure.

There is little doubt that social, economic, and institutional structures, and the many vested interests they engender, shape state policies. Indeed, the few available detailed studies of offshore jurisdictions invariably demonstrate that in each and every emerging offshore locale, there was a local alliance of private and public interests supporting legislation in favor of offshore or, alternatively, opposing legislation against it. For instance, as we have seen, the British government and the Bank of England supported policies they believed would make London the leading financial center in the world. These policies better explain the rise of the Euromarket than do the antics of Sir George Bolton (Burn 2000). But the problems with these theories were already identified by Johns: they ignore the structural conditions that gave rise to offshore in the first place and present it as a simple outcome of conflicting interests.

### THEORIES OF STRUCTURAL COUPLING

We need, therefore, a better way of linking structure and agency. Less deterministic structural theories of offshore draw on a principle that Bob Jessop called "structural coupling." Jessop argues that the capitalist economy is not wholly self-contained, or, to use Marxist jargon, it is not a totalizing "complex structure" (Althusser 1969). Rather it is "structurally coupled" to other systems with their own operational logic(s) or instrumental rationalities (Jessop 1987, 563). With this formula, Jessop seeks to create a space for negotiated and hence unpredictable historical outcomes in the evolution of the capitalist system. But Jessop does not want to lose entirely the sense of historical determination. He argues that the term "structural coupling" captures a certain ulterior logic which "involves blind co-evolution among coexisting systems and social spheres . . . changes in its environment are reflected in changes within capitalism"(1987, 563).[2]

According to this theory, the capitalist system goes through phases of crisis and growth. Periods of capitalist crisis, which normally take the form of falling rates of profit, are also periods of intense technological and political innovation as firms seek to raise their profit ratios. Such structural conditions serve to stimulate changes in the behavior of states and firms, but the precise changes they bring about cannot be predetermined.

For example, Fröbel, Heinrichs, and Kreye (1980) argued that the EPZs began to proliferate in the 1970s in response to the crisis of profitability experienced in the core capitalist economies from the 1960s onwards. This, combined with rising taxation and trade union belligerence, drove companies to relocate to Third World countries. EPZs were established and nurtured by multinational corporations seeking low-wage workers and higher profits. Agency-oriented studies may be able to identify certain individuals or companies playing important roles in the establishment of specific EPZs, but they miss the broader picture. Similarly, theories focusing on domestic class structure may be equally misplaced. Whatever the balance of domestic forces, Fröbel et al. argued, Third World countries were quite simply unable to resist the attraction of EPZs because of their chronic balance of payments deficits (1980, 295). With regard to the role of UNIDO in popularizing these zones (discussed in chapter 4 below), they concluded: "it is clear that UNIDO conceives of free production zones from the perspective of their function in the valorization process of capital" (1980, 296). In their view, the "enclave character" of EPZs served the "provision of a modern infrastructure" (1980, 297) for capitalist accumulation. "It is the function of free production zones to fulfill the requirements for profitable world market oriented industrial production in those places in the developing countries where unemployed labor is available and suitable for industrial utilization"(1980, 295). This point is reiterated by an International Labor Organization document which states that export processing zones "are the mechanism through which global production chains are elaborated" (ILO 1998).

Fröbel et. al. therefore accept the OECD's dating of the period that saw the proliferation of the offshore economy. They contest however, its findings about offshore's origins. Far from representing a market response to a surge in regulation and taxation, the proliferation of offshore jurisdictions and enclaves was a response to the crisis of capitalism. The same idea is echoed by Giovanni Arrighi. Although the origins of the Euromarket are earlier than those of other elements of offshore, he notes, "this amassing of liquid funds in Eurodollar markets became truly explosive only from 1968 onwards" (1994, 303). For Arrighi "the formation of the Eurodollar or Eurocurrency market was the *unintended outcome* of the expansion of the U.S. regime of accumulation" (1994, 301; my emphasis). At the same time, he notes, the late 1960s is significant because "this rapid growth was an expression of the new frontiers that had been opened up for the transnational expansion of U.S. corporate capital" (1994, 303).

These authors do not claim that offshore was set up to accommodate the needs of capital. Offshore locales were already in existence for reasons that may have had little to do with the crisis of the late 1960s, but were brought into wider use and began to proliferate when the need arose. The expansion of offshore was then functionally related to a specific set of needs. What started off as sets of unintended outcomes, proving a boon to firms and wealthy individuals seeking to reduce their tax bills, served also, and equally importantly, as organized means of deterring states from reimposing higher taxation and regulation and outflanking them if they did so.

DYNAMIC THEORIES OF STRUCTURAL CHANGE

It was convenient, of course, that offshore jurisdictions happened to be in place to greet with open arms the crisis of profitability of the late 1960s. And that precisely may be the problem with the structural coupling interpretation. Were these juridical innovations mere historical accidents? Or is there more to the story then meets the eye? This takes us back to some of the more intriguing aspects of the Marxist theory of the state. We need to dwell briefly on some aspects of this theory to understand the nature of an alternative interpretation of the rise of offshore. According to Marxist theory, the state serves its proper function in a capitalist society as long, and only as long, as it appears socially neutral—as if it is standing outside social relations (Holloway and Picciotto 1978; Poulantzas 1973). The reasons for this can be summarized as follows:

(a) A society based on contract is predicated on exchange between free individuals who are equal before the law (as opposed to, say, slaves or serfs).

(b) The modern state is composed of such free individuals, defined by the state as citizens. Indeed, the state ensures their status as equal members of society with equal rights and duties.

(c) A higher authority must define the nature of the rights and duties of the individual and the nature of economic contracts.

(d) Contractual economy only flourishes in a predictable and stable environment; the state is supposed to provide such an environment. Furthermore, the state institutes and controls change in an apparently stable and predictable manner; its decisions are conducted on the apparently impersonal basis of the law. The state, therefore, is both the origin and the subject of law,

(e) As the subject of law, the state is understood to possess a corporate personality.

(f) Sovereignty is the expression of the supreme authority of the state in law enactment.

This theory maintains that the capitalist state has to present itself as a body that is external to the conflicting interests in "civil society," so it represents itself as an ideal universal citizen pursuing the national interest. The state is understood therefore as if it exists outside social relationship—as the source of law. At the same time, the state is also the subject of law.

This brief summary of Marxist state theory is a necessary background to understanding one of the more interesting interpretations of the emergence of tax havens. Sol Picciotto identifies the apparent fiction of offshore as derivative from the nature of modern capitalism. It is not the case that the state is "real," while offshore is a fiction; rather, the truth is the other way around. Modern states are abstract entities, and they have forged a concomitant abstract space, offshore. According to Picciotto, the most significant factor in the chain of events that has led to the creation of tax havens in the early twentieth century is the reification of the state in capitalist society, as an objective entity as if it existed "beyond and outside social relations." But as we saw, the reification of the state "is itself the result of the development of specific forms of statehood, based on particular social structures and practices"(1999, 44).

In fact, not only is the concept of the state an abstraction, but modern states themselves are also abstract entities. Hence "the sovereignty of the state consists of an impersonal power, wielded by public authorities, and mediated by abstract concepts" (Picciotto 1999, 44). Sovereignty defines the juridical personality of the state. At the same time, sovereignty is wielded by public authorities. Policymaking is conducted, therefore, in the name of supposedly objective concepts such as the national interest, the public interest, and the people, so that there is an important gap between the abstraction of the state and the concrete reality of policymaking.

This gap implies, first, a certain space for interpretation. As a consequence policy has an essentially interpretative quality to it. But, second, the gap must be filled by mediating sets of ideas concerning the nature of power, sovereignty, and the practice of authority. These are narratives by which society tells itself about itself. These ideas are internalized and tacitly understood, if rarely verbalized on a daily basis. For example, to our medieval ancestors, such a mediating narrative, writes Jonathan Friedman, "is best expressed in the notion of the 'great chain of being.' a universal hierarchy stretching from God through the angels, to man, to animals, and, in some versions, to the devil, a hierarchy in which every separate form of existence has its established place" (1993, 217). This discourse pervaded medieval understanding of society and power: everything else was explained and "made sense" with reference to these mediating ideas. The twin concepts of nation and state, as we will see in chapter 6, play similar roles in modern narratives of order and change.

The historical confluence of capitalist rationality, the law, forms of state, and sovereignty has produced a vernacular of territorial power in which state sovereignty is exercised within territorial boundaries. It is an organizing or mediating narrative, telling us how to think about the relationship between nation, state, and society (or people). This narrative, as we will see in chapters 3 and 6, prescribes certain relationships between territoriality and the law, suggesting that state power operates exclusively within territorial boundaries. "However, the scope of effective exercise of states' power is far from being circumscribed in precise and mutually exclusive terms. As defined by their jurisdiction, which is the substance of their sovereignty, it is flexible, overlapping and negotiable"(Picciotto 1999, 45). Furthermore, "the existence of a world market generates private economic and social relations which transcend state boundaries, so that claims to the exercise of powers and functions by different states inevitably intersect" (1999, 46). Effectively a gap has been generated between, on the one hand, the discourse of state power, territoriality, and control, and, on the other hand, the practicalities of putting such a discourse into effect. Since power is wielded in the name of abstract concepts which are fluid and subject to inter-

pretation, the exercise of state power is adaptable and contestable, and
different states have historically sought to resolve the tension in different ways. Furthermore, "the elasticity of the state's claims to jurisdiction is even greater in relation to business activities, since they entail
another layer of fiction"(1999, 46). For Picciotto, offshore was not a predetermined result of the structure of the world economy, nor was it the
result of individual action. The structural properties of the capitalist
economy have produced certain "spaces of action," and as it happens,
these spaces were filled in historically by the formation of what today
we call offshore. This does not mean that offshore was the inevitable
outcome of the gap that Picciotto sees between the ideology of the
nation-state and the practice of statehood, it was merely one option
among many. The fact that certain options were chosen over others can
then be explained in terms of political power—an implication of Picciotto's theory. The existence of such space of action may be seen,
therefore, as a contributing, but not a determining factor in the establishment of the offshore economy.

Stephen Neff says more or less the same thing when he argues that
in the nineteenth century there was a "basic incompatibility, in the
economic sphere, between the traditional prerogatives of sovereigns
and the smooth functioning of the liberal economic system" (1990, 49).
This development was unfortunately overlooked, or so he thinks, by
legal experts seduced by the intellectual attraction of positive international law. But he fails to see that these sets of contradictions were not
accidental, but structurally inherent to the capitalist economy in the
nineteenth century. Thus, the incompatibility between the different
goals of "liberalism" in fact generated an enabling space which, as we
will see in chapter 3, gave rise to offshore.

In seeing the complexity and diversity of tax regulations as a clear
opportunity for business, Picciotto is careful to note—against a simple
Marxist interpretation—that business is not necessarily in favor of the
system of diverging regulations. And while he regards the different national tax regimes as offering great opportunities for tax avoidance and
evasion—something that business understands well and may support—
he also notes that business also likes stable and predictable regulatory
environments. In this way, offshore presents business with a dilemma.
In any case, he argues, we need to distinguish between the opportunistic use of divergent tax regimes and the original causes of their emergence. Business did not create the situation, rather the root cause was
"structural"—it was a context that emerged from the system of com-

peting sovereignties, in which each state advanced its own interpretation of the rules of taxation and regulation. Faced by diverging systems
and interpretations of business taxation laws, individuals and corporations were able to opportunistically relocate to take advantage of diverging systems. The problem was well recognized from the outset, and
indeed, there has been an important movement in the twentieth century to try to harmonize national business tax laws. But again, in a
world of competing sovereignties this is proving impossible.

### A HISTORICAL ANALYSIS OF OFFSHORE

It is difficult to argue against a holistic analysis of the sort offered by
Picciotto, except to the extent that methodological holism often serves
as a disguise for latent forms of functionalism. But Picciotto takes us a
long way from what Lipietz calls the "grand engineer" conception of
history (1987), the deterministic view that some cohesive, omnipotent
"ruling class" or "transnational elite" is able to impose itself on history. Here, on the contrary, we encounter an open-ended theory of history, but a theory which does not fall prey to its nemesis, subjectivism.

A layered conception of structure and its relation to agency is proposed. The international structural forms that emerged in the late nineteenth century contained a contradiction between the emergence of national states with mutually exclusive sovereignties, that is, insulation
of the state in law and attempts by a growing number of states to impose business taxation on the one hand, and on the other the commitment to the internationalization of capital. But this contradiction
should be considered as no more than a structured realm of possibilities. How actors on the ground would react to these opportunities could
not have been predicted. True, class structures in advanced industrialized countries ensured that the solutions that were sought would not be
incompatible with the quest for profit—effectively, with market expansion or what we call the internationalization of capital. But the exact
solutions, and their long-term impact were unpredictable. Policymaking, conducted in the name of abstract concepts, harnessed a whole
slew of specialists (lawyers, accountants, judges), as we will see in the
next chapter, to interpret these concepts in light of the contradictions
it faced. The result was that offshore appears to have been created by
nobody and for no apparent reason.

At this point we can take the analysis in two directions. First, we can
demonstrate how the apparent incompatibility between state and capital was itself a product of deeper structural forms; in fact a structured

outcome. The insulation of the state in law was not an accident of history, but should be understood in the context of much broader sets of transformations which saw the rise of nationalism and the emergence of the nation-state. The new nation-state saw itself as responsible to no one but its own population. It sought to demarcate its boundaries as clearly as it could, but it also gave support to the forces of internationalizing capitalism. Nationalism (of the nineteenth-century variety) served as an operational narrative legitimizing a particular type of state.

The value of such analysis lies precisely in showing how some of the by-products of that period, namely offshore and the commercialization of sovereignty, are emerging one hundred years later as one of the key factors in destabilizing the entire narrative construction of the nation-state. I discuss these matters in chapter 6.

At the same time, we can extend the argument in the opposite direction and ask, when presented with a particular dilemma involving offshore, how and why certain solutions were chosen. A simple answer would point to the social configuration of power and interest— suggesting that, as is often the case, those in power chose solutions that advanced their interests. A more sophisticated answer would seek to include the simpler one, and add to it the mediating role of ideas. Nigel Thrift, for example, shows that the concept of such interests cannot explain action. In fact, in contrast to the scripted theories of political economy, we should pay attention to "how tentative, tendentious and uncertain global capitalism really is"(1998, 162). "Capitalist business," he argues, "is based in a notion of 'theory' that is of a different order from more formal theory; it is based on problematizing and problem spaces." Thus, "practical order is constantly in action, based in the irreversible time of strategy" (1998, 164). In our analysis of the emergence and spread of offshore, we will pay special attention to this form of practical ordering and pragmatic policymaking.

This suggests that we need to locate the growth of the offshore world in a historical context, but we need to do so without losing sight of the specific political, institutional, and cultural conditions that shaped the nature of offshore. This approach is embedded in a broader methodology which takes the view that the present "reflects the influence of past arrangements and conditions in its subsequent evolution by shaping the options open to the [actors]" (Lukauskas 1999, 264). The point is brought home well by Badie and Birnbaum (1994). Writing in a different context (that of European state formation), they provide an apt statement of the theoretical predicates of institutionalist and historicist methodologies: "Putting the state back into historical perspective," they write, "meant conceptualizing it as a sociological invention derived from social practices which were themselves situated in a specific space and time and in a cultural context which gave it [the state] meaning" (1994, 154).

We can shift the application of Badie and Birnbaum's useful methodology from the formation of the state to the emergence of offshore, and use their predicate to deepen our temporal examination of the dual process of a break with the past and a creative venture. We can think, then, of the production of the offshore economy as a historical process located within specific time/space coordinates. Accordingly, our historical narrative must

1. Demonstrate that offshore locales were deliberate constructs or innovations; demystify, in other words, the origins of specific offshore locales, and seek out the historically specific conjunctures in which offshore innovations took place.
2. Link the innovation of offshore to the institutions of the state, the firm, and sovereignty; for offshore innovation does not take place in the abstract, but derives from existing social (i.e. institutional) practices.
3. Link the innovation of offshore to the broader historical context, including the dominant discourses of the time.

In our analysis of the emergence of the offshore economy, we will therefore endeavor to add an element—let us call it an analytical space—that integrates the notion that offshore must have evolved within an institutional framework, as an outcome of practices themselves rooted in an estimation of future developments. Thus, in the final analysis, my basic premise is that offshore was not a historical necessity as much as a chosen possibility, or rather, a series of chosen possibilities. A history of offshore must begin from the assumption that what may be described retrospectively as stages in the development of offshore came about because specific actors made particular choices based on the limited information they possessed; and moreover, that they were probably oblivious to the larger and longer-term impact of their decisions.

## THEORIES OF CUMULATIVE CAUSATION

The notion of policy as interpretative practice also draws on institutionalist theory. Evolutionary institutionalist interpretations seek to understand the formation of offshore, and its subsequent impact on state and society, not so much in terms of the grand gesture, but as a process of "cumulative causation" in which actors are viewed as mere "bearers" of history. Historical events and institutional forms come about through a series of developments and contested outcomes, often enacted pragmatically and for reasons that do not necessarily have a direct link to the eventual outcome.

In the institutionalist scheme of social change, entities such as the state are hierarchical and logically interrelated sets of institutions and structures, including the governing or "political" institutions which provide these entities with formal instruments of adaptation and change. "Nation," "people," "state," and so on are socially constructed; they maintain and reproduce themselves with the aid of identifiable social practices. Governing or political institutions are "thinking" or "policymaking" bodies that react or fail to react to events. They exist and reproduce themselves within formal and informal procedural frameworks, and are limited in their ability to react by their formal and informal social structures. They are knowledge-based interpretative and discursive institutions, but inasmuch as they are institutions, though, their discourse is not open-ended possibility but is contained by the concretely evolving institutional framework (i.e., their knowledge is situated).

But how are we to conceptualize such evolutionary change? We can draw at this point on theories of cumulative causation, which explain the dynamics of the process that produces "progressive" institutional change. In his discussion of Thorstein Veblen, Bush notes that "Technological innovation changes the objective circumstances of the community. The new set of circumstances alters habits of thought and behavior; these new habits of thought and behavior are projected into other areas of the community's experience, giving rise to further innovations in the arts and sciences, which, in turn, produce new technological innovations in the community's efforts "to turn material things to account" (1988, 152). Change is understood here as cumulative causation. Remove technology from the equation and we find a useful methodology here. For example, as we will see in chapter 6, the economic logic of the commercialization of sovereignty is fairly straightforward. But if we ask: What are the likely social and political impact of the commercialization of sovereignty? Then we immediately sense that the effects are likely to be quite profound on the way citizens perceive their relationship to government. Indeed, the entire ideological framework of the nation-state is destabilized, and this will have an "economic" effect, because it will to some extent constrain and determine government economic policies.

Our survey of the literature has revealed a surprising predicament. We should not confuse, as much of the literature has tended to do, the origins of the offshore economy with its proliferation. The former, as we will see in the next chapter, dates to the later nineteenth century. The latter began around the late 1960s, when something dramatic seems to have taken place to stimulate it. Indeed, if there is a lesson to be learned from the temporal separation between the origins and the proliferation of offshore, and from the principle of cumulative causation, it is that the future impact of the offshore economy cannot be projected linearly from the present. The likely impact of the offshore world has to be seen, therefore, in a broader context.

There are in effect two sets of questions that need to be asked: one structural, the other temporal. The first concerns the conditions that gave rise to offshore in the first place. The study of these conditions also provides an inkling of the deeper effects of the offshore economy on contemporary states and societies. This brings us back to Johns's structural theory. Johns argues, convincingly, that offshore is a condition attendant upon a transnationalizing economy operating in the context of competing sovereignties. But he accepts the two basic conditions, the system of sovereignty as well as the process of capital internationalization and the political support for it, as given. In his scheme, offshore originated simply in a paradox, but merely stating the paradox ignore the issue of timing. One of the main tasks of this book will be to unravel this paradox and ask: Why and when did these conflicting trends begin to operate, and why have they contributed to the rise of the offshore economy?

# CHAPTER THREE

# The Emergence of Embryonic Forms of Offshore

In order to understand the origins of the modern offshore economy, we need to be clear about its distinctive characteristics. As we have seen, the offshore economy is often associated with the rise in regulation and taxation in the advanced industrial countries in the 1960s and 1970s. This has a superficial plausibility about it: as we will see in chapter 5, the 1960s and in particular the 1970s were indeed years that saw a tremendous expansion of the offshore economy.

There are, however, two problems with this thesis. First, offshore in its modern form emerged much earlier than its recent proliferation.[1] Second, it is the virtual character of the offshore world that is at the core of its spectacular success. The offshore financial market, as we saw, is primarily a virtual market, a convention and an accounting device. Tax havens like the Cayman Islands or Bermuda are used primarily to funnel money into the international financial markets (see fig. 1). Whatever the aspirations of tax havens might be, their core business consists of charging rent or license fees in return for granting firms a right to incorporate in their jurisdictions. If companies and individuals were required to completely relocate to tax havens, or if shipping companies had to relocate to flag of convenience states, then interest in taking advantage of tax havens or flags of convenience would have remained relatively insignificant. In contrast to other forms of competitive deregulation, whether at the municipal, national, or international level, in the case of tax havens and flags of convenience often only a purely juridical residence is sought.[2] The principal attraction of offshore jurisdictions, including the Euromarket, and the main cause for their spectacular success lie, therefore, in their ability to provide protection from national regulation and taxation without the need to physically relocate.

Figure 1. Major Net Interbank Flows in 2000, Q1.

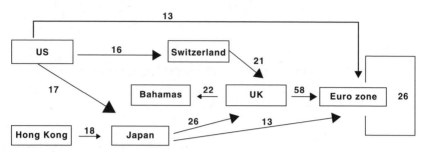

*Source:* BIS 2000.

Here we come to the crux of the matter. What lawyers call "international tax planning " comes down to a plethora of accounting strategies aiming at exploiting legal loopholes that allow individuals and companies to shift residence without actually moving. If we want to understand the origins of offshore, we need to understand therefore where and how these loopholes emerged in the first place. Their origins are to be found not in the 1960s or 1970s, but rather in the late nineteenth century, a period that saw the emergence of what can be described as embryonic forms of offshore.

For reasons which will be discussed partly here and partly in chapter 6, the nineteenth century, and in particular the second half of the century, was a period characterized by intensifying efforts at nation-state construction (Hobsbawm 1975). These states required increasing amounts of money to finance their operations, and they began to increase individual and corporate taxation in a systematic and organized manner. But throughout the century, the effects of the first Industrial Revolution, combined with the revolutions in transportation and communications and the emergence around the 1860s of the first modern multinational corporations, saw what many regard as the first phase of internationalization of capital. The emergence of nation-states and the internationalization of capital were somewhat in conflict. However, the advanced industrial states of the time wished, on the whole, to pursue concomitantly the policy of nation-state building, and that of international economic expansion. The tension between the two had to be resolved somehow—principally by a series of bilateral treaties, of which the Cobden Treaty of 1860, regulating commerce between Britain and France, is considered the most important. But some of the ideas and

principles that were introduced at the time contained potential loopholes, which subsequently were exploited by the offshore economy.

### ECONOMIC SOVEREIGNTY

To understand the history of the legal loopholes that opened up space
for the subsequent emergence of the virtual economy, we need to dwell
first on the often misunderstood relationship between sovereignty and
the market. The term "market" was introduced to the English language
in the twelfth century, ultimately from the Latin *mercatus*, meaning
"trade" or "place of trade." In the sixteenth century "market" began to
be used for buying and selling in general. In the nineteenth century
economists added the idea of the market as an abstract price-making
mechanism that is central to the allocation of resources in an economy
(Swedberg 1994, 256). The modern market is understood, therefore, as
an arena for the contemporaneous exchange of goods and services spanning the entire globe.

Such exchange does, of course, take place, but the traditional emphasis on goods and services can be misleading. Modern market exchange consists primarily of contractual relationships, or exchanges in
title rights. Indeed, a considerable portion of international exchange
nowadays is purely exchange in title rights, dispensing with the physical exchange of goods or services that is assumed to follow. I am not referring simply to the spectacular growth of trading in futures and derivatives, including financial futures, but more fundamentally to the
characteristics of a global contractual economy. As Sheila Dow explains:
"The distinguishing feature of a modern capitalist economy is that it
rests on contracts. For example, production is organized by means of
labor contracts, with payment in arrears because production takes time.
More important in relation to the financial system, investment and
production are often financed by borrowed funds which require debt
contracts. In this way, the whole system of financial intermediation
rests on contracts denominated in money" (1999, 33). The contractual
nature of market relationships reminds us that the capitalist market is
essentially "an endless chain of legal relations" (Pashukanis 1983, 85).

The distinction between exchange in goods and services and exchange in contract or title rights may appear of little importance. But
that is incorrect. Exchange in consumable goods or services is certainly
facilitated by, but does not necessitate, a formal system of law. In early
medieval Europe, for instance, the famous "land peaces" compensated
for the lack of clearly demarcated political sovereignties and a robust

system of contractual law (see Fisher 1989). Similarly, during the Renaissance and the baroque period traders relied heavily either on family ties or on their compatriots (the premodern concept of the nation) in lieu of formal contractual relationships (Braudel 1979). But the modern capitalist economy, which consists of a complex web of contractual exchanges, requires the kind of systemic support that can be provided only by a stable system of law. Capitalist society is therefore a society regulated by law; it is a society that operates within the bounds of a system of rules, historically backed up by the power of the state.

To what extent is the institution of the state an absolute prerequisite for the effective creation and reproduction of the institution of the contract? For Picciotto (1992) this is a historical relationship as the state in effect "nationalized" various laws, placing itself both as the source and guarantor of the law. Whether contractual relationships can survive the (projected) decline of the state system is a matter for speculation—I think not (Palan 2002). Notwithstanding, the institution of sovereignty serves nowadays two closely related functions. First, it functions as a constitutive code of the international states system, assigning roles of behavior and functions to sovereign states. Sovereignty is viewed therefore as the juridical expression of the principle that divides the planet into clearly demarcated lines of authority and responsibility. Secondly, sovereignty also serves as the foundation of the national and international law of contract, specifying that each individual exchange or contract must be located in a sovereign realm. In fact, each and every international commercial transaction must specify not only the choice of law—i.e. the location of the contract—but also the choice of forum of the contract. The choice of law is simply the choice of which legal system will govern the contract; the choice of forum specifies whether courts, arbitration, or other means of dispute resolution are to resolve a potential conflict (Dowling 1995). Needless to say, each of these choices opens further avenues of calculated use and abuse of law.

Far from serving as a purely political or juridical concept, the institution of sovereignty defines the unity of the political system with the economic system, for it defines not only the powers of the state but also the sanctity of contract. Differently put, the sanctity of contract is secured by the principle of sovereignty. Contractual relationships, now spanning the entire globe, are rooted, therefore, in the system of sovereign states. The state provides the security and predictability required by the economic system, but not in a mechanical or static manner. On the contrary, the law courts, as arms of the state, lay down the working rules and thus interpret the nature of the contract (Commons [1924] 1959). The centrality of contractual relationships in modern capitalism therefore places, the state and the institution of sovereignty at the very heart of the global market, because the state is "essential to the creation and guaranteeing of the property rights that are traded" (Picciotto 1992, 80).

This dual role of sovereignty suggests that however global the market may appear, it is in the true sense of the word *inter-national*. The global market does not inhabit a homogeneous juridical space—as is sometimes assumed in economic literature—but a patchwork of national systems of laws joined together by a set of bilateral and multilateral agreements. It follows that the intensity of global exchange witnessed nowadays could have evolved only once some sort of transnational infrastructure of law was in place. There is, therefore, a history, yet to be fully told, of the ways in which such a transnational infrastructure was erected. We know enough about the process, however, to be able to say that it was long and bloody (Ferro 1997). Nevertheless, by the second half of the nineteenth century market relationships were sufficiently normalized within the geographical core of the capitalist world economy to be replaced by less violent processes of legal homogenization. The embryonic forms of offshore emerged during this phase, as we will see below, because the dual role of sovereignty, as the source and guarantor of the sanctity of contract and the expression of territorial power evolved concomitantly and in a largely mutually supportive manner over a period of three hundred years or so. But the two sets of principles embedded in the concept of sovereignty came into conflict in the second half of the nineteenth century. This conflict expressed itself as a contradiction between the demand for sovereign exclusivity and the requirement for a transnational system of law and norms supporting capitalist expansion. But, as Friedman notes, "in the conflict between the supremacy of national will and the supremacy of international order, the former was an easy victor" (1964, 76). The contradictions between national legal systems which were becoming ever more insulated and discrete, and rapidly internationalizing capital were resolved in a pragmatic manner. One among four types of legal solutions to these contradictions were embryonic forms of offshore.

## FROM SOVEREIGNTY TO SOVEREIGN EXCLUSIVITY

Paradoxically, therefore, the increasing mutual insulation of legal systems, in other words the insulation of the state in law, was a major unintended cause of the emergence of offshore. Indeed, as we saw in chapter 2, the offshore economy relies heavily on universal adherence to a particular interpretation of the concept of sovereignty, which confers upon the sovereign an exclusive right to make law within a delineated territory. Such an interpretation of sovereignty is not as common, and certainly not as ancient, as is normally believed. No doubt it evolved over a long period of time, but one of the reasons that offshore emerged only in the nineteenth century was that this strict interpretation of sovereignty was a product of the same century.[3] I do not want to overemphasize only this side of the equation. The appearance of corporate taxation and the emergence of multinational enterprises was equally significant. Nevertheless, how and why sovereignty evolved in the nineteenth century in ways that produced this "basic incompatibility, in the economic sphere, between the traditional prerogatives of sovereigns and the smooth functioning of the liberal economic system" is an interesting one to ask (Neff 1990, 49). For Neff, as we saw, it was an unfortunate development, overlooked by legal experts at the time who were seduced by theoretical arguments from positive international law. I believe, however, that processes that brought about the increasing insulation of state in law just at the time capital was spilling over borders had deeper causes. It was a culmination of a broad historical process echoing the manner in which states evolved in the European context.

There is a lively debate over whether the concept of sovereignty can be traced back to Roman times or to the late medieval period (Badie 1999; Mairet 1997). Bertrand Badie (1999) argues that while Roman emperors claimed ultimate power—which does seem to be sovereign power—they did not recognize the sovereignty of competing polities, and hence, in his view, the Romans had no concept of sovereignty. The modern concept of sovereignty evolved, he argues, from about the thirteenth century and only gradually became formalized as the basic ordering code of international affairs. The states of Europe emerged through a process that combined the internal subjugation of dissent and the forging of an alliance between the bourgeoisie and the European monarchs with external "liberation" from the Holy Roman emperor and the Catholic Church (Ranke 1840; Rubin [1928] 1989). But at this stage, claims to sovereign exclusivity evolved not as a rebuff to Christian ethics but as an extension of principles already enshrined in medieval thought. Under the new doctrine, the prince was understood to be the "servant of God," and consequently sovereign laws were still embedded in a universal ethical theory (Oakley 1991). So although states were claiming sovereignty, they still viewed themselves as part of a universal Christian order founded on natural law.[4] As Kenneth C. Cole observes, "What each sovereign could reasonably claim as a prerequisite for effective local government was a finality of decision on all issues arising within his realm"—but *"insulation of the nation-state in the matter of law enforcement is a very different thing from insulation as respects law itself"* (1948, 17; emphasis mine).

No doubt, during this long period of transition, the concept of sovereignty became increasingly associated with territorial power. But although the relationship appears to us nowadays natural and necessary, the territorial principle has in fact a somewhat different history. After the fall of the Roman Empire, different tribes inhabited the same territorial space. In this state of affairs, the rule arose from the seventh and eighth centuries that every man carried with him, so to speak, the personal law under which he was born. Thus, "wherever he went, the Frank lived under Frankish law, the Visigoth under Visigoth law, the Roman under Roman law" (Schmitthoff 1954, 19). Under feudalism, however, the opposite occurred with the establishment of an uncompromising territorial conception of the law. From the twelfth century, Italian jurists, followed by their French, Dutch, and Swiss colleagues, began to develop the modern notion of municipal law, thus linking territoriality with sovereignty. In some important respect, therefore, the territorial principle matured prior to the universal acceptance of the concept of sovereign exclusivity, and that led subsequently to some confusion. The former emerged from around the twelfth century; the latter matured only in the nineteenth century.

This raises the question why states waited until the nineteenth century before they began to construct strict territorial boundaries. Although the association of territoriality with sovereignty has a much longer history, it does not seem that by itself it explains the reasons for the establishment of strict territorial spaces. Part of the answer must lie with what today we call the broader discursive context of human interaction. It is worth dwelling briefly on the epistemological foundations of modern sovereignty, so as to help explain the reasons for the development of insulation of the state in law in the nineteenth century. Contrary to current thinking in international relations, the novel aspect of the emergent concept of sovereignty, at least in the seventeenth and eighteenth centuries was not necessarily the insulation of state law, but the underpinning of concepts of law by a relativist epistemology. Medieval thought held to a "rational and moral—but static—conception of . . . order" (Richardson 1998, 81) within an, unchanging, hierarchical universe. Its cosmology, however, came under increasing pressure from the Renaissance onward, particularly during the baroque period. Heidegger shows beautifully how Newton signaled a decisive epistemological break from the orderly medieval world (and indeed, from Greek thought) in which everything had its preordained place (1993, 284). In the old epistemology, things were considered different because they belonged to different realms and hence possessed different qualities (earthly as opposed to heavenly bodies, etc.). But in the relativist epistemology of Newton, primordial differentiation collapsed and all material things, from earthly matter to the stars, were now assumed to consist of similar matter and obey similar rules.

The modern concept of sovereignty emerged during this period of changing epistemology. In the new epistemology, instead of being united in their distinctness, polities, like Newtonian matter, were now viewed as essentially similar but located in separate geographical areas. In this emerging understanding, polities were placed in relation to each other and not, as previously, as components of a hierarchical universal order.[5] But as a result of being placed in relation to each other as similar entities, states came to be not only differentiated by their territorial claims, but also placed in relations of competition with each other. Conflict was understood to result from the expansion and contraction of territorial spaces.[6]

Underpinned by this relativist epistemology, modern sovereignty contributed in time to the production of identities based on the territorial principle—or the doctrine of "natural harmony" idealized by baroque thinkers. This relativist conception was energized by a plethora of mechanical metaphors that proved significant in the construction of territorial identities. As polities were now understood to be similar, they were also visualized as material bodies, or "bodies politic." This had partly to do with the new conception of space, time, and matter, but it was also due to other related changes. One implication of the collapse of medieval cosmology was that in the Enlightenment imagination, nature became separated from society: the natural and, increasingly, the social realm were understood as distinct, self-regulating mechanisms. But as nature became separated, it could also serve as a model for social organization. With the struggle for emancipation of new disciplines such as anatomy and medicine, and as philosophers began to grasp the incredible complexity of nature, they sought to obtain comparable symmetries and harmonies in human society. A movement that sought to closely imitate the work of nature in society is in evidence. Grotius and Pufendorf, for instance, developed their theories of sovereignty and the state on the model of living organisms (Gettell 1924, 399). Such metaphorical associations chimed well with the visualization of societies as corporeal bodies, as the persistent use of organic and mechanical metaphors postulated a world divided into well-organized, bounded communities. The advent of liberalism, with its emphasis on "individual" sovereignty, coincided with a conception of the state as possessing a personality of its own (Hobbes [1651] 1951, 81). Territory was viewed increasingly as a material expression of the corporeality of the unity of the "body politic."

With the epistemological underpinnings of sovereignty located increasingly in the territorial unity of the state conceived as a "body politic," the world was increasingly viewed as divided naturally into political communities. This, in turn, gave rise to two further tendencies. On the one hand, there was the "nationalization" of various laws such as the law merchant and contract law (Barret-Kriegel 1986; Lindholm 1944; Tigar 1977). Secondly, political communities, modeled or aspiring to be modeled, as philosophers had argued, on organic entities, began to take the very shape they aspired to imitate. Both these tendencies produced a concern with the necessary spatial delimitation of the "body" of the body politic—its territory.

This took a long time to mature. Throughout the period of state formation in Europe we witness a very gradual process of putting these ideas into practice in the form of the gradual shift from frontiers to borders (Kristof 1969).[7] This shift began in connection with changes in the understanding of the nature of the body politic itself. The question arose, as we saw in chapter 1, of the extent to which political authority stretched beyond the physical boundaries of the state land onto the sea. Perhaps more importantly, however, from the late fifteenth century onward, a number of crude attempts (crude in comparison with similar efforts in the nineteenth and twentieth centuries) were made to unify and homogenize territorial spaces. These took the form of cleansing the body politic of foreign elements, the best known of which are the deportation of the Jews and the Moors from Spain (Maraval 1995). Homogenizing the territory became a goal all rulers aimed at. Foreigners were placed under surveillance and housed in special quarters, if possible near the ruler's palace. Relativist epistemology, combined with the practice of absolutism helped shape a newly rational conception of space and a theory that gradually placed a premium on the insulation of states from each other.

## THE NATIONALIZATION OF SOVEREIGNTY

I do not wish to give the impression that the insulation of the state in law and the creation of boundaries can be reduced to discursive processes. I am stressing this dimension because it helps explain the legal implication of insularity that eventually led to the formation of offshore. While absolutist states prepared the way, the emergent capitalist economy structured on contractual relationships forced changes in the institutions of state, society, and sovereignty in the late eighteenth and early nineteenth centuries, culminating in the advent of what Michael Mann calls the "infrastructural state"(Mann 1984). Prior to the nineteenth century, sovereigns certainly claimed a right to finality of decision on issues arising within their territorial realms, but formal adherence to the principles of natural law could be construed as limiting the purview of sovereignty. Only with the decline of natural law were the last vestiges of transnational ethical morality removed and states fully insulated from each other in law. Historians agree, therefore, that this was accomplished only during the nineteenth century. Only then did sovereignty began to express "the exclusive, unique institutionalized and strictly public dominance over a territorial national ensemble and the effective exercise of central power without the extra-political restrictions of juridical or moral order which characterized the feudal state" (Poulantzas 1973, 162). In fact, writes Frederik M. Van Asbeck, "since the nineteenth century we have been confronted with a new historical situation, viz., the existence side by side of isolated states, between which there is no moral or spiritual bond" (1976, 190). Only during this period did the sovereign people come to be viewed as the ultimate source of rights and duties and hence of the law, as the state effectively nationalized the rule of contracts (Medwig 1992). The strongest advocates of the new principles were American jurists. Chief Justice Marshall of the United States declared in 1812. "The jurisdiction of the nation within its own territory is necessarily exclusive and absolute. It is susceptible of no limitation not imposed by itself. Any restriction upon it, deriving validity from an external source, would imply a diminution of its sovereignty" (quoted in Neale and Stephens 1988, 10). Increasing insulation of the state in law found expression in legal theory through the rise of positive international law;[8] a doctrine that maintained that the practice of government, rather then theories about it, is the source of international law. Originally the function of positive law was to attach penalties to violations of natural law, and by doing this, to remove arbitrariness from authority (Sabine and Shephard 1922, xxiii). But in the nineteenth century positive law gave ultimate authority to the state.

Institutions do not exist in isolation; they interact with other institutions. The rising fortunes of positive international law parallel the increasing acceptance of the doctrine of popular sovereignty (first promulgated by the Fronde movement in France in the seventeenth century) (Mairet 1997). The theory of popular sovereignty changed the degree to which sovereignty was seen to imply exclusiveness, suggesting that "once a nation-state is formed . . . a "natural" organic whole has come into existence, which seems to function as a closed actor" (De Wilde 1991, 33). We witness the development of an interesting conflict between the path-dependent evolutionary development of an institution (sovereignty) and its need to adapt to a changing external reality. Veblen describes how sovereignty underwent a profound transformation at the beginning of the nineteenth century—a transformation that rendered it, strictly speaking, *non-sense*:

> In the course of this era of state-making, the prince became a "sovereign" by Grace of God, with tenure in perpetuity. . . . The prince became a sovereign; that is to say, all men became subject and abjectly inferior to him, in the nature of things; and to him, for no reasoned cause, all men thereupon owned unquestioning and unqualified obedience and service, in the divine nature of things. This notion of "sovereignty" is essentially a proposition in theological metaphysics, according to which some sort of immaterial superiority is infused in the person of the sovereign by divine fiat. . . . When and in so far as the democratic commonwealth has displaced the Monarchical State, this theologico-metaphysical attribute of sovereignty is conceived by the experts in political law and speculation to have passed over intact to the Nation. . . . The democratic Nation, therefore, is a sovereign by the Grace of God, whatever other blessings it may enjoy. But the democratic Nation has no personal existence except in the several persons of its citizens. So the experts in political speculation have drawn the logical consequence, to the effect that these democratic citizens are vested with this princely sovereignty, each and several, unalienable and in perpetuity. That is to say, these democratic citizens, each and several, by Grace of God hold sovereign dominion over the underlying population of which they each and several are abjectly servile components. So also it should apparently follow by force of the same metaphysics that each of these sovereign citizens, being at the same time a loyal member of the underlying population, by Grace of God owns unqualified and unalienable allegiance to his own person in perpetuity. (Veblen [1889] 1994, 25–26)

All this, Veblen concludes, "seems foolish of course, but it has the merit of consistency" ([1989] 1994, 27). Veblen, in effect, questions the pathos of rationality of poststructuralism. For him, consistency is valued more than rationality, so that an institution can survive despite being, strictly speaking, non-sensical—as long as it works in terms of the broad discourse of the day.

But what does "as long as it works" mean, when applied to the rise of popular sovereignty in the seventeenth century? Institutional continuity, and the logical functioning of the system of rationalities which has to incorporate a multiplicity of institutions and beliefs into some pretended coherent "whole," rendered the whole, the dominant ideology, workable only if sovereignty was reinterpreted in terms of popular sovereignty. The logic of the instrumental value system is that of efficient cause, so that instrumental values are validated in the continuity of the problem-solving process. The institution of sovereignty was now reinterpreted so as to detach it from the divine right of kings (effectively vis-à-vis the nobility, the Church, and the Holy Roman Empire) to the divine right of the people, the latter assumed to be a spiritual unity. "Sovereign" was increasingly taken to mean "functions without external interference." Popular sovereignty worked because it validated the broad transformation in state and society witnessed in the early nineteenth century.

Thus, there was no one single cause for the increasing insulation of the state in law. But by the early nineteenth century a specific historical event had generated momentous transformations. Due to the tremendous impact of the Napoleonic wars, in the course of which the entire population residing in a specific territorial location was treated for the first time (at least theoretically) as equal members of the state, the people who resided within the territorial state were now considered "citizens." The idea of citizenship, again, can be traced to ancient times. But as much as concepts such as citizenship evolve historically, it was reinterpreted in the nineteenth century within a broader discourse that assigned to it a specific meaning. Poulantzas notes that during the early years of the nineteenth century, the concept of citizenship essentially implied "the atomization of the body-politic into 'individuals'—that is, juridical-political persons who are the subjects of certain freedoms"(1978, 63). This view of individuals as bearers of rights and duties constitutes, as well as being constituted by, a conception of the state as organizer of social life. In this way, the territory of the nation-state is reinscribed in a new conception of politics, founded on a systemic conception of the social order.

Thus, it was only during the early years of the nineteenth century that territorial sovereignty was detached from Christian morality and attached to the act of governance of the people by themselves. From being a jealously guarded prerogative of the monarch, territorial sovereignty became an instrument of governance—one that could be negotiated, reformed, and improved (Douglas 2000). Consequently, although this systemic conception of social order remained latent, in the new democratic politics the nation-state was viewed increasingly in tacit system terms, that is, as a form of relationship of interdependence between units and the whole. Thus, "[m]odern individuals [are viewed as] the components of the modern nation-state" (Poulantzas 1978, 104). In this conception, state and power became homogeneous, and sovereign exclusivity becomes a central instrument of governance.

This systemic conception of the state and the attendant organic view of the state/society complex proved to be very significant. Systemic theories, although implicit at the time, generated an interesting disjuncture: on the one hand, nationalism maintained that communities were the outward expression of a deeper, primordial bonding of the "people"; In the words of Ernest Renan, nations were "une âme, un principe spirituel" (1996, 240).[9] But at the same time, societies were increasingly perceived as agglomerations of individuals held together by artificial means—by the "political system" or the state, the law, and the police. The artificiality of existing political boundaries inherited from the period of dynastic politics contrasted sharply with the pathos of the "will of the nation," and led to angry calls for the construction of political entities modeled on the ideals of nationhood. The implications of such latent systemic thinking were that system closure, translated into crude measures of territorial closure, became in the mind of contemporaries an urgent political project vital to ensure the smooth running of self-governing societies and the well-being of spiritual national entities.

### THE EMERGENCE OF A THREE-DIMENSIONAL NATIONAL CAGE

Ideas about the functional necessity of insulating states from each other for the purposes of self-governance, still implicit in the late eighteenth century, became explicit in the early years of the nineteenth century as the concept of exclusivity vis-à-vis the Church, the nobility, and the Holy Roman Empire was replaced by the concept of exclusivity in the affairs of states in relation to each other. These principles, carved out in the midst of what was, in effect, a trans-societal space of economy and society, were then expressed materially in the formation of stricter state borders—as replacements for the more amorphous *frontiers* that had constituted the boundaries between states. Theories of national exclusiveness were now put to the test, so to speak, and became policy. Consequently, parallel to states' monopolizing the means of violence and representation, by the early nineteenth century some were beginning to adopt the principles of totality and exclusivity by physically demarcating their borders.

Epistemological assumptions about the nature of state and nation, combined with new techniques of power, naturally informed state practice. During the early nineteenth century European states began in earnest to define and guard their territories and to control and regulate their populations.[10] "Over much of Europe" writes Sidney Pollard, "frontiers gelled into economically meaningful barriers" (1981, 253). Remnants of extraterritorial jurisdiction principles that had survived into the early nineteenth century were swept aside (Liu 1925). Not only were boundaries established between one state and another, but also a clear distinction was created in international law between national spaces and international spaces (Kish 1973). Similarly, by the early nineteenth century the principle was coming to be recognized that nationality and flags could be granted to ships by states other than those of their origin (Carlisle 1961, 154). Likewise, the origins of domicile laws can be traced to the late nineteenth century (Graveson 1977, 160).

The shift to clearly demarcated boundaries required an increasingly rigid interpretation of the relationship between sovereignty and territoriality as well as a new conception of the sovereign space (Liverani 1990). But as states demarcated their territories with greater rigor, they encountered a series of "technical" obstacles. For reasons partly to do with technology and later with the weakening of the colonial empires, and in parallel with the extension of the law of the sea into space, the historical context in which boundaries were established had to evolve pragmatically as countries sought to demarcate their boundaries more strictly. The principles enshrined in the law of the sea served as the model for demarcating boundaries of sovereignty: "The power of the land ends where the power of arms ends" was the motto (Bynkershoek, quoted in Kish 1973, 6). However, technology in particular posed new challenges to the discrete concept of national space. As states claimed new powers over different territories and spaces, the danger of conflagrations due to the lack of clear boundaries arose. From foreign invasion to satellite communications, the defense of the national space raised a practical question: What is the precise boundary of the national space? As technology has increasingly become detached from territorial constraints, the conception of the national space has been extended to define intangible boundaries or "shores."

Stricter boundaries founded on the principles of positivist international law engendered tensions that began to manifest themselves in earnest in the late nineteenth century in four key jurisdictional areas: ensuring that contracts signed in one country would be binding in another; conflicts between the principle of absolute sovereignty and taxation; (3) identifying the fiscal location of intangible commodities (witnessed today in software and services); and (4) the erosion by one state's rules and regulations of the sovereignty of another (Neale and Stephens 1988, chap. 1).

These tensions exercised some of the best legal minds of the era, and jurists' solutions were not straightforward. Considerable evidence indicates that in some areas of the law these tensions eroded the insulation of national territory in law. This is particularly true in the case of human rights and the limited acceptance of individuals as subjects of international law (Cutler 1997; Van Asbeck 1976). Yet the process also had the seemingly paradoxical effect of creating juridical boundaries that were "fictional" three-dimensional "national cages" of sovereignty. A state's sovereign territory extended laterally into the seas to the extreme range of a cannonball, or three nautical miles, and was later extended to twelve miles. This twelve-mile zone became the norm in the early nineteenth century (Prescott 1975, 37),[11] and generated internationally accepted horizontal lines separating one state from the another. When hot air balloons and eventually aircraft began to fill the skies, national boundaries were extended vertically up to the so-called Von Kármán line of 50.550 miles. The line determined the upward limit of jurisdiction in the atmosphere, effectively extending the sovereign space to fill a three-dimensional volume. More than ever before, sovereignty was seen to reside within—and only within—this three-dimensional national cage. The principle also applied to the entire subsoil of national territory, to the center of the earth (Kish 1973).

Faced by the problems of the movement of "intangible goods," states relied on these same principles to extend their boundaries into "imaginary" spaces, that is, to extend the national cage into the purely juridical dimension. We see this first with regard to patent laws, then with the introduction of passports and passport controls during World War I, and then with the delimitation of intangible forms of property rights.

Paradoxically, even as the sovereign nation cage (or territoriality) evolved, the increasingly discrete state system was faced with momentous expansion and integration of the world economy. Technological advances in land and sea transportation contributed to the emergence from around the 1850s of a much more integrated world economy (Hobsbawm 1975). More significant to our subject was the emergence of a new type of enterprise, the modern corporation. Until the 1840s, writes Alfred Chandler, "traditional enterprise remained as all-pervasive in production as in commerce" (1977, 5). But from around that time, a new type of company emerged, which was to have a profound impact on the nature of the global political economy. International companies were certainly not a new phenomenon. The East India companies (Dutch and English) are perhaps the best-known examples of traditional multinational enterprises. But, writes Christopher Tugendhat, "to list these examples is to evade the issue. The present situation is quite different from the past. . . . The most striking characteristic of the modern multinational company is its central direction. However large it may be, and however many subsidiaries it may have scattered across the globe, all its operations are coordinated from the center" (1971, 10). These companies were internally integrated, centered in one of the leading nation-states, but with subsidiaries spread around the globe—a problem, no doubt, for the fledgling territoriality principle. The first modern multinational enterprises began to expand beyond their home countries in significant numbers in the 1860s. Among the first industrialists to cross borders were Friedrich Bayer, who took a share in a plant at Albany in New York State in 1865, two years after establishing his chemical company near Cologne; and the Swedish inventor of dynamite, Alfred Nobel, who set up an explosives plant in Hamburg in 1866. In 1867 the U.S. Singer sewing machine company built its first overseas factory in Glasgow (Tugendhat 1971, 12).

Although the big expansion of multinationals took place only after the end of World War I (Chandler 1990, 157–61), the principles of the international legal framework that was supposed to deal with the potential disputes arising from the conflicting principles of territoriality and internationalism evolved in the late nineteenth century. It was generally recognized that the authority of a sovereign over a subject's allegiance does not cease when the subject leaves the state territory (Neale and Stephens 1988, 10). How, then, were states supposed to bridge the two principles? In dealing with this problem, two ideas proved to be nonnegotiable: the principle of exclusive sovereignty (or the territoriality principle) which evolved in response to the broader restructuring of capitalism and the state; and the strong support by governments of the major industrialized countries of the time—Germany, the United States, and the United Kingdom—for business and the internationalization of business (Picciotto 1992, Neff 1990).

Faced by these contradictory demands, jurists were not surprisingly unable to come up with a neat and clear-cut solution to the problem. As a result, the tension between the two principles remains at the roots of many present-day disputes about jurisdiction (Neale and Stephens 1988, 13). The solution, or rather the various solutions proposed and implemented, were therefore of a tactical and pragmatic nature. By "tactical" I am not implying that they were transitory or unimportant; on the contrary, the major industrialized powers were experimenting with a number of ideas. But these ideas never added up to a clear and uncontested set of principles; rather they evolved and changed over time—and are still changing today. The patchwork of international laws evolved, first and foremost, through what was then called "municipal" (that is, national) legislation governing foreign affairs and the law of treaties. International law developed gradually as the core states of the emerging economy clarified the way in which they would treat foreigners and extrajurisdictional contracts.

The principle of "comity," according to which two nations would allow each other's legislative, executive, and judicial acts to take effect to a certain extent within their territories provided one basis for dealing with these matters. It was viewed as a matter of both international duty and convenience (Neale and Stephens 1988, 14).

A second layer of rules was gradually added to this, through a host of bilateral treaties designed to harmonize laws concerning the treatment of aliens. At this stage, the universality of international law was not yet assumed, and treaties frequently discussed the extent to which "international law" was applicable outside "Western Christendom" (Jenks 1958, 29). Commercial treaties became the most important species of international convention. The most significant of these was the 1860 Cobden Treaty, which became the model for numerous subsequent commercial treaties and produced what Nussbaum calls an "interna-

tional bill of rights." (1961, 203). Under such treaties, nationals of each
signatory country were granted a series of rights in the other: personal
and property protection; free sojourn; admission to trade and industry
including the right of permanent establishment of business activities;
protection from discriminatory treatment regarding taxation and similar imposts; free access to courts; freedom of ownership; and exemption
from military service (Nussbaum 1961, 204). Many of these treaties
were supported by stock clauses, such as the "national treatment
clause" which promised the nationals of each country some of the same
rights as those enjoyed by the nationals of the other. Some treaties were
signed for mutual assistance in the enforcement of national law among
governments and "among courts of civilized nations" (Nussbaum 1961,
212). The most important type of bilateral treaty, perhaps, was that
which established uniform principles in the "choice of law"—that is,
that each contract must specify its location for jurisdictional purposes.

In addition to the layers of municipal laws and bilateral treaties,
states allowed companies to develop their own "law." Jean-Phillipe
Robé notes that as "state lawyers have found great difficulty in agreeing
and formulating amongst themselves rules which apply to international commerce they preferred to leave the initiative to traders themselves" (Robé 1997, 50). This has allowed the growth of a hotly disputed
branch of private international law: the *lex mercatoria*, or law merchant—a branch of law that traces its origins to medieval times and already at that time was being used as the basis for the treatment of con-
sular representatives (Nussbaum 1961).

Because the legal solutions to the tension between the territorial
principles of sovereignty and internationalism were not set up centrally
with a clear view of the long-term implications, but rather emerged
haphazardly in different forums, certain loopholes were inevitable, and
some of these were later exploited by the offshore economy. The more
integrated the world economy, the more visible the tensions will be,
and the more apparent these loopholes will become. That was not yet
the case even in the nineteenth century, but the competition that char-
acterizes the offshore economy was foreshadowed in the one state that
achieved integration of its economy within the context of a loose federal structure, the United States.

### THE DELAWARE CORPORATION

The competitive dynamics that eventually produced offshore were already in evidence during this period within the federal structures of the

United States. The modern tax haven caters to a varied clientele, including wealthy individuals, multinational enterprises, financial corporations, and insurance companies. It does so by providing a whole host of laws (or a lack of laws) to attract their business. But today's tax havens are in effect an amalgam of strategies that originally evolved separately in response to niche demand. For example, the earliest evidence of strategic lawmaking of the kind that we associate with offshore emerged in the laws of company incorporation in the United States.

Modern incorporation laws came relatively late to the United States.[12] A forerunner of the close binary relationships that characterize many tax havens such as Luxembourg and Belgium, Monaco and France, Liechtenstein and Switzerland, the Channel Islands and the United Kingdom, and Panama and the United States (discussed in chapter 4), New Jersey's corporation law was intended to attract business from its richer neighbor, New York. And just like many tax havens, from Monaco to the Cayman Islands, metropolitan lawyers brought in the idea of creating specially designed tax laws.

The first comprehensive general incorporation law in the United States was the 1846 Iowa act (Larcom 1937, 2). But following the American Revolution "the individual American states were jealous of the sovereign right to create corporate bodies, and insisted upon examining each application upon its merits" (Lindholm 1944, 46). By that time, New York and Massachusetts were already the homes of some of the largest corporations in the world. During the 1880s, New Jersey was in dire need of funds. A corporate lawyer from New York persuaded Governor Abbet to back his scheme to raise revenue by imposing a franchise tax on all corporations headquartered in New Jersey. The scheme provided that New Jersey should "liberalize her laws regarding corporate regulation to an extent that would make it advantageous for all corporations to be organized under her protection"(Lindholm 1944, 57). When the Delaware legislature debated the drafting of a new general incorporation act in 1898, it sought to emulate the success of New Jersey. Here again, a group of lawyers from New York played a prominent role in drafting the proposed act (Larcom 1937, 9). It was obvious at the time that Delaware was enacting "liberal" laws to attract corporate business (Larcom 1937, 17). A contemporary study of the practice argued that "the sale of corporation charters at bargain prices by a state was always questionable from an ethical point of view and has not become such from a financial standpoint"[13] But as Lindholm (1944, 160) notes, by

1902, 1,407 corporations were incorporated in Delaware and by 1919, 4,776. In fact between 1916 and 1926 incorporation fees and the annual franchise tax provided more than 40 percent of Delaware's state revenues. Today Delaware is still home to half of the New York and American Stock Exchange listed companies because of its business-friendly environment (*Lectric Law Library Lawcopedia* 2002).

### THE BEGINNING OF OFFSHORE

Although the smaller American states competed by offering "liberal" incorporation laws, effectively utilizing principles that we still associate with offshore, they were still the real homes of these companies. The principle of purely fictional incorporation for tax purposes, which had a far more profound impact on the development of the offshore economy, originated elsewhere. This had to do again with the tension between the territorial principle and internationalism.

Sol Picciotto traces the origins of the practice to a series of rulings of British law courts. In the last quarter of the nineteenth century, problems involving the tax liability of British companies whose activities took place abroad began to surface. The British government handled the issue with the aid of the courts. In 1876 the issue of extrajurisdictional corporate taxation was brought before the Exchequer courts. In *Cesena Sulphur Co., Ltd. v. Nicholson* and *Calcutta Jute Mills v. Nicholson,* the courts held that although the activities of these companies took place abroad, they were under the control of persons belonging to a governing body located in England. They were therefore resident in Britain and liable to the national tax regime. Aware that many shareholders were foreign, the court contended that if they invested in a British company they were liable to pay British tax (Picciotto 1992; Schmitthoff 1954, 382–86).

The courts later established the further principle that British-registered companies could not escape potential liability for income tax on their trading profits unless the whole of their activities and all their management and control took place abroad. The precedent for this was the 1929 case of *Egyptian Delta Land and Investment Co. Ltd. v. Todd.* It was demonstrated that although the company was registered in London, "The business of the company was entirely engaged and controlled from Cairo where the directors and secretary permanently resided; the seal, minutes and books of accounts and transfer were kept, transfers were approved [before being registered in London], and dividend was declared and paid. . . . [Consequently] the House of Lords held that the company was ordinarily resident in Egypt, and not in the United Kingdom" (Schmitthoff 1954, 384). The court effectively set a limit on the principle of nationality of British companies, by reference to the degree of real links to the territory of the British state. By doing so, it allowed for the proposition that some British companies were not subject to the nationality principle because of their tenuous links to British territories. This case created, argues Picciotto, "a loophole which, in a sense, made Britain a tax haven" (1992, 8). Companies could now incorporate in Britain and be assumed elsewhere to be British, but avoid paying British tax. The ruling proved significant because it applied not only to the United Kingdom but also to the entire British Empire, a point later exploited by jurisdictions such as Bermuda and the Bahamas and perfected in the 1970s by the Cayman Islands.

Modern bank secrecy laws, in contrast, evolved in Switzerland. Strictly speaking, these laws belong to the next phase in the evolution of offshore described in chapter 4. Nonetheless, the story of modern bank secrecy laws helps bring into sharp relief the effects of the tension between territoriality and internationalism. Bank secrecy is an old and well-established principle. Swiss bankers began offering secrecy to aristocrats for a fee during the French revolution, and *comptes anonymes,* numbered bank accounts, were invented at the end of the nineteenth century (Robinson 1995, 133). The Swiss developed these practices further, so that as early as the 1920s Switzerland became the preferred location for asset protection (Fehrenbach 1966, 49). At that time, Switzerland was the only country in Europe not imposing restrictions on foreign exchange. In addition, the Swiss Supreme Court had ruled much earlier that, unless customers specifically authorized them to do otherwise, banks were under a binding obligation to preserve secrecy. Not surprisingly, many wealthy families moved their assets to Swiss banks. Around the 1920s, too, the Swiss began experimenting with the idea of the "offshore corporation," drawing on the experience of the United States (Fehrenbach 1966, chap. 3; Faith 1982). A number of Swiss cantons, emulating Delaware and New Jersey, competed with one another by deliberately writing their company codes to allow incorporation of as many firms as possible. Swiss lawyers created corporations with dummy Swiss directors, whose shares were held by personal holding companies, with the identities of their owners kept secret under the banking secrecy laws. In this way, the Swiss created companies that under international law were deemed to be completely Swiss and therefore protected by Swiss and international law, but whose assets were located in other countries.

Threatened by the depression of 1929 and in particular by the series of bankruptcies in Austria and Germany in the early 1930s, the Swiss parliament began to debate an amendment to the bank law to safeguard the Swiss banking system. Contrary to the original intention of this reform, the Swiss financial industry managed to persuade the authorities to adopt stricter principles of bank secrecy than ever before. In 1934, for "the first time in history the principle of bank secrecy was put under the official protection of the penal law" (Fehrenbach 1966, 73). It became a criminal offense for bank officials to divulge any information regarding a customer's identity, even to the Swiss authorities, and the protection was extended to protect foreign nationals as well.

In offering this protection to nationals of other countries, the Swiss simply took advantage of the international norms that had evolved in the nineteenth century, under which foreign nationals were accorded the same level of protection as citizens. But these norms had evolved to facilitate interaction among citizens and companies of different countries. Now, however, the norms were used specifically—although the Swiss denied this vigorously at the time, and later claimed that the law was intended to protect victims of Nazi persecution—to attract the business of foreign nationals.

Many countries viewed the Swiss law as an act of aggression. In fact, in some countries—such as Spain—owners of Swiss corporations could be jailed! (Fehrenbach 1966). The United States, in particular, put great pressure on the Swiss over divergent interpretations of the principle of sovereignty, but to no avail. The problem was exacerbated when the Bahamas, Liechtenstein, Lebanon, soon devised their own bank secrecy laws. A steady supply of bank deposits found its way to these havens from people—including criminals, money launderers, and tax avoiders—who for one reason or another sought to escape scrutiny in their own countries. Swiss law became the benchmark, and any newcomer had to up the stakes. Whereas the Swiss invented the numbered account, insisting that at least two bank officials know the identity of an account holder, Luxembourg took the idea a step further by providing that only one bank official should know the account holder's identity. Austria then took the principle to its logical conclusion: according to that country's banking law, no one needs to know the identity of an account holder. Consequently, as other countries followed suit, the struggle to restrict bank secrecy became far too difficult to pursue. Even if Switzerland had relented and changed its banking laws, there would still have been sixty-eight other tax havens to deal with. In the end, the United States abandoned the struggle and joined the ranks of offshore jurisdictions by creating its own variant of the low regulation environment, the international banking facilities.[14]

The inauspicious, eclectic beginning of the modern system of tax havens is not only a historical curiosity; it also alerts us to an important distinction between the origins and the later diffusion and growth of the phenomenon. Although development of tax havens is naturally of great interest to financial regulators, their origins are what international relations scholars find interesting, not least because of the importance attached to a system of states, particularly a system of sovereign states, that appears to have encouraged the experimentation with and innovation in state laws that produced tax havens.

### THE DENIAL OF THE UNITY OF THE SUBJECT

Some amendments to national laws enshrined principles whose implications apparently were not entirely understood at the time. The way the British state stumbled upon tax havens and the Swiss government enacted its banking secrecy laws were simply instances of the use of courts and legislatures to handle the tension between the internationalization of capital and the sovereign rights of states. The solutions of the British and Swiss governments, however pragmatic they may have appeared at the time, were radical and innovatory. In extending the new banking secrecy laws to foreigners, which as we have seen was a principle well enshrined in international law, the Swiss government reaffirmed its claims to sovereignty over accounts "held" in its territory. In so doing, the Swiss government indicated its adherence to principles that were already accepted in British law—namely, that the location of intangible assets is determined by the place where transactions physically take place. This meant that, initially, the physical act of opening an account was sufficient to offer sovereign protection to account holders, wherever they might live or whatever citizenship they might possess. Later, with the advance of technology, the physical act itself could be dispensed with, since interacting face to face with a bank clerk located in a tax haven is no longer necessary.

In applying its protective laws to foreigners, the Swiss government, in effect, followed the British example and extended the notion of territoriality into a fourth juridical dimension. At the same time, the Swiss banking laws of 1934 denied any sovereign claims over foreign accounts by the holders' real countries of residence. The Swiss government instead claimed a sovereign privilege to write its own laws. In so doing, the Swiss in effect legislated that individuals could be separated from their money; account holders could reside in one country and, for all intents and purposes, be under the sovereignty of that country; but their money, when deposited in a Swiss bank in Switzerland, was deemed to be under Swiss sovereignty. It was, of course, entirely in accordance with the principles of territorial sovereignty for the Swiss government to devise laws that (1) "extend the courtesy," as Paul Fehrenbach puts it, and provide foreigners with the same protection Swiss citizens were enjoying in Swiss courts; and (2) as a consequence, protect those foreigners from their own governments' sovereign claims.

Now, if we probe deeper into the Swiss law of 1934, we notice that the Swiss government proposed to resolve the tension between the insulation of the state in law and the internationalization of capital by questioning the legal unity of the subject in law. Individuals, as citizens or as corporate entities, could reside in one capacity in one jurisdiction, and in another capacity in another jurisdiction. And since "real," living individuals cannot spread themselves physically over different jurisdictions, they were offered fictional or juridical location in Switzerland.

To resolve the taxation difficulties posed by the activities of multinational enterprises, the British state proceeded similarly: A series of court rulings from 1880 onward allowed for the division of the legal unity of enterprises: they could be incorporated in the United Kingdom but reside elsewhere. The U.K. courts insisted on evidence for real residence of companies as opposed to fictional residence. Other states, which were not as concerned with material evidence of corporate activity, used the same principle as mere bait by which they were able to sell companies "off the shelf" to any interested party. The effect of these rulings was to create a new international principle that allowed legal persons to divide themselves among different jurisdictions. This, to my mind, is the origin of offshore!

These rulings have had some startling consequences. Because of the discrete nature of insulated "national" laws, multinational enterprises do not exist in law. As Robé (1997) argues, "*de jure*, the multinational enterprise, as differentiated from *the corporation*, does not exist in law"! Yitzhak Hadari substantiates the argument, noting that "the MNE is a business and economic creature, and the usage of that term is presently found only in those fields. Properly viewed the MNE is not a single *legal* entity, but rather a group of corporations throughout the world sharing a single underlying economic unity" (1973, 754). The patchwork of international as opposed to truly global law creates what Richard Johns calls "the potential for government-induced frictions and factor immobility" (1983, 2). But far from being a hindrance, "the separation of the enterprise into distinct legal entities enables corporations to achieve greater efficiency. It can provide a convenient vehicle through which a single group can manage much different business" (Hadari 1973, 758). Thus, "the "greatest challenge to state sovereignty comes from organizations which have no existence in law!" (Robé 1997, 52). "Although the economic or political reality of the existence of enterprises such as IBM, Toyota, Elf Aquitaine and the like is not questioned by anyone, *the enterprises themselves do not exist as such in positive law*" (Robé 1997, 52; emphasis mine).

Although Robé uses language too strong for most jurists, there is broad agreement that the legal status of the multinational enterprise is ambiguous. There are certainly ways and means by which different legal systems have sought to clarify their positions with regard to the nationality of corporations, not only for the purpose of taxation but also for diplomatic protection and inclusion in bilateral and multilateral treaties.[15] More specifically, in most countries income tax statutes contain specific provisions under which tax authorities may fully or partially disregard the separate existence of a corporation in a multicorporate structure, if this is necessary in order to prevent tax avoidance or tax evasion. Courts also try to distinguish between real and sham corporations (Hadari 1973). Nonetheless, the variations among different statutes and interpretations, including the marked difference between Anglo-Saxon and continental laws, muddy the waters considerably (Leben 1980). Combined with the proliferation of tax havens and the practice of "treaty shopping," multinational enterprises have managed to obtain considerable freedom from national laws.

The dissection of sovereignties can reach absurd proportions. In 1953, in *Lauritzan v. Larsen*, the U.S. Supreme Court determined an issue of jurisdiction over foreign-registered ships by postulating the possibility of seven jurisdictions: the place where a wrongful act was committed, the law of the flag, the allegiance or domicile of the injured party, the allegiance of the ship owners, the place of contract, the accessibility of the foreign forum, and the law of the forum (Carlisle 1961, 160). The denial of the legal unity of corporate personality makes perfect sense from the perspective of national sovereignty, sovereign equality, and national self-determination, but it has created huge problems for the regulatory capacity of the state. Under the circumstances of the growing insulation of the state in law and the internationalization of capital, it was logical to extend the same principle of demarcation into a new imaginary analytical space in which foreigners were presumed to reside in some capacity within the territorial boundaries of one state and in another capacity in another state. Furthermore, each state developed its own principles of demarcation.

There was a price to pay for dividing the legal subject in law in order to accommodate a stricter notion of territorial demarcation and thus to uphold and even strengthen the fiction of the discrete juridical unity of the sovereign state. The fiscal subject was divided: in the fictional world of sovereign equality, its activities were placed under various jurisdictions, each representing a spatio-analytical (for want of a better term) territory. But while the fiscal subject was denied full legal unity, the real subject—whether corporate or individual—remained whole. With the complicity of a growing number of governments, these juridically dispersed subjects have learned to take advantage of the fiction of their fragmentation by rearranging their legal existence in whatever ways they see fit.

Since individuals and corporations were given the opportunity to spread themselves into different localities, they understandably went "shopping" for those localities that offered them what they considered to be the best arrangements. The ambiguity of the law, and the diverging and insecure interpretations of legal and fiscal jurisdictions, ensured, however, that for the sake of prudence many corporations avoided the more scandalous tax havens. But the practice of jurisdiction shopping—or commercialized sovereignty—has spread. This is the true meaning of the term "international tax planning"; it is the planning of whichever aspect of their "reality" corporations or wealthy individuals are prepared to reveal at which location.

In this chapter I argued that it is not enough to recall the history of the first instances of offshore legislation. Offshore did not spring spontaneously from the will of certain individuals or states, but required a prior phase which saw the establishment of what I call "spaces of action"—the legal and political infrastructure that later supported the offshore economy. That original phase, which took place in the nineteenth century, was not intentionally connected with the subsequent development of offshore. It came about because of the pragmatic and concrete manner by which different states sought to resolve the basic contradiction between the insulation of the state in law and the internationalization of capital. There is little evidence that jurists and policymakers at the time had any inkling of the future possibility of offshore, yet it is difficult to describe that original phase without also discussing the later actual development of offshore.

It is in the denial of the juridical unity of the corporate subject, a ploy that certainly helped resolve in the short term the contradictory developments of capitalism in the late nineteenth century, that the origins of the offshore economy lie. This suggests, as argued in chapter 2, that offshore was simultaneously an intended but also a structurally determined outcome. In the broadest sense, the origins of offshore can be linked to important contradictions in the basic institutional structure of modern capitalism, namely, the expansion of market relationships within the context of a particularistic state system. And this suggests, in turn, that offshore cannot be relegated to the status of a peripheral or subsidiary after-effect, but must be seen in the context of the general development of capitalism.

Clearly, the insulation of the state in law could work only as long as subjects did not move between states. Because as long as they stayed put, there was no distinction to be made between subjects "in" the territory and "of" the territory, that is, those who were physically located in the territory and those who were legally citizens of that territory. When subjects began to move between territories, or to own properties in other territories, states were forced to reconcile their claims for exclusive sovereignty over subjects "in" and "of" their territory, and that reconciliation always took the form of a compromise. The need for compromise was clearly understood by jurists and policymakers, as the Cobden treaty and other bilateral and multilateral treaties demonstrate. The compromise was viewed at the time (and even now) primarily from the perspective of the state. It showed that claims for sovereign exclusivity were not, and could not be, absolute. It was less obvious at the time that the sort of compromises hatched by jurists also had important implications for subjects, individual or corporate, who could not be considered under the exclusive sovereignty of one state. This gray and murky area of near, but never absolute exclusive sovereignty, created therefore a parallel gray and murky area in which the assumed unity of the subject in law could not be upheld. This was a successful and workable compromise. For unless states were prepared to accept the principle of relative sovereignty and the relative unity of subjects, these subjects could not move from one place to another.

The compromise was not viewed as particularly problematic at the time. On the contrary, the underlying assumption was, as Ian Goldman (2001) shows, that each state wanted to give the best privileges to its own citizens, individual and corporate, to the detriment of citizens of other countries. The Cobden treaty and other similar treaties simply sought to offer a higher degree of protection to foreigners. No one could have predicted that some states would wish to reverse the logic and offer privileges to foreigners they might not offer to their own citizens! But that remote possibility was inherent in the legal and political agreements established in the nineteenth century. Growing integration of the world market and advances in communication and transportation technologies tipped the balance for some of the smaller jurisdictions in favor of offering privileges to foreigners, using that strategy to harvest revenue from the world economy.

In spite of having emerged in the late nineteenth century in the context of stricter territorial demarcation of the state at a time of growing internationalization of capital, offshore then remained dormant for about fifty years. Save for the antics of some of the smaller U.S. states, deliberate offshore legislation is witnessed only after World War I, and even then the offshore economy evolved only slowly and in a haphazard manner. Different jurisdictions stumbled upon different aspects of the modern tax haven strategy such as bank secrecy laws, low taxation, "liberal" corporation laws, and these attributes appear to have originated in different places and at different times. It was only by the 1930s that a small number of tax havens, including Switzerland, Liechtenstein, the Bahamas, and Bermuda, began to integrate the diverse elements into a core component of their developmental strategies. Then, like a gigantic jigsaw puzzle, the various elements joined together around the 1970s to produce a coherent offshore economy.

# CHAPTER FOUR

# The Growth of an Offshore Economy

A well-known principle of the history of the diffusion of scientific innovation is that of supervening social necessities. Once prototypes are in place, observes Brian Winston, "general supervening social necessities now work on these prototypes to move them out of the laboratory into the world at large" (1998,6). The development of offshore appears to have followed a similar pattern: once prototypes or embryonic forms of offshore were in place by the 1920s, supervening social necessities helped diffuse the principle around the world. With the diffusion of these innovations, a second phase in the development of an integrated offshore economy began. Then, from the 1960s onward, the still diverse and disparate innovations were competitively emulated by yet more states, until the offshore economy was transformed from a mere potentiality to an everyday reality.

Of course, this rise of the offshore world was part of broader trends in economy and society, and the relationship between offshore and the wider capitalist world economy changed over time. From the 1920s to, say, the mid-1960s, the offshore economy evolved slowly, and did not play an important part in shaping the development of the capitalist world economy. Furthermore, while the new offshore jurisdictions took advantage of the legal principles that had been put in place in the late nineteenth century the conflict between the principles of territoriality and internationalism did not as yet play a significant role. Around the late 1960s however, things began to change. From then on, the offshore world became an attractive alternative to businesses battered by the scourges of rising taxation, regulation, and labor unrest at home, and a general decline in profitability associated with the collapse of Fordism (Aglietta 1979) and the onset of stagflation in the 1970s. This period saw a massive expansion of the offshore world. At the same time, we begin to witness a more political use of offshore as a threat to taxing and regulating governments.

The innovatory potential of anachronistic social formations is nowhere better demonstrated then in the case of the European tax havens. Switzerland, Luxembourg, Liechtenstein, Monaco, Andorra, Gibraltar, and the Channel Islands—these were all small jurisdictions that failed, by their admission, to move with the times (Fehrenbach 1966). Each of these formations boasts its own unique history and sense of survival, and they all ended in one way or another exploiting their oddity for pecuniary gain. Their spokesmen argue, of course, that they never set themselves up deliberately to garner rent from their neighbors by adopting permissive legislation. Rather, it was the other way around: the world around them was launched on a course that led to an unprecedented rise in taxation and regulation.[1] In the words of Colin Power, Jersey's top civil servant, "It is not the island that has made itself more and more attractive, it is the relatively high tax structures of the main industrial countries that have made them relatively unattractive" (Jeune 1999).

The long-term context of the rise of these places as tax havens was the advent of so-called mass society. The introduction of scientific methods of production (Taylorism) and the conveyor belt (Fordism) during the early years of the twentieth century contributed to an unprecedented rise in productivity. There were, however, no social mechanisms able to absorb the massive increase in goods and no concomitant mechanism ensuring that demand for these products would rise in proportion to the rising supply. This contributed to the general crisis of overproduction which marked the beginning of the Depression of the 1930s. The crisis was eventually resolved as New Deal types of social regulation spread throughout the advanced industrialized countries leading to a drastic rise in taxation and social regulation (Aglietta 1979). Faced by such momentous changes, the small feudal leftovers in Europe did not follow suit, not least because they were neither producers nor important consumers of mass goods. They remained wedded to the past. Soon, and according to their rulers, to their chagrin, they found themselves in receipt of "hot money" in search of low-tax, no-questions-asked jurisdictions.

### Anachronism and Innovation: The Cases of Monaco, Andorra, and Liechtenstein

The smallest among these anachronistic jurisdictions (five square miles in size) was the Grimaldis' Monaco,[2] which remained until very recently a specialist asset haven, where wealthy foreigners placed their savings. Monaco, which traces its origins to medieval times, would have disappeared during the Napoleonic wars but for the fact that Talleyrand was a personal friend of the Grimaldis and wrote in pencil on the margin of a draft project, that ultimately became the Treaty of Paris (1814), the words "and the Prince of Monaco will be restored to his State" (Smith 1912, 103). Monaco remained poor, however, and in 1856 Prince Charles III sought to alleviate poverty by establishing the famous Monte Carlo casino. Charles was impressed, no doubt, by the successful examples of small German states, Wiesbaden, Baden-Baden, and particularly the principality of Hesse-Homburg. The prince, in fact, imported a certain Mr. Blanc, who worked for the Homburg casino, to set up the Monte Carlo casino.[3] Not that the government of Monaco was in favor of gambling—of course not. In a self-righteous explanation, rather typical of the pronouncements of contemporary tax haven governments, an official document from that time lays down Monaco's position:

> As a matter of principle, we do not approve of gaming houses, and the governments who suppress them act wisely. Established in large centres of population, they constitute a permanent excitement, stimulating the spirit of cupidity, and bring about the demoralization and ruin of unfortunate people who, attracted by the false hope of gain, press passionately round the green baize. But when such games are established a long way from the large towns, and when the distance is such that the cost of the journey can only be met by rich foreigners, one may accord them the benefit of extenuating circumstances, for they do bring an element of prosperity amid the native population, who are themselves severely excluded from the gaming saloons. Such are the conditions enforced at Monaco: everything is so arranged as to safeguard the morals and the money of the inhabitants, while conferring on them the material advantages resulting from the sojourn in their midst of numerous tourists. (Smith 1912, 117–18)

In any case, following the construction of the railway to Nice, opened 25 October 1868, the Monaco casino proved to be a great success. Soon after, Charles III abolished "with one stroke of the pen all direct taxation" (Smith 1912, 125). He did so, according to sympathetic historians, because he was fearful of the tax revolts he had seen in his youth, and was anxious to show that he was not profiting from the casino. Nevertheless, since revenue from the casino paid for the entire public affairs of Monaco, low taxation and the Mediterranean climate attracted many wealthy visitors and residents, and Monaco became the model of a cheerful, fabulously rich tax haven. It took about half a century, however, for Monaco to develop a veritable tax haven strategy.

Other European tax havens originated in equally exotic circumstances. Andorra, established as an independent country by Charlemagne, still pays small feudal tributes to France and to the Bishop of Urgell (Spain) to whom it was ceded in 1133. Recently it has become a magnet for tourists who, as its official Web site boasts, are "attracted by Andorra's duty-free status and by its summer and winter resorts. The banking sector, with its 'tax haven' status, also contributes substantially to the economy."[4] Similarly, Liechtenstein took its name from its rulers since 1719, the princely house of Liechtenstein. Following World War I, its independence was confirmed by a special memorandum attached to the Peace of St.-Germain, "Liechtenstein's existence was practically unknown except in the German-speaking states," so that "An historical introduction was therefore necessary" (Raton 1970, 55). Liechtenstein adopted Swiss laws when it broke its former links with Austria and associated itself with Switzerland, but it "perfected" the Swiss system of bank secrecy laws with regard to company ownership. As Peillon and Montebourg wryly comment: for Liechtenstein "secrecy proved to be the principal source of economic development" (2000, vol. 1). In the words of Jules Stewart (1996):

> The Anstalt is widely considered the ultimate in banking secrecy. Unlike in Switzerland, where bankers are legally obliged to be aware of account holders' identities, this is not required in Liechtenstein except where there may be legitimate suspicion of criminal activity. A lawyer signs a due-diligence agreement with the Liechtenstein authorities, and when both are satisfied that the money involved is clean, the customer is referred to one of the local banks.

The Anstalt has been a great success. The number of such companies is simply unknown. Peillon and Montebourg (2000) estimate them at thirteen thousand. In any case, the results are impressive. This minute jurisdiction, "free from any socialist tendencies" (Stewart 1996), now enjoys an average annual income of more than thirty-five thousand dollars, making the thirty thousand Liechtensteiners richer than their Swiss neighbors.

*Tax Havens: The Case of Switzerland*

Switzerland is by far the bigger and most important among these social formations. Swiss writers such as André Siegfried like to emphasize the Swiss "democratic way of life" and the long tradition of scientific culture and mathematical science to explain the extraordinary success of the Swiss insurance business. He acknowledges, however, that the country has "an exceptionally large amount of capital at its disposal . . . which enters Switzerland to find a refuge from fiscal persecution or currency instability" (1950, 108–9). Switzerland was traditionally a place of refuge, for French Protestants as well as Bolshevik revolutionaries, but "at the beginning of the twentieth century the introduction of a closer fiscal control in various countries, and particularly in France, led to a new emigration, this time of a fiscal character" (Siegfried 1950, 111).

A supervening social necessity played a role in the conversion of Switzerland into the world's premier tax haven. As with the Euromarket, which had a lot to do with the difficulties British banks specializing in foreign lending were experiencing in 1957, so Swiss offshore evolved originally to protect the Swiss banking industry. Due to the country's generally stable political system, Swiss banks had served as asset havens for centuries. But during the 1920s the country evolved further, actively legislating to attract business into its territory. This was stimulated in part, no doubt, by the introduction of income tax laws in France and Germany (Braithwaite and Drahos 2000, 93). But the main reasons are to be found elsewhere: by the end of the nineteenth century, Swiss commercial and private banks grew to an enormous size by relying on international business for the bulk of their business.[5]

The mercantilist atmosphere of the 1920s, however, combined with severe restrictions on capital mobility in Europe, threatened to starve the Swiss banking and insurance sectors of the funds they needed. But Switzerland possessed some advantages over its neighbors. During the 1920s, it "failed to move with the times" and did not prohibit the import of gold or currency. Furthermore, in Switzerland in contrast to its neighbors, tax evasion was considered an administrative problem (Fehrenbach 1966, 48). The unique federal system based on the cantons, which had already established a solid reputation as the preferred refuge for endangered foreign funds, proved to be irresistible to German industrialists. Fearing inflation, political unrest, and Reparations, "virtually every German corporation doing business abroad opened a Swiss bank account and channeled most of its foreign exchange there" With the connivance of the Weimar Republic, German firms began to utilize the cantonal corporation laws and the secretive Swiss banking system to "get round Allied Reparation demands, and [thus] created a solid finan-

cial basis for German industry in spite of the social and political disso-
lution in Germany" (Fehrenbach 1966, 54).

Another nowadays immensely popular tax evasion technique developed in the 1920s was that of buying companies "off the shelf." Fehrenbach (1966) describes how a Swiss lawyer, Streuli-Schmitt, working
with one of the big three banks, helped an unnamed but, Fehrenbach as-
sures us, famous Italian family to evade their country's taxes. Streuli-
Schmitt set up two chartered companies, both under nominated
dummy directors who were clerks in his office. The two companies
were given Swiss residence; indeed, Streuli-Schmitt used his own home
for that purpose. A transfer was then effected between one of the Swiss
companies, Ajax AG, which bought five million dollars worth of the
shares of the Italian family's company with money pledged from the
other Swiss-chartered company. Ajax AG, on paper worth five million
dollars now belonged to the second dummy company, which was
owned by the very same Italian family, with the papers held in the
vaults of the unnamed bank that was Streuli-Schmitt's confederate. In
this way, "the assets themselves did not even have to leave Italy. They
could remain where they were—but under international law they were
now completely Swiss, protected by Swiss and international law"
(Fehrenbach 1966, 61). The Swiss bank was not required to reveal
names, the amount of the transaction, the owners of the two companies' shares, or anything else in its vaults, indeed later laws prohibited
the Swiss bank from revealing any of this information even to its own
government. There was no way, therefore, to demonstrate that the Italian family owned the second chartered company that owned Ajax AG.
The bank and the lawyer charged steep prices for "managing" the affairs
of this company.

But this was only the beginning. Switzerland became a fully-fledged
tax haven with the enactment of the secrecy amendments to its banking laws in 1934. Bank secrecy laws were already of long standing and
were general throughout the Western world, but they did not protect de-
positors against the tax man. In this respect, the 1934 bank secrecy laws
made Switzerland different from all other countries. The myth is that
the laws were enacted to protect Jewish accounts from the Nazis (see
among others Fehrenbach 1966), but Nicolas Faith (1982) does a good
job in demolishing the myth. The Swiss banking law, which took two
years to draft beginning in early 1933 until its acceptance in October
1994, could not have possibly been drafted in response to the Nazi
takeover only months before the Swiss deliberations began. The impe-

tus for the law came from the great financial difficulties experienced by the Swiss banking community following the collapse of the Austrian Credit-Anstalt and other Austrian and German banks. In addition, in 1932 the Paris offices of a Swiss bank, the Basles Handelsbank had been raided and various tax evasion scams had been revealed. The raid played an important role in a number of court rulings in 1932 and 1933 paving the way for the enactment of the bank secrecy laws. As a result, the bill contained many "ill thought compromises," as Faith puts it, between the Swiss authorities and the banks, and served very clearly to advance the interests of the latter, including the reinforcement of the existing secrecy laws. The Swiss banking secrecy laws of 1934 may be considered, therefore, an intentional policy decision—although here again we find that special interests have influenced state policy.

### Flag of Convenience: Panama

Just as with other types of early offshore, precedents for the use of flags of other countries abound in the nineteenth century and even earlier.[6] But these were not flags of convenience in the modern sense, for they did not take advantage of laws specifically aimed at outflanking taxes, labor protection laws, and other forms regulation. Again as with other types of offshore, the development of the flag of convenience in Panama drew on existing Panamanian law—inherited, incidentally, from Colombian law. The Panamanian fiscal code allowed for the registry of vessels through Panamanian consuls in foreign countries. This feature of Panamanian law, as with similar laws in Guatemala, Honduras, and Nicaragua was originally not intended to attract foreign ship owners so much as to encourage the development of an indigenous fishing fleet by allowing Panamanian citizens to purchase ships abroad.

Following the familiar pattern of binary relationships, the establishment of Panama's flag of convenience benefited to no small extent from the country's supposed special relationship with the United States. U.S. ship owners, perhaps mistakenly, felt protected by the United States even though their ships carried Panamanian flags. Here again we find that Panama's success was paradoxically the result of its failure to "move with the times" by introducing stricter labor and tax legislation. During and after World War I, the U.S. government was particularly concerned to maintain a strong merchant fleet. To achieve this the United States Shipping Board was established in 1915, and subsequent legislation gave it extensive powers. Meanwhile, a number of laws were enacted to extend to seamen some social benefits. Although the Shipping

Board would not allow the transfer of major vessels to the flags of other countries, a loophole in the administration of this policy proved to be the basis for the establishment of the Panamanian flag of convenience. The Shipping Board had responsibility for merchant vessels of the Central Powers that had been taken over during the war or handed over under the Versailles treaty. The Shipping Board then entered into financial arrangements with private firms to charter these vessels, but with the surplus of merchant ships in the early years after the war, these private operators were losing money. The board therefore felt obliged to sell the ships but felt that under its charter it could not put the ships up for sale to U.S. owners: as a result of the shipping surplus, they would fetch very low prices and this would in effect amount to a subsidy from the Shipping Board. The board decided that the way out was to sell the ships to U.S. owners but stipulate that the ships would be transferred to a foreign flag to work on routes where they would not compete with other U.S.-owned ships (Carlisle 1961). The eventual buyer of these ships, Pacific Freighters, chose Panamanian registry because, as one of the line's officers frankly stated, "the chief advantage of Panamanian registry is that the owner is relieved of the continual but irregular boiler and hull inspections and the regulations as to crew's quarters and subsistence. We are under absolutely no restrictions, so long as we pay the $1 a net ton registry fee and 10 cents years a net ton tax."[7] Within three or four years, Panama revamped its registration laws and developed into a flag Of convenience state.

The attraction of Panama to U.S. owners was quite simply that it did not impose the various restrictions and regulations that the United States and some European countries were beginning to adopt after the war. Thus it seems that the United States played a prominent role in the growth of flags of convenience. Similarly, during the same period an American company, United Fruit, created the Honduran registry with the connivance of U.S. officials to ensure the cheap and reliable transport of its bananas.

By the 1930s the use of Panamanian registry became well established. When the Metaxas government in Greece (1936–41) raised social security contributions and enforced other laws on its ships, this contributed, as predicted at the time, to a massive transfer of Greek shipping to the Panamanian flag. Rodney Carlisle tells the story of how Aristotle Onassis's "vessel, the *Onassi Penelope*, was immobilized in Rotterdam because the local Greek consul would not issue clearance papers until Onassis replaced an assistant cook, who had fallen ill, with another Greek cook. . . . after telephoning and telegraphing all night, the next day [Onassis] switched registry to Panama" (1961, 59).

### Export Processing Zones: The Case of Puerto Rico

As with other offshore facilities, historical parallels can be drawn between export processing zones and the free towns and ports of medieval Europe and the entrepôt centers of the British Empire such as Singapore and Gibraltar. Many authors date the origins of the EPZ phenomenon to Puerto Rico in 1947–51 when the government there developed the first modern duty-free industrial parks with standard buildings ready for occupancy for export industries. Puerto Rico may, however, have drawn on the experience of the first U.S. special economic zone, set up in Staten Island in 1937. With its special relationship to the United States, Puerto Rico too, is a classic case of the binary relationship that is so typical of the phase of accidental innovation of offshore. It is also typical in its anomalous status regarding taxation. Under the island's political arrangement with the United States as it evolved after 1898, Puerto Ricans were U.S. citizens with complete freedom to move to the mainland, but could not vote in federal elections if they were resident on the island. Hence, under the principle of "no taxation without representation," island residents were free from U.S. taxes. Of course, there were Puerto Rican taxes to be paid, but under the new laws, export industries attracted to the island were exempt from these, at least initially. As Mayne observes, "Puerto Rico enjoys a free tariff access to the United States mainland market so it was early deemed desirable that this opportunity be exploited through an active promotional campaign in the United States" (1961, 41).

Puerto Rico also had a long history of economic planning. In 1942 the government Planning Board and Budgetary Board were formally organized, with the specific aim of promoting industrialization and tourism. Promotion in the United States was spearheaded by an office in New York with a staff of over a hundred people. "To assist the campaign," writes Mayne, "a variety of incentives have been provided, such as 10 years tax exemption from all taxes . . . provided the industrial activity is the type which has been determined to be desirable for Puerto Rico" (Mayne 1961, 42). The promotional campaign in the United States was able to draw on the Individual Tax Exempt Act of 1948 and the Industrial Incentive Act of 1954 (Stead 1958). The Puerto Rico Industrial Development Company (PRIDO), set up in 1950, established an elaborate system of zones of development which may be regarded as precursors of EPZs. By 1961 PRIDO had promoted over seven hundred plants with a combined investment of $465 million, or half of the manufacturing infrastructure in Puerto Rico (Mayne 1961, 43). Seven years later Colombia established the Barranquilla Export Processing Zone (Abbott 2000).

A different route to the EPZ model emerged in Ireland as an extension of the idea of the duty-free shops. Shannon airport developed because of its geographic location; it was the first suitable landfall for long-distance aircraft traveling from the United States to Europe. A vibrant aviation infrastructure developed around the constant and growing international traffic. Advances in engine technology and aircraft design steadily extended flying range, however, and by the late 1950s, it was clear that Shannon's strategic role would soon be eclipsed. This imminent and unwelcome change in Shannon's fortunes was the catalyst for the formation of the Shannon Free Airport Development Company (Shannon Development) by the Irish government in 1959. Its role was to develop an alternative basis for a continuation of air transport activity at Shannon.

The company set about its task by seeking to simultaneously and speedily develop industrial and tourism infrastructures in the region of the airport. The company began to innovate by extending the existing duty-free status to embrace the operation of manufacturing industry within a designated zone. In this way, the original duty-free system evolved further on the basis of the concept of bifurcation of the sovereign space for tax purposes. UNIDO and UNCTAD were impressed by the success of Shannon and PRIDO and used them as a general model to be promoted in developing countries. But as late as 1966 there were only two export processing zones in developing countries, one in India and one in Puerto Rico.

PHASE TWO: COMPETITIVE EMULATION:
THE BAHAMAS, THE CAYMAN ISLANDS, LIBERIA

Having originated somewhat accidentally, relying on existing institutional and legal structure and driven by supervening social necessities the offshore economy entered a stage of diffusion through competitive emulation. It is difficult to make a fast and hard distinction between the stages of accidental innovation and competitive emulation. In the latter case either states followed an already existing blueprint or private operators discovered a new territory whose laws and geographical location were somewhat similar to those of existing offshore locales. In any case, at this stage the strategy became conscious, and was often pursued under the guidance of roving lawyers and accountants acting as advisers to governments of these small jurisdictions (Naylor 1987).

The extension of the tax haven idea to the Caribbean follows the pattern of competitive emulation. Here, the Bahamas took the lead, and once again, an existing institutional arrangement played a key role—in this case, the establishment by the United States during World War II of two well-equipped airbases, which, together with overcrowding in Florida and revolution in Cuba, made possible an influx of tourists attracted by "the comparatively unspoiled charm of 'old' Nassau" (Craton 1962, 279). But soon these tourists discovered the real charm of the Bahamas: with no income or corporation taxes and only a nominal 4 percent probate tax "the Bahamas enjoyed what has been called 'a salubrious financial climate.' Catering for tax refugees has become the most lucrative Bahamian industry"(Craton 1962, 281). The Bahamas was on its way to become one of the world's premier OFCs.

Meanwhile, a flag of convenience magnate, D. K. Ludwig, spent $2 million on a three-hundred—foot dock in Freeport. In this ideal location, the Freeport Bunkering Company began providing tax-free fuel to ships in the early summer of 1959. "In the first three weeks of operation, Freeport Bunkering sold 2 1/2 million gallons of fuel oil and there were often queues of ships waiting to discharge or take fuel" (Craton 1962, 281). Subsequently, the Bahamas government developed a series of successful export processing zone in Freeport as ancillaries of the already existing tax haven strategy. A similar process is now in evidence with regard to Hong Kong, while Ireland has gone in the opposite direction, as its EPZs served as the model for the extension of financial laws in the 1990s.

The spoils of the huge tourist/financial real estate development in the Bahamas were not shared at all, leading to political turmoil there. But this only gave other Caribbean islands a chance to compete, with the Cayman Islands taking the lead. Unlike many of its neighbors, the Cayman Islands' competitive advantage was firmly established when it refused to go for independence and remained a British colony. That gave the islands the political stability and organized legal system investors yearn for. The Cayman Islands started its activities in the 1960s with "a fairly lax" regulatory regime (Stewart 1996). But this developed rapidly and today the Caymans are the world's fifth biggest financial center. Other "juridical anachronisms" joined the fray including the Channel Islands, employing their peculiar constitutional arrangements that originated from the medieval English monarchy's possession of Normandy to good effect.

Flags of convenience diffused in a somewhat similar pattern. The development of the Liberian registry after World War II was due to the U.S. government's desire to stabilize the territory. Like Panama, Liberia had a special relationship with the U.S., dating from its foundation in 1822 by black American settlers. Its flag of convenience started with a scheme hatched by Edward R. Stettinius Jr. for a system of privately directed economic aid to Liberia. A former secretary of state, in 1947 Stettinius organized Stettinius Associates–Liberia, Inc., which in turn set up the Liberia Company together with the Liberian government. Stettinius was then approached by a number of shipping companies wishing to register under the Liberian flag. Some of his associates in the Liberia Company set up another company, the American Overseas Tanker Corporation, which bought five tankers and promptly leased them to Esso. By 1949, Stettinius and his associates, many of who were former State Department officials, with the help of Esso lawyers drafted the Liberian maritime law. The Liberia Company meanwhile began to advertise the new law widely, and it proved a great success (Carlisle 1961). The Liberian registry grew from two ships totaling 772 gross tons in 1948 to 975 ships with 10,078,778 gross tons in 1958, outstripping Panama's 602 ships and 4,357,800 gross tons. The United States has developed the Marshall Islands flag of convenience in a similar way (Van Fossen 1992).

The diffusion of EPZs followed a somewhat different pattern. As Emadi-Cofin points out, in this case international agencies such as UNIDO and UNCTAD actively sponsored the new development. This has led to a tremendous diffusion of EPZs, so much so that by the early 1990s, half of the countries classified as "developing" by the United Nations had active EPZs (1996, 142). To begin with, a Puerto Rican government expert, Alexander Firfer was provided to Taiwan in 1960 to review its industrial development plans, and endorsed a plan to turn an artificial island in Kaohsiung Harbor into Taiwan's first EPZ. Another Puerto Rican, Hu Barton, later advised the government of Indonesia to turn Batam Island, just offshore from Singapore, into a free zone linked to that city. Many visitors from developing countries, especially in the Caribbean, came to Puerto Rico to see how success was achieved. The consulting firm of Arthur D. Little, Inc., which was under contract to Puerto Rico as development adviser continuously from 1942 to 1962, also spread EPZ knowledge to many countries in later years, including

Jamaica, Cuba, Venezuela, Mexico, the Central American countries, and the Dominican Republic (Abbott 2000).

Another contribution of the Puerto Rican experience was the accustoming of U.S. industry to offshore operations. Many companies first learned how to operate offshore in Puerto Rico and became confident of their abilities—making them good candidates for further expansion overseas. Conrad Hilton, for example, went international with his hotels based mainly on the enormous success of the Caribe Hilton at San Juan, built by PRIDCO as an attractive hotel for potential investors. In addition, plant managers from Puerto Rico spread to other regions as their companies developed. The Rockwell integrated circuits plant at Mexicali, Mexico was managed by a man who began his career at sixteen in the GE plant in Puerto Rico and spent twenty-five years moving up through the ranks (Abbott 2000).

### PHASE THREE: OFFSHORE BECOMES A KEY FACTOR IN THE INTERNATIONALIZATION OF CAPITAL

As we have seen, states such as Monaco, Switzerland, the Cayman Islands, and Liberia served as the springboard for the development of offshore not as instruments of advanced capital but precisely because they were out of step with the times. Consequently, they could not possibly have served, even unintentionally, as the "epitome of capital." And yet, there is little doubt that offshore is intimately linked to the politics and practice of capital in the twentieth century. How can we bridge these apparently conflicting facts?

My answer is based on a variant of the regulation approach. A strong variant of the regulation theory suggests that the crisis of Fordism, or mass production technologies, was at the heart of the emergence of a new global post-Fordist economy. I propose here a softer variant, according to which Fordism was contradictory at all levels, including the international level. The offshore economy remained largely insignificant until the late 1960s but proved to be particularly important thereafter, because, for reasons that had little to do with offshore in itself, the world around it changed. The general crisis of corporate profitability which began to be felt from the late 1960s, combined with the secular development of the Euromarket, and improvement in communication and transportation technologies, all rendered offshore jurisdictions a viable and attractive alternative to heavily regulated and taxed states. The discovery of offshore exacerbated, therefore, already existing contradictions in the international dimension of Fordism. Consequently, we witness mutually reinforcing developments from the 1970s, as the offshore economy facilitated the internationalization of capital, and this in turn, further facilitated the integration of the offshore economy.

Much has been written of the regulation school and hence I need not discuss this in great detail. I emphasize here the international aspect of Fordism or the so-called politics of "embedded liberalism" and American hegemony (Kolko and Kolko 1972; Van Der Pijl 1984). According to this view, the politics of the New Deal in the United States and social corporatism in Europe was matched by a unique, if somewhat contradictory international order, structured around a modified form of liberalism, or embedded liberalism (Ruggie 1982). With the establishment of a global market as their ultimate goal, American foreign policymakers and their allies set about to create an international institutional structure predisposed to business interests. But this transnational order, whose institutions emerged at the end of laborious negotiations at San Francisco and Bretton Woods, turned out to possess four distinctive characteristics potentially fraught with difficulties:

1. It was grounded in the principles of "free trade," that is, the lowering of tariffs and the progressive removal of barriers to trade and productive capital investment. This stimulated in time the globalization of the world economy and led gradually to blurring the distinction between the national and the world economies. Free trade implied a commitment by the key capitalist states to the transnationalization of their and other societies' economies.
2. This, in turn, raised the possibility that the national economies might eventually be subordinated to the world market. These principles were written into the Bretton Woods and GATT agreements, and also, later on, into the charter of the NATO alliance.
3. However, for historical as well as practical reasons, the transnationalization of the economy had to be accommodated by the existing system of states. Indeed, the system of states itself seems to have gained a new lease on life with the commitment, written into the United Nations charter, to sovereign equality and the right to self-determination.
4. Furthermore, the underlying "corporatist-liberal" social bargain, as Kees Van Der Pijl (1984) called it, which underpinned the commitment of America and its allies to free trade, placed heavy stress on the state as the regulator of social and economic activity. Thus, the Pax Americana saw a widespread and massive increase in state intervention. As a result, the transnationalization of the world economy took place hand in hand with the expansion of national planning.

Thus, the transnational order contained contradictions that expressed themselves in a growing spatial incongruity between the economy and the polity. Whether alternative and better solutions were feasible or attainable at the time is a contentious issue. Although the International Monetary Fund was established to help eliminate short-term capital imbalances, it could not by itself resolve the inevitable conflict that resulted from embedding national policy in an increasingly international environment. Not surprisingly, "the discussion [at Bretton Woods] revolved around the degree of autonomy countries should be permitted in pursuit of domestic economic policy" (Cooper 1974, 67). But the accord required a delicate balancing act as governments were supposed to adopt policies of welfare and growth, and yet subordinate these when needed to the broader principles of the Bretton Woods system. The system encouraged intergovernmental conflict, which could be averted only if states were willing to exercise a considerable degree of what Aubrey (1966) calls "discipline"—something, he suggests, that they either lacked or the exact meaning of which was hotly debated.

The contradictions of the Bretton Woods system faithfully reflected the broader theme of the disjunction between politics and economics in the postwar international order. The architects of the postwar order were naturally cognizant of these difficulties. They were aware that a transnational economy required a concomitant overlapping transnational politico-juridical system so that contracts would be honored, trade routes protected, foreign investment secured, and so on. They were also keenly aware of the disruptive influences arising from the fact that states were bound to try to gain unfair advantages from the system. Against this background, a series of measures, some formal and some not, were devised so that an operative and coherent globally encompassing political superstructure would be brought into existence.

First, although it is very difficult to prove the point, it appears that the key capitalist states accepted the anomaly introduced by the spatial incongruity between politics and economics on the implicit understanding that the "invisible hand" of the world market would shape the social forces that gained from free trade in each and every country, and generate positive effects in the new global arrangement. The World Bank, the IMF, and later on the variety of aid programs were intended to integrate Third World states into this vision by furnishing them with adequate means for "development," which inevitably would take the form of evolution of social classes and political interests favoring their countries' integration into the world economy (Kolko and Kolko 1972; Van Der Pijl 1984).

Second, it was understood from the outset that the key capitalist countries were to undertake concerted measures to circumvent the worst excesses of a potentially anarchic international system of states. A key aspect of this was to be an entente among the wartime allies, the Soviet Union, Britain, and the United States. These states were supposed to share, through the agency of the United Nations, the burden of running the world economy. The United Nations was viewed, therefore, from the outset as a club, a meeting place of states that shared in the governance of the world economy. The United Nations, and in particular the Security Council, were supposed to be the linchpin of a complex and intricate system of rituals by which capitalist countries sought effectively, although it was not discussed at the time in such terms, to create a governing structure that would encompass the entire globe. Needless to say, the idea that the Soviet Union would go along with the U.S. plans proved very quickly a chimera and as a result, the United Nations never played the role it was supposed to play.

Third, the United States took upon itself the role of the guardian of the emerging Pax Americana. It is important to appreciate that U.S. foreign policy was founded on a clear distinction between the pursuit of self-interest and the use of violence. American commentators understood very well why the United States resorted at times to policies that might have been potentially damaging to its allies, putting these policies under the headings of "competition" and "restructuring." Such policies, however, had to be carried out peacefully—they had to remain in the realm of "economic" competition and not spill over into military shows of force. The enormous firepower of the United States has been reserved in the past fifty years only for what American policymakers deemed to be "universal goals": to guard and maintain trade routes, strategic raw materials, and regimes that were friendly to the trading system. America's military might was not used, therefore, simply to project and enhance its national interests wherever such interests were deemed under threat (as opposed to the covert activities of the CIA which apparently were employed more liberally in defense of these interests), nor did U.S. military power evolve simply in response to a real or imagined Soviet threat. On the contrary, the Soviet threat was perceived as one of the many challenges to the liberal trading system.

In spite of these precautions, the Bretton Woods system was vulnerable to internal contradictions that led to its collapse in the early 1970s, and indeed it held together as long as it did probably only because of the Cold War. Above all, just as the technology of mass production (Taylorism and Fordism) informed the emergence of a particular form of state, the crisis of the state contributed to the crisis of the international economy. Just as postulated by Hirschman (1970), an assault on the Fordist state evolved simultaneously at the political level as "Voice," dissatisfaction expressed through neoliberal parties, and economically through "Exit," as capital explored alternative locations to the Fordist state. The neoliberal onslaught accelerated the trend toward relocation of production. This contradiction within international Fordism or "embedded liberalism" generated not only a post-Fordist state but in fact a post-state mode of regulation, a new type of geography of regulation.

The offshore economy, still modest in the early years of the 1970s, proved to be the main vehicle for the economic strategy of exit. One of the key factors that led to the collapse of Fordism was the advent of a truly integrated and largely unregulated global financial market. Helleiner (1994) demonstrates that strict limitations on international movements of capital had to be imposed in order to protect the new national macroeconomic planning measures of the 1930s. Furthermore, he demonstrates that contrary to the common assumption, the United States did little to use its powers to open up the financial markets of other countries (and indeed its own) until the early 1960s. Embedded liberalism, or the international dimension of Fordism, required, in other words, strict capital control.

The Euromarket was the principle vehicle for financing the expansion of the exit strategies of the multinational enterprises (see chapter 2); the tax havens, with their plethora of shell corporations, were critical for diversification, tax avoidance, and the management of internationalization of capital; the export processing zones were particularly attractive to capital evading heavy taxation and regulation and relocating in search of cheap and docile labor (Fröbel et al. 1980); flags of convenience grew tremendously to support this new phase of globalization. This was the critical point in the development of offshore. From a marginal developmental strategy, offshore became a central dimension in the internationalization of capital.

The collapse of the Bretton Woods agreement did not lead, as forecast by some, to total breakdown of the transnational sociopolitical formation that we associate with the Pax Americana. On the contrary, falling rates of profit at the end of the 1960s, combined with improvements in management techniques, communications, and transportation, and the Euromarket have led to a massive shift of production facilities from the center to the periphery. Initially this benefited a number of so-called semiperipheral states: Greece, Yugoslavia, Spain, and Portugal in Europe; Brazil, Argentina, Venezuela, and Mexico in Latin America; Hong Kong, South Korea, Singapore, and Taiwan in East Asia. This phase of globalization was characterized by a huge increase in foreign direct investment, financed and mobilized through the Euromarket. In the five years down to 1989 FDI rose by 29 percent a year, three times higher than international trade (UNCTC and UNCTAD 1991). Greater capital mobility in conjunction with globalization of the financial system has produced a marked-driven environment and a shift in the perception and goals of state policy. As a result, states are increasingly seeking to attract investment into their territories and to improve their position in the international division of labor. They find themselves in the grip of a "beauty contest," seeking desperately to attract production facilities, capital, and trade to their shores. As we will see in the next chapter, tax havens and other offshore jurisdictions are caught nowadays in this competitive game.

This chapter lends support to one of the central contentions of this book as presented in chapter two, namely, that offshore locales were deliberate constructs or innovations whose origins must be sought in a historically specific conjuncture. As we saw in this chapter, while the legal and political infrastructure that supported the offshore economy emerged earlier, and in an entirely different context, the period between the end of World War I and the collapse of the Bretton Woods agreement in the early 1970s saw the gradual development of the offshore world economy from a mere potentiality to a verifiable integrated economy spanning finance, shipping and Third World manufacturing.

Interestingly, the steady rise in taxation in advanced industrialized countries in the 1950s and 1960s does not appear to be the main cause for the emergence or proliferation of offshore jurisdictions during this period. On the contrary the causes for the appearance of bank secrecy laws, relaxed corporation laws, flags of convenience, and export processing zones, were far more varied and contingent than conventional thinking would make us believe. Slowly, and only very gradually, the idea that these different techniques might be used as a developmental strategy by small states began to develop. Furthermore, it was not necessarily the rate of taxation or regulation as such that persuaded many banks and companies to take advantage of the emerging offshore economy, but rather the crisis of profitability of the late 1960s which forced companies to look for ways of reducing costs and raising profits. It was only at this point that the Euromarket was truly "discovered" and the concept of export processing zones became popular.

# CHAPTER FIVE

# Offshore and the Internationalization of the State

The collapse of the Bretton Woods system was accompanied by important changes in the patterns of international trade, leading to a new phase of internationalization of capital. The trend towards relocation and internationalization of the multinational corporations led to the establishment of a distinctively global mode of capitalism (Michalet 1976), accompanied by a rapid expansion of the offshore economy. In fact, during this period the offshore economy became an integral part of an increasingly global world economy. But as the offshore economy expanded further, it reached saturation and a complex "race to the bottom," that is, towards regulatory laxity, started up in the 1980s. From then on we witness a process of internal differentiation, as the shrewder jurisdictions began to pursue niche strategies.

Throughout this era of globalization, the direct impact of the offshore economy was less significant than the indirect impact. A growing offshore economy fed the perception—no doubt seized upon by interested parties—that states could no longer afford to continue to try to control their economies in the same way that the Keynesian or Fordist state had done. States shifted from so-called demand side to supply side management of the economy, or from the Fordist to the competition state. The true impact of the offshore economy was felt, therefore, indirectly, magnified many times as advanced states began to adopt some of the principles of offshore, such as deregulation and lower taxation, throughout their territories.

## EXPORT PROCESSING ZONES AND NEW PATTERNS OF TRADE

From the early 1970s, a small number of Third World countries, the so called newly industrialized countries (NICs), began to develop their industrial capacity by attracting export-oriented mass manufacturers from older industrialized regions (Ernst and O'Connor 1989). There was much talk at the time of a "new international division of labor" (Fröbel et. al, 1980). In retrospect, the new international division of labor never materialized, and foreign direct investment remained much as it had always been, within the triadic core of the United States, Europe, and East Asia (Hirst and Thompson 1996). Nonetheless, the changes in the pattern of trade contributed to the transformation of the Third World, if not its elimination as a plausible concept (Palan and Abbott 1996). Whether the emergence of Third World manufacturing in general, and the EPZs in particular, had such a catastrophic impact on the manufacturing base of the triadic core as is often claimed is a matter of dispute. It appears that it has not. But as is often the case, facts are insufficient to explain historical change. The myth of the decline of the manufacturing base of industrialized countries faced by cheap Third World manufactured products—most of which originated from the EPZs and were produced by multinational corporations from the advanced industrialized countries—was widely believed. The perceived threat of relocation and decline, whether real or not, was seized upon to rationalize and restructure power relationships in the center.

Faced by the growth of EPZs, advanced industrial countries reciprocated by establishing regional development organizations and began to offer their own brands of industrial sweeteners and tax holidays. These did not take the form of EPZs—and hence cannot be considered offshore—but they aped the offshore principle. The phenomenon reached such proportions that in the 1990s, the OECD commissioned two comparative studies to examine the shift towards what it described as "precompetitive" subsidies—targeted subsidies in the form of tax holidays and sweeteners aimed to attract investment (Ford 1990; Goenenc 1990). These studies suggest that industrial subsidies and handouts were on an upward trend. Ford estimates that the subsidy, paid out as a percentage of sectoral value, added reached around 2 to 3.5 percent of GDP by 1990 (Ford 1990, 6). Goenenc (1990) believes that these figures understate the true rate of support. Even so, these conservative estimates represent considerable sums of money. They would amount in today's figures to between $500 to $800 billion a year transferred from taxpayers to shareholders in the advanced industrialized countries (Palan 1998b).

It would be foolish to argue that EPZs are the sole or even the main cause for the rise of precompetitive subsidies in advanced industrialized countries, but they certainly played an important role in what may be described as the politics of redistribution. They have contributed to the blurring of the distinction between offshore and onshore not by raising offshore regulation and taxation, but rather by relaxing onshore regulation.

## THE EUROMARKET AND FINANCIAL DEREGULATION

The deregulation of national financial markets and the formation of a truly global financial market (Stopford and Strange 1991, 40–41) complemented changing patterns of production. The term "financial deregulation" refers to a medley of regulations that contributed, on the whole, to the reduction, and sometimes the elimination, of barriers in domestic and international financial markets. Financial deregulation is normally associated with the neoconservative onslaught on the Fordist state. It appears as one of the more successful instances of "rolling back the frontiers of the state." Experts disagree however as to the root causes of the trend. There is a school of thought that maintains that the debt strategies of the United States, the United Kingdom, France, and later on Germany and Japan stimulated international financial deregulation (Ruehl and Hughes 1986; Sassen 1991). Others take the view that deregulation was driven by technological innovation (Mason 1987). Some argue that the key factor pushing for deregulation in the United States was high and volatile interest rates (Harrington 1992), while others contend that many of the financial innovations and the new government regulations were aimed to bolster the competitive positions of embattled national financial sectors (Allen 1994). As in the case of the relocation of manufacturing and production facilities, we soon discover that the perceived threat from offshore proved to be as important, if not more so, than any real threat. As a Bank for International Settlements report notes:

> Deregulation has also been a response to the reality that previous regulations were being circumvented by technology in various ways. Unauthorized operations were simply being carried out offshore, with foreigners getting the business. Viewed from the perspective of either what is desirable, or what is feasible, re-regulation of domestic financial markets would not seem to be the preferred solution to any new problems posed by internationally integrated financial markets. (BIS 1995, 6)

It is difficult, if not impossible, to disentangle fact from fiction in this highly ideological debate. The truth probably is that financial deregulation was driven by practical considerations in combination with ideological and political interests. The seeds of financial deregulation were sown, according to Mason (1987), in the early 1970s with the collapse of Bretton Woods. Gary Burn (1999), however, is probably correct in stressing the important role played by the Euromarket. The Euromarket punched a hole, he argues, through the entire regulatory matrix of the national state and proved the futility of capital controls and regulation. Ultimately, the unregulated and competitive Euromarket could not but spell the end of national controls (Helleiner 1994). But the true impact of the Euromarket took a while to be felt. Susan Strange identifies the introduction of certificates of deposit (CDs) in the early 1960s as one of the key innovations that in conjunction with the Euromarket led toward financial deregulation. CDs are short-term negotiable instruments issued by banks with terms of maturity of mostly up to one year. Banks in New York first issued them in 1961. They were, in the words of Harrington:

> An imaginative response to the constraints on the New York banks. It was a means of competing with U.S, Treasury bills in that it too was a liquid negotiable instrument. Because they were negotiable they could be sold and there could be no way of limiting holders to any geographical area. In effect they were means of getting round restrictions on deposit taking; they could be sold via dealers in the whole country so NY banks could compete for wholesale trade in the entire country. (1992, 37)

The growth of CDs fed the growth of the so-called secondary money markets, or parallel wholesales money markets, which emerged in the United Kingdom and United States (Moran 1986, 10). Actors in these markets, with little government control over them, took advantage of the expanding bond market in the 1970s and began to compete effectively with the traditional banking sector (Khoury 1990). Governments tolerated the activities of these secondary institutions because they helped to absorb growing public borrowing in the 1970s. The established banks, however, felt hampered in competing with these nimble market operators and demanded, and got, a certain freedom from regulation so they could respond effectively by offering new products. Growing government debt in the 1970s, therefore, stimulated fierce competition in the financial markets and led to a snowball of financial innovations and deregulation. Competition in the international financial markets produced further deregulatory momentum among countries traditionally operating strict regulatory regimes, so that their financial sectors would be able to hold their own (Goodman and Pauly 1993).

The Euromarket proved to be the driving force of financial deregulation. The disruption that it caused to domestic financial regulation was widely recognized and spurred the Federal Reserve and the U.S. Treasury into action (Helleiner 1994, 135–45). In April 1979, the United States proposed that the Bank for International Settlements establish a committee to consider the imposition of reserve requirements on bank operations in the Euromarket—effectively seeking to re-regulate the market and bring it back onshore. Unsurprisingly, the United States met with stiff resistance from the Swiss and the British governments as well as from—and this may have proved more significant—its own banking establishment (Hudson 1999). By 1981 the United States conceded defeat and retaliated by establishing the international banking facilities (Helleiner 1994). Alan Hudson shows that the New York banking fraternity, led by Chase Manhattan, used the real or imagined threat posed by the Euromarket and the Caribbean tax havens (which the same banks had of course helped establish as large financial centers in the first place) to achieve their aim of more liberal financial laws. He quotes a U.S. Treasury official who says: "the large U.S. money center banks had been down here for five years previous asking us to do it. They had this grand vision that London was going to migrate to New York" (Hudson 1999, 146). It did not take long for the Japanese to emulate the U.S. response. The Japanese Hosomi plan imitated the New York IBF in order to "spur domestic liberalization by exhibiting to domestic bankers what unrestricted market transactions actually meant" (Ruehl and Hughes 1986, 28).

As in the case of the EPZs, the effects of financial deregulation has been to blur the distinction between offshore and onshore finance. In the words of a BIS report, "The setting-up of offshore facilities in the United States [IBFs] and Japan [JOM], whose exemption from most domestic regulations makes their operations akin to Eurocurrency business, and, more generally, the growing intertwining of domestic and foreign currency business, have considerably reduced the importance of the distinction between these two segments" (1995, 7). The blurring of the distinction between offshore and onshore is sometimes interpreted to mean the decline of offshore. For example, an IMF report argues that

The role of OFCs began to be challenged. During the last 15 years, the financial industry has experienced massive deregulation—particularly in the OECD countries—capital and financial controls have been dismantled, markets opened, tax rates reduced, and international cooperation improved. As a result, the regulatory and fiscal environments of domestic financial centers have converged with those of offshore centers and significantly reduced the comparative advantages that OFCs once had. (Cassard 1994, 1)

In fact, however, far from signaling the decline of offshore, financial and manufacturing deregulation must be interpreted as the embedding of offshore in the global political economy.

### OFFSHORE AS A SERVICE ECONOMY

While the offshore economy fed the forces of financial deregulation and internationalization, the emergence of an integrated global financial market stimulated the further growth of the offshore economy. In the period of declining profitability and stagnation in the late 1970s, firms found it difficult to finance expansion from conventional sources, and resorted to the fledgling Euromarket (Arrighi 1994; Swary and Topf 1992). So far we paid attention to the tax and regulatory advantages offered by the Euromarket and tax havens, but as the Euromarket expanded, linking the OFCs with the IBFs, the new offshore financial market began to offer some additional advantages. Financial specialists stress nowadays the logistical convenience of operating offshore. A modern financial market requires a sophisticated and costly infrastructure, including communications, air transportation, and accounting and legal services. It would be cost-inefficient, Park notes, "to establish an elaborate infrastructure of international finance in each country to service just one national market. So there is an economy of scale" (1982, 32). The unique nonterritorial location of the Euromarket allowed for such economies of scale by integrating different locales into one market.

Operating through a combination of regulatory realms, including London, the United States, Japan, and, of course, tax havens, the Euromarket also offered other important advantages. From around 1962 Euroloans (followed later by Euronotes) proved to be effective mechanisms for transforming short-term loans in the interbank market into medium- to long-term loans. The Euromarket facilitated bond issues underwritten by international banking syndicates subject to no one country's securities law. This led to a rapid and widespread syndication of bonds, and that, in turn, made huge sums of money available for investment, leveraged buyouts, and mergers and acquisitions. The result was that corporate and business groups were increasingly assembled from around the globe, in "tax neutral structures [where they] can be organized for the benefit of all participants" (Le Breton 2000). This, in turn, helped the process of relocation and investment—and hence also the spread of EPZs—as companies could now draw on an international market to finance their plans. This happened especially in Third World countries lacking the financial infrastructure to support inward capital flows (Stopford and Strange 1991, 43). In this way, the promise of a ready-made infrastructure combined with low labor costs, loose social legislation, and low taxation offered by the EPZs, together with the new techniques of financing developed in the Euromarket, played an important role in altering the patterns of international trade during the 1970s and 1980s. The offshore economy became, far more integrated with the global economy than is generally assumed, as an emerging global financial market teamed up with the EPZs (and flags of convenience) to accelerate the trend toward the relocation of basic manufacturing to these zones.

Thus, the removal of capital controls and other impediments, a pervasive business-friendly culture, and modern technology, together ensure that the offshore economy has become part and parcel of business life. It sets the scene for what the Diamonds (1998) call the "century of offshore investment."

The offshore financial market is now serving a worldwide clientele, lessening the importance of physical location and national financial systems. The nonregulatory benefits of the Euromarket extended initially only to cases where banks and other financial institutions intermediated between two nonresident borrowers and savers. This narrow legal exception became the major reason for the integration of the tax havens as active nodes in the global financial system. As residents of tax havens, banks and companies could appear as nonresident wherever and whenever they wished. Buying companies "off the shelf" had the effect, therefore, of releasing practically anyone who wanted to from the restriction of the onshore financial market.

## COMPETITION AMONG TAX HAVENS

Once co-opted into the very heart of the global financial market, a number of tax havens ceased to be marginal formations and began to view themselves as financial centers. The number of viable offshore centers, however, is probably limited. An unseemly struggle has developed between many of them, with glossy marketing brochures and international conferences on the rise. Competition evolved in a fairly sophisti-

cated manner: "The Isle of Man is competing against the Channel Islands, and even the more sedate Jersey and Guernsey are at each other's
throats, hiring public relations firms and holding presentations in London, Paris and other leading cities to gather potential business" (*Economist* 1994). Fierce competition has led simultaneously to the proliferation of tax havens, whereby jurisdictions actively compete and
emulate each other's laws. It has also led to differentiation and adaptation as different centers seek to attract certain portions of the financial
sector. Large accountancy firms play an important role in identifying
and defining the niche strategies of tax havens. Price Waterhouse, for instance, advises Gibraltar, while KPMG Peat Marwick "helps" Malta
and Trinidad and Tobago (*Economist* 1994).

Offshore centers closer to U.S. time zones have sought to tap into the
flow of funds from that country. Bermuda and the Cayman Islands are
the most successful recipients of U.S. money. The Cayman Islands was
the first offshore jurisdiction to enact a mutual fund law, back in 1973,
which, combined with its money laundering laws, proved a successful
recipe for attracting institutional business. The year 2000 saw a 32.7
percent increase in the number of funds, the highest single annual increase in the Caymans' history. There were 3,014 registered funds at the
end of the year, with more than $250 billion in assets (Bounds 2001).
The Cayman Islands have poured money into the infrastructure to maintain their success. The other successful Caribbean haven, Bermuda,
gained in particular from the Hong Kong exodus, as the colony was
about to return to Chinese sovereignty. Like many of the more successful tax havens, Bermuda pursues a dual strategy. On the one hand it
caters to the super-rich and has gained in particular from the decrease
in the British individual income tax to a maximum of 40 percent—
paradoxically releasing additional liquid funds to be used offshore. On
the other hand, it also specializes in the captive insurance business. By
1993, Bermuda was home to some thirteen hundred captive insurers, or
one-third of the world's total (*Economist* 1993). It maintains its position
to this day (Booth 2000).

Switzerland's specialty is private banking for the super-rich (*Euromoney* 1996). It takes advantage of its solid reputation and location at
the heart of Europe. It has built a considerable expertise, with some five
thousand experienced fund managers and client relationship officers.
Fears that Brussels could exert pressure for increased disclosure and
harmonization has led Swiss banks to operate through the Channel Islands. Swiss banks now channel approximately £130 billion every year

to the City of London through Jersey, and account for more than 40 percent of Guernsey deposits (*Economist* 1998).

The Channel Islands, in turn, play an integral if supportive role in the City of London, Luxembourg, and Swiss banking strategies. The islands present themselves as the acceptable face of the offshore industry. Supposedly, the strict regulatory standards and the political stability offered by the islands are prime factors in gaining the confidence of both banks and their clients (Stuart 1990). Due to tremendous pressure on land and real estate, the Channel Islands are interested in attracting large businesses with little personnel. The islands' laws therefore cater to high-volume corporate business, with Guernsey in particular competing head-on with Bermuda for captive insurance (*Economist* 1996). Guernsey is Europe's biggest domicile for offshore insurance and is a leading fund management, banking, and fiduciary center. The financial services sector accounts for one-third of Guernsey's economy (Boland 1999).

The pressure exerted by Brussels and the United States on Switzerland only works to the advantage of Liechtenstein, which according to a Price Waterhouse employee "is primarily for those clients who want an additional element of secrecy and protection for their assets. It is very strong because of its proximity to Switzerland, which is the world's leading offshore center. The principality tends to serve traditional wealth more than the new money coming out of places like Latin America" (*Economist* 1994). Similarly, after the German authorities introduced a withholding tax in 1994, some DM 90 billion flowed into Luxembourg by 1997 (*Economist* 1996). In fact, Luxembourg has stolen Switzerland's crown among institutional investors. One particular disadvantage of Switzerland vis-à-vis Luxembourg was its hefty stamp duty, which considerably increases the cost of stock market transactions. In addition, Switzerland adopted restrictive laws regulating investment funds (Euromoney 1996). By 1998, Luxembourg had more banks and bankers then Switzerland, and was the home of some three thousand equity, bond, and currency funds and subfunds which managed investment capital in excess of £200 billion. Taking into account cash on deposit in Luxembourg's more than two hundred registered banks, the total comes to well over £500 billion. By comparison, the Channel Islands have only £175 billion (Euromoney 1998).

Since 1989 Dublin has been making a determined effort to give Luxembourg a run for its offshore money. The International Financial Services Centre (IFSC) has over the past four years built up regulated funds to a total of \$35 billion. The south coast of Ireland has experienced an unprecedented real estate boom, and Dublin attempts to specialize in catering to "high net-worth individuals." "IFSC officials claim that major advantages of setting up in Ireland include lower start-up and operating costs than in Luxembourg, with the same ability to market products into Europe with an EU passport" (Stewart 1996). As there is fear that Switzerland, Luxembourg, and Dublin will eventually succumb to European Union pressure, a second-tier group of centers, linking the City of London, Zurich, Luxembourg, the Channel Islands, Gibraltar, and Liechtenstein, has emerged and behaves like one big integrated financial center. Many banks and corporations maintain a number of subsidiaries in all of these havens in order to take advantage of specific laws that each of them offers, and as a way of complicating and masking their operations behind a multitiered range of subsidies.

In fact, there is a new game in town, competition for corporate headquarters. Many countries, including those not traditionally associated with tax havens, have began to tailor their tax rules to attract corporate headquarters because they believe that these create employment, particularly in services, and may encourage other local investment. "Tax authorities have been prepared to apply transfer-pricing rules on the provision of group administrative services on the basis of a profit mark-up element charged over the cost of providing the services to group companies" (Schwartz 1994). The manner in which the arrangements are provided varies enormously. The United Kingdom, for example, attracts the highest number of headquarters operations in Europe, but has no formal rulings process. Belgium, a newcomer to this game, established in contrast a Coordination Center, which has a formal legal basis (Schwartz 1994). In addition, a number of states are now competing for the privilege of serving as homes for holding companies. The Netherlands has historically dominated this market, with other countries such as Luxembourg or Austria playing a very much secondary role. The passing of the EU Parent Subsidiary Directive has, however, opened up the playing field considerably. The directive requires EU member states to eliminate withholding tax on dividends to parent companies in other EU states. As corporations globalize they now seek to locate their treasury operations in tax-favorable jurisdictions, Jersey has attracted a number of these banks, such as Morgan Grenfell, Kleinwort Benson, and Citibank.

Another aspect that has become particularly significant in the past few years is the establishment of trusts in tax havens to avoid severe inheritance laws and the heavy cost of litigation (Diamond and Diamond 1998). Bermuda, in particular, is aggressively pushing for this lucrative business.

### THE COMPETITION STATE

As in the case of the EPZs, it is difficult to disentangle the real and the imagined threats posed by the offshore economy to national economies. There is no shortage of scholars who pronounce with great authority and confidence that offshore was the cause for liberalization, and claim to have discovered a direct correlation between technology, power or state, and the changing patterns of global capitalism. The situation, however, is far more complex than this view allows; in fact, it is simply impossible to disentangle cause and effect in the rise of offshore. In some instances, there is little doubt that offshore played an important role in dismantling key instruments of national power. Radio broadcasting from the offshore pirate stations completely undermined national broadcast monopolies, demonstrating the futility of government attempts at controlling the airwaves. But the direct impact of the offshore economy, substantial as it may have been, proved in practice less significant than the indirect impacts. The fact of the matter is that the growing offshore economy fed the perception that states could not afford to continue to try to control their economies. The true impact of the offshore economy is felt, therefore, indirectly, magnified many times by some important changes in the nature of the state—changes that were to some degree brought about because of the offshore economy.

One thing is clear: reductions in regulation and taxation have become part of conventional thinking about the role of the state, a change that evolved, at least in part in order to combat the (real or imaginary) threat of relocation to the offshore economy. "Was there a revolution in international political economy in the 1980s?" asks James Boughton in an authorized history of the International Monetary Fund. "To a great extent, the silent revolution of the 1980s resulted from a shift in economic philosophy toward a new classical synthesis in which government has an indirect role in, but not a direct responsibility for, ensuring national economic prosperity; in which private economic activity is promoted through good governance and the development of physical and social infrastructure" (2000, 5). Eric Helleiner does not think the revolution had anything to do with a shift in philosophy; rather, the rise of a business-friendly culture was brought about by the policy of the

United States (1994, 115). For the contributors to Alesina and Carliner (1991), the changes were due largely to the complexities of the domestic political process in the United States. For others it was an awakening to the realities of the international market faced by the crisis of stagflation of the 1970s. These, I submit, are not necessarily incompatible theories, as much as theories emphasizing different dimensions of a multifaceted process.

On the one hand, a "new classical revolution" in economics was clearly in the making. More significant perhaps, these changes induced transformation in the policies and aims of states. Lipietz already noted that by the early 1970s "each country strives to improve its competitiveness at the expense of the domestic purchasing power" (1987, 70). Similarly, Stopford and Strange observed that "structural change in the international political economy has altered the nature of the game by affecting the actions and response among firms and states"(1991, 4). Strange postulated that rather than competing for power and prestige, states were now increasingly "competing for world market shares as the surest means to greater wealth and greater economic security" (1987, 564). These new models of state intervention, dubbed by Philip Cerny (1990) the "competition state." reinforced, in turn, the offshore economy.

There is no generally agreed definition of the competition state, but broadly it comprises three elements. The first is a pervasive belief in national competitiveness as the means for generating economic growth and higher standards of living. This idea is certainly not new, and can be traced back at least to later mercantilist thought. Nonetheless, national competitiveness has become a central ideological plank guiding policy. Second, market integration has rendered demand side policies unreliable, leaving governments with little option but to concentrate efforts on supply side measures. Third, the distinction between national and international policies is no longer tenable (Palan and Abbott 1996).

In the competition state, governments think strategically about the place of their national economies in the world economy. A populist version of such theories serves increasingly to justify policy. Meanwhile countries that, in the language of an OECD (1995) report, "provide economic agents with a framework which gives them confidence and encouragement to move forward" are likely to be rewarded by lower interest rates on their borrowings and a higher volume of foreign direct investment (Sinclair 1994). Others may experience capital flight. In theory, competition states are able to borrow heavily in global markets, thus accelerating their rates of economic growth. Conversely, those that fail to adopt prudent financial policies may experience a drastic reduction in investment. For all these reasons, trade theory places great stress on the active role of the state in encouraging growth.

The new model of state incorporated the offshore economy into its very structure. As we saw, a variety of legislation that went under the heading of financial deregulation was justified explicitly by reference to the offshore economy. Similarly, an array of special regional incentives, tax holidays, special bilateral trade agreements, and the like were enacted in response to the export processing zones. The competition state adopted, in other words, techniques that were developed originally in the offshore world, such as deregulation, liberalization, and market integration, to advance its interests. The removal of capital controls and other impediments to the movement of capital, in turn, encouraged capital to make further use of the offshore economy. Paradoxically, if not at all surprisingly, in spite of the supposed blurring of the distinction between offshore and onshore, the trend of firm formation in offshore jurisdictions failed to slow down in the least—indeed, quite the contrary. A study of recent trends is still to be conducted, but all the evidence suggests that the offshore economy is in healthier shape than ever. The Cayman Islands posted a 51 percent increase in the number of offshore entities (a broad category that includes financial and nonfinancial entities including companies bought "off the shelf") in 1999. Mauritius recently announced that there are fourteen thousand offshore entities on its territory (Panafrican News Agency 2001). In 1999 Bahrain declared an increase of approximately 10 percent in operating assets in its offshore banking units (Reuters 2000).

The rise of the competition state is often justified on an empirical basis; as trends in state policies are observed, but also on a theoretical level, as a justified response to changing technology and patterns of capital accumulation. It is clear, however, that the offshore economy has been a key factor contributing to and facilitating these changes. But as states increasingly reorient their policies toward what they take to be global capital—much of it in effect operating through the offshore economy—they reinforce by their action the legal and political infrastructure that supports further globalization. Thus, the principles embedded in the offshore economy become institutionalized into the very fabric of the state system.

## THE OECD CAMPAIGN AGAINST HARMFUL TAX COMPETITION

The expanding offshore economy in the later part of the twentieth century was unquestionably viewed with some consternation by, among others, the governments of Germany, France, and the United States. Nonetheless, as we saw, until fairly recently advanced industrialized countries sought to resist the attractions of offshore mainly by relaxing their domestic regulations and taxation. But growing concern with issues of money laundering, drug trafficking, and harmful tax competition has propelled the offshore economy to the top of the political agenda. Spates of important studies have been published recently, grabbing the headlines and giving the impression that the offshore economy is facing its most serious challenges yet.

The IMF began the trend by publishing two important reports, one specifically on the growth of offshore financial centers (Cassard 1994), and the other on the role played by offshore centers in the East Asian financial crisis (Errico and Musalem 1999). The two reports, notes Paul O'Neill, the U.S. treasury secretary, "take a notably condemnatory tone with respect to the issues addressed, and the advocacy of internationally coordinated action against targeted countries represents an approach that is more aggressive than is typical for the OECD" (U.S. Treasury 2001). The reports were followed by a series of unilateral and multilateral headline-grabbing measures against OFCs. The U.S. Treasury is rolling out its "national money laundering strategy 2000" (U.S. Treasury 2001). "UK targets offshore tax evasion," trumpets a headline in the *Financial Times* (2000a). The European Union is putting pressure on several member states, especially Luxembourg to abandon its bank secrecy laws (tax-news.com, 2000, April 3). Most notably, the French Assembly commissioned a series of unusually candid and thorough investigations of European tax havens. So far it has published strongly condemnatory studies of Liechtenstein, Monaco, Switzerland, the City of London, the British dependencies, and Luxembourg (Peillon and Montebourg 2000a–b, 2001a–b, 2002).

But arguably the most significant measure with regard to OFCs, however, began in 1998, when the OECD launched its harmful tax practices initiative, commissioning a report that set out criteria to attempt to define harmful tax practices and provide a framework for future work to address such practices (OECD 1998). Following that report, and in conjunction with the growing concerns about the role that OFCs might play in destabilizing the international financial system, the OECD established a subsidiary body, the Forum on Harmful Tax Practices, which, in turn set up a permanent body, the Financial Stability Forum (FSF). The Financial Stability Forum published an influential report in June 2000 (FSF 2000). The report identified thirty-seven countries as tax havens, and forty-seven additional countries as offering potentially harmful preferential tax regimes. The report relied exclusively on data from and discussions with government officials of offshore jurisdictions. It never consulted independent experts, lawyers, and practitioners in the field. But it gave details of the supervisory and regulatory arrangements in each jurisdiction, making recommendations for change. The report provided a one-year period for the identified tax havens to enter into commitments to eliminate their harmful tax practices by the end of 2005. It also provided that jurisdictions that did not make such commitments would be included on a list of "uncooperative" tax havens which was to be published in July 2001. Thanks to intense lobbying by tax havens and politicians from advanced industrialized countries (such as Hillary Clinton, for instance) the second report has not been published at the time of writing.[1]

The Financial Stability Forum campaign for transparency appeared to have made headway during 1999 and 2000. Switzerland, Luxembourg, Gibraltar, Liechtenstein, Bermuda, and the Cayman Islands are some of the more important tax havens to have responded by enacting what they claim are broad reforms in their financial legislation. "Sweeping legislation passed at the end of 2000 ended an era in banking in the Bahamas," was a typical report in the *Financial Times* (2001). Liechtenstein had announced that it is prepared to cooperate with the FSF over the issue of money laundering. Antigua and Barbuda have established an executive team to prepare for a review of money laundering by the Paris-based Financial Action Task Force.

However, following the accession of the new administration to the White House, the United States no longer supports the OECD campaign against harmful tax competition (U.S. Treasury 2001). Indeed, I would argue that considering the delays in publication of the FSF second report, the change of heart of the United States, the ambiguous policies of other OECD countries, and the lack of independent assessment of the true effects of recent policies, the time is not right to attempt an informed assessment of the true impact of the new legislation. Indeed, it appears that the offshore world is not at all in decline. The Caymans' position as "the second biggest offshore mutual fund jurisdiction" has been if anything strengthened in the past year. The biggest

annual rise in numbers of its offshore entities came, notes Andrew
Bounds, "during a year in which the Cayman Islands were blacklisted
by . . . the Financial Action Task Force" (Bounds 2001). We have already
seen that many jurisdictions have experienced record growth in the
number of offshore entities licensed in their territories since the publication of the FSF report.

Ian Goldman (2001) argues that the impression of an overall assault
on offshore is somewhat misleading. Whereas the issue of opacity (bank
secrecy laws, corporate ownership, etc.) is being tackled by the OECD
governments, the legal use of offshore for the purpose of tax avoidance—of much greater significance than illicit use—continues apace. In
a similar vein, in a detailed examination of the OECD's policies
Michael Webb reaches the conclusion that "only those forms of tax
competition which can be shown to be inconsistent with neo-liberal
ideology were targeted in the 1998–2000 agreements, and even there international cooperation had a limited impact" (2002, 3). The FSF was
never really concerned with offshore as much as with financial instability. Soon enough it found that offshore financial centers "do not appear to have been a major causal factor in the creation of systemic financial problems" (FSF 2000, 5). Nonetheless, it acknowledged that
some OFCs were, in its own diplomatic words, "unable or unwilling to
adhere to international supervisory standards" (FSF 2000, 5). But the
FSF was never against OFCs as such. It acknowledges that offshore is
used primarily for tax and regulation avoidance, and secondly as asset
protection (FSF 2000, 14), but it goes on to state: "The term 'offshore'
carries with it in some quarters a perception of dubious or nefarious activities. There are, however, highly reputable OFCs that actively aspire
to and apply internationally accepted practices, and there are some legitimate uses of OFCs" (FSF 2000, 12). So by implication, then, the
emergence of OFCs is, generally speaking, a positive development, and
the FSF's aim is to promote what it takes to be "reputable" offshore centers. Thus, the report's aim is in fact to support the development of offshore activities, believing it is in the interest of all to achieve certain
standards.

Similarly, the IMF and BIS have no objection whatsoever to the offshore economy as long as it does not affect financial stability. The IMF
was encouraged to investigate offshore financial centers in the wake of
accusations following the East Asian crisis. Unsurprisingly, perhaps,
one of the IMF reports came to the conclusion that offshore finance may
have accelerated some aspects of the crisis, but was not the cause of it

(Errico and Musalem 1999). The basic message seems to be that the principle of integrated, "efficient," unregulated money markets is a good thing. We need, therefore, to read the promising announcements made by some OFC governments in this light.

This leniency of international economic and financial organizations towards offshore is not at all surprising. As we have seen, since the 1970s the offshore economy has dug deep roots into the very fabric of the contemporary international political economy. Some argue, as we saw, that the very boundaries of the offshore economy are being eroded. But they tend to forget that the boundaries between offshore and onshore are being eroded because the principles governing the offshore economy such as low taxation and light regulation have infiltrated the state. The changes brought about by the offshore economy—to be contrasted with the phenomenon itself—are palpable, decisive and, I would add, irreversible. In that sense offshore is not only symptomatic of an array of transformative practices that are shaping modern capitalism, but, more controversially, offshore has proved to be a central restructuring agent in this transformation. It is, as Leslie Budd (1999) suggests, forcing the shift towards "global neoclassicism." The offshore economy, therefore, has already infiltrated and shaped the state system to such an extent that recent policy initiatives can only make slight differences at the very margins. The focus on policy issues simply misses the big picture.

CHAPTER SIX

# Offshore and the Demise
# of the Nation-State

Not so long ago Switzerland, the Cayman Islands, the Bahamas, and Liberia were considered aberrations. Knowledge of their role and functions within the offshore world, indeed, any knowledge of the offshore world, was scarce, and that world remained the preserve of the super-rich. But in the past decade or so, offshore has opened its arms to the masses. Private banking used to be the preserve of a select few. Not many banks would have considered managing portfolios of less than $1 million; indeed, many insisted on at least $5 million in their clients' accounts. But now postal and Internet offshore accounts accept deposits as low as $500; offshore debit cards, betting shops, and so on abound. The Internet is proving to be a great universalizing force, offering practical demonstration of the advantages of offshore to growing numbers of people worldwide. The offshore economy, therefore, is no longer merely integrated into the practice of business, but is rapidly becoming part of daily life, as more and more people participate in it directly or are becoming aware of its existence through the media and by word of mouth. How does this expansion of offshore affect the nature of political life? What are the likely effects of offshore on the nature of the social bond in societies intent on commercializing their sovereignty?

It would be foolish, of course, to try and quantify or pretend to offer an accurate prediction of the long-term consequences that commercialized sovereignty may have for the state and politics. What does seem likely, however, is that increasing awareness of the commercialization of sovereignty will destabilize not only the concept of popular sovereignty—the dominant understanding of sovereignty in the nineteenth and twentieth centuries—but also the entire discourse of the nation-state; and that this awareness will contribute to the rise of a new discourse of statehood and a new type of politics. My argument is predicated on a particular interpretation of the nature of the discourse of the nation-state and its relation to the concept of popular sovereignty, drawn primarily from the work of two prominent French sociologists, Nicos Poulantzas (1978) and Dominique Schnapper (1998). Neither author has achieved great prominence in the Anglo-Saxon world; Poulantzas is arguably the better known, but his last book where he developed these ideas never had the impact of his earlier works. Much of this chapter is therefore devoted to the relationship between popular sovereignty and the nation-state.

## COMMERCIALIZED SOVEREIGNTY AND THE REORDERING OF THE DISCOURSE OF THE STATE

When it comes to considering the likely societal effects of the commercialization of sovereignty, we should consider these in their totality—not simply in economic but also in cultural and social terms. It is not simply a matter of how much is gained by offshore jurisdictions from practices such as the sale of license fees, but also of what sort of legitimacy can be attached to states that engage in these practices, and of how the subject perceives his or her place in states and societies that have commercialized their sovereignty. But these questions apply not only to the citizens of tax havens and other offshore jurisdictions. Today we all inhabit a world of commercialized sovereignty—in which states routinely employ their sovereign right to make law, and the exclusive right of citizenship, something that was viewed not too long ago as an expression of the sacred association between citizens and their nation—for commercial purposes. Commercialized sovereignty is not simply legitimized, by whatever means—rather, as it is practiced, felt, observed, sensed, it shapes the subject's perception of his or her social world. A subjective cognitive process goes on whereby the subject internalizes this collective behavior and constructs a worldview that normalizes it, renders it unproblematic. But such normalization must take place within a broader systemic reordering of the legitimizing landscape, which not only allows for the internalization and legitimization of commercialized sovereignty, but also, in turn, affects the politics of participation.

To put it in the context of our discussion: a particular interpretation of sovereignty, say the theory of divine right of kings or the concept of popular sovereignty which replaced it in the early nineteenth century, evolved in a context of a broader system of meanings that assigned roles and functions to power and agency. Such global meaning, in turn, was operative within what may be described as a political economy of governance (Foucault 1979). The theory of the divine right of kings, for instance, would make sense only in the context of an agrarian, nonsecular society, in which the prince's claim to sovereignty was advanced and legitimized because secular rule was viewed as an expression of God's will on earth. That broader historical context, which explained and made sense of the practice of rule, therefore drew upon the dominant discourse of the time which presented a fairly coherent story about the nature of social life. But how, then, was the discourse of divine right of kings replaced by that of popular sovereignty? According to discourse theory, change in discourse comes about only rarely in a linear manner. Often, "practices . . . work upon existing discursive structures. . . . Discontinuity occurs in the form of mutations and redistribution rather than discoveries or complete breaks" (Colebrook 1997, 43). This was the case with the changes witnessed in the early nineteenth century which, as we saw in chapter 3, took the form of a mutation in the discourse of sovereignty that rendered it, as Veblen argues, a non-sense. Yet the mutation in the concept of sovereignty took place in the context of a broader discursive reordering that greeted the rise of the modern world. The concept of sovereignty survived this reordering, but it survived in a new form.

This is an evolutionary type of change. If we apply the same methodology to our case here, then, in order to understand the impact of commercialized sovereignty, we need first to sketch out the general parameters of the discourse of the nation-state, and in particular, the role of the concept of popular sovereignty. Then we must ask how commercialized sovereignty is likely to destabilize the discourse of the nation-state and how a new system of meaning is likely to emerge. Here again, we find that offshore is not the sole or even the main cause of change. But the expansion of the offshore economy, taking place at this particular time, is reinforcing precisely the tendencies associated with the rise of neoliberalism.

## THE GRADUAL RISE OF THE EUROPEAN NATION-STATE

Benedict Anderson (1981) put forward a well-known argument about the constitution of an imaginary entity, the "nation," and links its appearance to a number of technological and cultural innovations, particularly the printing press and the spread of vernaculars. The nation, or more appropriately, the nation-state, is a narrative; in fact, a plurality of "historical narratives that naturalize a particular, territorially oriented view of sovereignty" (Shapiro 1997, 17). The concept of the nation serves as a transcendental fiction (not unlike the ancient cult of the dead) imputing to certain social practices a particular meaning as manifestations of collective or "public spirit." In fact, the discourse of nationhood and public spirit constitutes precisely the very subject it assumes. Nationalists, of course, tend to present the nation as an ancient, primordial spiritual unity, which discovers its "true nature" in a revelatory moment. Thus Michelet argues: "France was born and started into life at the sound of the cannon of the Bastille. In one day, without any preparation or previous understanding, the whole of France, both cities and villages, was organized at the same time" (cited in Kohn 1944, 97). He believes, like other nationalists, that a "nation" or "people," possessing certain attributes, existed at least "in potential"—and that it came to life at a particular moment in time. But as Sandra Halperin (1997) demonstrates, what was presented as an already constituted, assumed nation and its associated meaning was nothing but a political program aimed at creating the nation. Yet the assumed nation begot certain assumptions about how people should regard the state and the social environment, and informed their views and practices. That is why early nationalists, like Johann Gottlieb Fichte, paid great attention to education: the aim of the "new education," he declared, was to make a man moral and strong which, he assured his readers, was the only way by which the German nation could live ([1808] 1981, 80).

But how did this discourse evolve? In line with Claire Colebrook's remark about the importance of practice in the construction of discourse, I suspect that the consciousness of nationhood evolved over a long period of time. In what follows, I narrate selected key points in the transition from the absolutist state to the nation-state. I highlight those aspects that proved important in the establishment of today's flexible institutional structures which are bracing themselves to adapt to globalization. My argument is that from the early nineteenth century, the principle of nationality has been repeatedly deployed as a new principle of territorial rationalization.

*Centralization and Homogenization of Power*
The critical preparatory period for the rise of the nation-state was absolutism (Poulantzas 1978). Absolutist rulers sought to homogenize and rationalize their territories in the belief that diversity encouraged factionalism and feuds (Schnapper 1998, 115). Thus, the expulsion of the Moors and the Jews from Spain—to which we can add the Thirty Years War concluding with the Westphalian compromise, as well as the ex-

pulsion of the Huguenots from France—all fall within this broad trend of political homogenization. These policies had the result of establishing what Dominique Schnapper calls "a substratum of national consciousness" (1998, 98).

The slow process of homogenization and centralization of power, combined with the enclosure movement in England and rising market and contractual relationships, contributed in time to the breakdown of the traditional village communities. In addition, the economic slowdown experienced from the 1630s onward and the disastrous pan-European wars of the seventeenth and eighteenth century led to the emergence of a mass movement of vagabondage. As a result, issues of social control and of the reproduction of social order became the stuff of high politics (Baumann 1992). Foucault argues that the security problems led rulers to become preoccupied with the category of the "population," and traces the origins of the modern conception of the sovereign individual to this preoccupation. This is debatable. More important, however, was the emergence of "population as datum, as a field of intervention, and as an object of governmental techniques" (1979, 8). States began to adopt an array of techniques of incarceration and control to handle this mass of people. Louis XIV's edict ordering the homeless to be placed in workhouses proved in retrospect to be a significant development in social control—both by getting the state directly involved and by educating the cadres of capitalist labor.

As the category "population" makes its entrance in history, the state increasingly sees its role as the protector of its collective interests. But as social order was increasingly viewed as "mechanical" and imposed, the state came to be understood as a technique for "organizing" the life of the people. The reforms of Frederick William of Prussia (1620–88) and his successor were designed, writes Brian Chapman, to create a tightly organized and rigorously administered state "dedicated to three purposes: the protection of the population, the welfare of the state and the improvement of society" (1970, 5). In France, establishment of the *grandes écoles* for administration and engineering in the early nineteenth century diffused techniques of control learned from military barracks to the hospital and the prison (Foucault 1977).

The slow breakdown of village and regional economies, combined with the rise of the new money economy, and the post-Renaissance conception of individuality, fed into a changing conception of space. There was evidence for a shift from "the verticality of the premodern, medieval map [to] a spatiality centered on the 'individual' as a moral subjectivity tied to national boundaries, to a horizontal, bordered world, which determines levels of autonomy and obligation" (Shapiro 1997, 21). This abstract spatiality was closely tied to the rise of capital- ism, which entailed the development of "a specific space that is *con- tinuous, homogenous, symmetrical, reversible and open*" (Poulantzas 1978, 100; emphasis in original). The state thus inscribes the nation in space: the nation becomes coextensive with a particular territory. This modern conception of space was particularly significant, as we saw in chapter 3, in the emergence of embryonic offshore.

Thus, the very atomization of the body politic, as Poulantzas (1978) describes the process, places the state in a privileged position as organizer-in-chief of the population, soon to be assigned a new meaning as "the people." Indeed, by the late eighteenth century, the mass of the people was replaced by a theory of a more coherent nation as social philosophers began to advocate a role to the state in organizing and serving the unity of the people. The "social sciences" had an important role to play in this movement.[1]

It is interesting to note at this juncture that the word "organization" is etymologically linked to "organism." This is no accident. Social philosophers in the late eighteenth century took "organisms" as the ul- timate, perfectly "organized" machines to be emulated by society. The idea that the state was to "organize" society was predicated on the no- tion that the state was to achieve perfect harmony and balance in soci- ety as an expression of divine will. Countless studies therefore explored the relationships between the social whole and the organic entities that composed it. Likewise, the state was to bridge the gulf between the "natural" and the "social" or "artificial." The term "artificial" tends to be used pejoratively nowadays, but in the era of the French Revolution this was not the case. The term is etymologically derived from "art," and it was not understood as meaning "contrived" or "unnatural," but on the contrary as the quality of a work of art that attempts to recreate heavenly order on earth. The romantic tradition therefore insisted that the state was to be an "artifice," a unique work of art emulating the or- ganic unity of nature (Aris 1965).

Since the state's function was to organize and to adapt "society," the state had to adopt the new system of "rationality." Natural law theories of universal and unchanging hierarchical orders were losing popularity, to be replaced by dynamic and evolutionary theories. Smith, Kant, and Hegel, supported by a host of social theorists, were key spokespersons for the transition to modern "epistémé." During this period, social theory shifted from questions of justice and ethics to questions of logistics and strategy; from theories of order and change to more pragmatic discussions of procedures and the organization of the "body politic." Comparativists like Tocqueville expounded the merits of the American federal system of checks and balances, as a self-regulating but dynamic system wherein change was institutionalized and contained.

### The Great Historical Journey of the Nation

These developments prepared the way for the modern practice of the state, a practice sustained by the ideology of nationalism. Nationalism, however, appears on the face of it somewhat unrelated, an ideology and a practice that simply burst on the scene in the early years of the nineteenth century. As a theory, it appears to suggest that the nation is not the sum total of the individuals who happen to reside in a particular territory, but something that transcends such an aggregation. Hegel declares: "The rational is that which has being in and for itself, and from which everything else derives its value. It assumes varying shapes; but in none of them is it more obviously an end than in that whereby the spirit explicates and manifests itself, in the endlessly varying forms which we call nations" (1975, 28). Once the "nation" exploded onto the scene, it prescribed certain relationships between subjects and the collective. Since the nation, the "people," is "the spiritual individual" (Hegel 1975, 96) it must practice itself and empirically organize as a spiritual entity. The nation needs the state: for "world history takes account only of nations that constituted themselves into states" (Hegel 1975, 96). "In some respects the state is to the nation what the machine is to man. The machine may reproduce many of the capacities inherent in man, and even extend them, but it is nevertheless artificial and soulless" (Schonfield 1970, 181).

Jacqueline Stevens is correct in saying that "political societies constitute the intergenerational family form that provides the pre-political seeming semantics of nation" (1999, 9). In other words, the nation draws discursively on familial concepts, presenting itself as a large family. Nationalist narrative advanced a view of a shared destiny of this extended family, "the people." According to this doctrine, the nation is no mere arbitrary aggregation of individuals who happen to reside within a certain geographical location; rather, it is a soul, a spiritual principle. "A nation," writes Ernest Renan, "is a great solidarity, created by the awareness of sacrifices the people have made, and of those which people are prepared to go on making" (Renan 1996, 240). In each of the great Western democracies—in England, the United States, and France—a sense of uniqueness, and hence of the "grandeur" of its political project, sets in (Schnapper 1998, 42). At the heart of the formation of nations there is a "notable and lasting political event" that communicates a sense of the historical task of the nation. The nation is a historical entity; it undergoes a great journey of discovery and spiritual renewal. So France discovered its origins in the misty days of the destruction of Troy, no less (Beaune 1985), and the German Romantics discovered their medieval past in the Teutonic hordes.

The nation is founded, therefore, not on domination and hierarchy but on a sentiment of love. As Fichte taught: man has to do things through love; love is the motor of his desires. The nation is predicated on the assumption of a shared responsibility to the inherited culture of the forebears. The presumption of shared destiny of "the nation" begets, therefore, an assumption of social responsibility. While the nation "presupposes a past; it resumes itself in the present by a tangible fact: the consent, the clearly expressed desire to continue life in common" (Renan 1996, 139). During the French revolution, one proclamation read: "Society is obliged to provide for the subsistence of all its members either by giving them jobs, or by assuring the means of subsistence to those who are incapable of working" (quoted in Schnapper 1998, 127). The modern concept of the social is invented (Donzelot 1984).

### Nation and Democracy

The pursuit of national renewal and growth is the major task of the nation. Since the imaginary absence, the nation, unlike the previous imaginary absence, God, is immanent to itself, it must take control over its shared destiny. The nation becomes therefore "a daily plebiscite, as the existence of the individual is a perpetual affirmation of life" (Renan 1996, 241).

God-fearing people are likely to entrust their destiny to God and therefore to His emissaries on earth, so that political choices are seen as moral choices about following His injunctions or not. God-fearing polities like the medieval state or modern Iran are hierarchical; they are predicated on an act of subordination to the eternal laws of God. God's emissaries, the ruler and his associates, merely interpret this eternal law for the benefit of the community; they mediate between God and His people. A national community, however, cannot rely on eternal laws and must make choices as a community. Consequently, "in the age of nations, the political principle replaced the religious or dynastic as the unifier of men" (Schnapper 1998, 3). As members of a nation, not only do people have responsibility toward the collectivity, but also the nation has to organize itself so that its spiritual aims are fulfilled. The nation must therefore evolve procedures for anticipating and effecting choice.

The narrative of the nation had unmistakable implications for the politics of the nineteenth century. Politics is now seen as a structure and a process that "mediate" between the nation and its governing body, transmitting the collective will. No longer seen as an autonomous set of activities centered on court intrigues, politics is now defined in statist terms as purposeful social activity whose ultimate aim and function is the formal organization of society. This is at the heart of the modern concept of "domestic politics."

Since members of the nation share a mutual destiny, states are viewed as the functional arm ensuring the welfare of these mutual aid societies. The state emerged from the French Revolution as an organization that was supposed to respond to the "needs" of the people who inhabited a particular territorial space. As Easton puts it, although typically without the necessary historical perspective: "All social activities directly involving the 'authoritative allocation of value' at the societal level are carried out by a single decision center—the state itself—no matter how internally differentiated and extensively ramified those activities might be" (quoted in Poggi 1978, 92). The nation-state is viewed, therefore, in systemic terms, as a self-organizing family. The state is given the task of maintaining peace and harmony at home, and defending the territorial integrity of the nation. There are, naturally, diverging interpretations of the mechanisms that will ensure such a beneficial outcome. Conservatives are happy to leave such practical matters to the great and the good, while liberals place their hopes in the democratic process which requires constant communication between rulers and ruled. Notwithstanding these debates, nationalism tends to assume that rulers and ruled are locked in a systemic relationship and that their mutual relationship is an expression of their transcendental unity.

But as the nation is portrayed as a self-organizing egalitarian community, the question must arise: who belongs to the community? And dealing empirically with the question of who belongs also raises the more fundamental question: Who belongs to what? Consequently, the struggle for suffrage turns out to be a battle in which imaginary identities are constantly formulated and contested. As Schnapper notes: "The uniqueness of the modern nation lies in the integration of all populations into one community of citizens and in the legitimating action of the state, which is its instrument . . . it therefore implies the principle of universal suffrage—the participation of all citizens in choosing their governors and judging their methods of exercising power" (1998, 35).

The concept of citizenship had significant implications, in turn, for the concept of state closure. The nation, in the words of Anthony Smith, presented its closure analytically: "The new imagination pictures the nation as a homogeneous body of individuals, who are generalized equals or 'citizens,' and whose connections are impersonal and fraternal" (1986, 170). The geographer Friedrich Ratzel saw also the practical implications of such view. As Prescott notes, his spatial "Conception of states followed logically from his belief that the state was like a living organism which grew and decayed. The boundary and the adjacent territory, which is called the border, formed the epidermis of this organism and provided protection and allowed exchanges to occur" (1965, 8). States then set out to construct this epidermis by establishing physical boundaries supported by juridical perimeters.

Furthermore, the concept of citizenship was also reflected in the idea of national self-determination, which became a constitutive feature of the "international system" combining in practice the concepts of nation and sovereignty. National self-determination underwent two important if subtle changes. In the first phase the suggestion was that the unity of a people was ethnically based: belonging meant sharing certain "cultural" attributes. But by the early twentieth century a second phase was in evidence as sovereignty came to denote "the exclusive, unique, institutionalized and strictly public dominance over a territorial national ensemble and the effective exercise of central power without the extra-political restrictions of juridical, ecclesiastical or moral order which characterize the feudal state" (Poulantzas 1978, 162). This second phase, most clearly illustrated in the formation of the United Nations system, represented what may be called the "territorialization" of the nation.

The nation-state, therefore, is not an accidental coupling of two tangentially related sets of belief systems, but a historically specific form of what Foucault (1979) defines as "governance." Only during the phase of territorial rationalization was a unique and uncompromising relationship between political authority and territory postulated. Equally, only during this phase was the state seen as a historical entity, or a social body representing the "will of the people." The state sought to symbolize this merged relationship not only in its institutions, but also in investing its geography and architecture with meaning so that the state became a "living map" symbolizing the spirit of its people.

## COMMERCIALIZED SOVEREIGNTY

The discussion above also sheds light on the issues raised in chapter 3, of why the insulation of the state in law was achieved only in the early nineteenth century and not in the seventeenth as often assumed; and why this happened within the context of the rise of positivist international law. These can now be seen as components of the rise to dominance of the discourse of the nation-state.

In the discourse of the nation-state, the relationship between state and nation is understood as one of exteriority: the state is clearly the servant in this relationship, attending to the needs and welfare of the spiritual unity, the nation. Hence the nation, and not the state, becomes in the mind of contemporaries the primary force in history—hence, incidentally, we speak of "inter-national" relations or affairs, rather than of "inter-state" relations or affairs (Palan and Blair 1993). This discourse then guides the state to try to strive, as we saw, to "isolate" itself from other states in the name of protecting the nation, constructing an epidermis around this alleged spiritual unity of the "people." Practices and institutions, as much as the topography of the "insulated" state, then serve to affirm the theory of the nation—affirming the commitment of the state founded on the "will of the people" and the unity of the "people." Within this grid of meaning, the function of sovereignty is to assert the principle of the autonomy of politics.

We can see now how systemic relationships are established between different categories, and how these categories become "real"—or as real as the discipline of international relations which is only too happy to accept the unity of the state and the "national interest" as an indisputable fact. Thus, the imaginary closure of the nation-state does not remain simply aspirational, but informs practice, politics, and administrative goals, as the state seeks to shape the nature of the "body politic" by creating and shaping boundaries out of frontiers.

The personality of the "nation," representing a true collectivity and acting as a true actor, also affects the notion of sovereignty, which shifts during the nineteenth century, as we saw, from the monarch to the "people." This shift is associated with the rise of the doctrine of popular sovereignty, which, as Emerson observes, is "the right or power not of any individual or sum of individuals but of the whole conceived as an organic unity with a real personality of its own" (1928, 11). The concept of popular sovereignty does not simply imply a shift of power from the monarch to the nation, but represents therefore the mythical unity of the nation which is the ultimate arbitrator of human life.

Consequently, the concept of popular sovereignty, however ridiculous strictly speaking it is, as Veblen has wonderfully demonstrated,[2] makes sense in the grid of meanings embedded in the general concept of the nation-state: sovereignty has "shifted" to the "people." This not only implies that power and democracy ultimately lie with the imaginary discrete national entity, the nation-state; as we have seen, it also implies a certain type of politics, the politics of co-responsibility that members of this spiritual unity feel toward their forebears, their children, and each other. In that sense, there is something "sacred" about popular sovereignty. The sovereignty of the people has not simply "shifted" for unknown reasons from monarchy to the people. The shift consecrates "the people" (but also the state) as the locus of power, but also, as we saw, as a moral entity expressing a higher mode of individual "freedom." Popular sovereignty becomes the most important and enduring element not of power, but of the self-expression, the self-belief of the people. It becomes the foundational myth of the state.

Here we begin to sense that those processes that are leading to the commercialization of sovereignty may be of great significance. When governments opt to use this "sacred" instrument of power, sovereignty, in such a cavalier manner as a commercial asset, they cannot help but raise doubts in the mind of their peoples about the nature of the bond between government and people. The widespread practice of commercialized sovereignty destabilizes, therefore, the discourse of popular sovereignty—it renders the concept and the ideas that underpin it, less credible in the mind of the people. But in this way, governments help destabilize not only the concept of popular sovereignty, but also the concept of the "people" or "nation" that underpins it—nationalism may not decline, but is transformed into new forms. Popular sovereignty, as we have seen, is the juridical expression of the proposition that the "people" or the "nation" is a spiritual unity and hence power should reside with it. But the state now serves not only the "nation"— which, after all, is supposed to have a historical relationship with a particular territory—but also a host of virtual citizens, with whom it establishes relationships of a commercial and utilitarian nature. Indeed, in many cases, the state offers advantages to these foreigners far and above what it offers its own people (Goldman 2001). Some of the "natural" citizens may begin to question their relationship with their state, and consequently, their relationship to their nation. The very idea of national life predicated on mutual responsibility, which is at the heart of the modern concept of popular sovereignty, is itself questioned.

Thus, if Elizabeth Taylor is able to buy her way into Swiss citizenship simply in order to reduce her tax burden, then obviously the relationship between the Swiss government and its people—which now includes the virtually present Miss Taylor—is not one of "sacred" unity. On the contrary, the Swiss government sees its role as that of offering services for which it taxes its citizens, and it advertises itself accordingly. In this way it implicitly suggests that its right to rule is not founded necessarily on the "will of the nation," but also on the fact that it offers a better bundle of regulations to its citizens, including those who acquire citizenship for pecuniary reasons, than other governments. The relationship between government and citizens is a business proposition. The problem is, of course, that implicit in the deal is that government and people are no longer united by some transcendental spiritual link. The concept of the "Swiss people" no longer expresses deep familial and cultural links to a particular place. The "Swiss people" may consist, as the government of Switzerland is clearly suggesting, not only of those who happen to be born in Switzerland but also of those who chose Switzerland because of its bundles of regulations and laws.

This sheds new light on one of the less-noticed aspects of the Tiebout paradigm, which, as we saw in chapter 2, informs much of modern thinking about business taxation. Tiebout's "extreme model" was based on the assumptions that voters, i.e. citizens, are in fact consumers—"consumer-voters are fully mobile and will move to that community where their preference patterns, which are set, are best satisfied"; and that "there are a large number of communities in which the consumer-voters may choose to live" (Tiebout 1956, 4). In other words, the relationship between subjects and "communities"—whatever that term might mean—is purely utilitarian.

Tiebout was writing about local communities and the politics of city incorporation in the United States, and his model certainly appears far more extreme when applied to the relationship between states and their citizens. But what appeared extreme in 1956 is no longer so: the concept of voter-consumer underpins, as we saw in the introduction, the ideology of global constitutionalism. The vague and ambiguous link between offshore and global constitutionalism becomes, then, surprisingly, obvious and clear.

A study that traces the way one myth of the nation-state is replaced by another is still to be written, but I would argue that the growing popularity of utilitarianism, rational choice theories, and the "new political economy" is an expression in academicspeak of deeper movement in society. Here, Weberian "empiricism" is mobilized apparently unwittingly in support of a controversial state theory, but the theory in turn is employed to legitimize the new type of consumer politics. Auster and Silver were pioneers in this supposedly "hard-edged," nononsense state theory. The state, they argue, "is usually surrounded by a powerful mystique. It is not viewed as simply another of the myriad institutions contained in any society, owned of necessity by certain individuals and not by others. The state is seen in other ways; often it is viewed as the expression of some transcendental force: the 'leader,' the 'nation,' the 'workers,' the 'general will,' or divine will" (1979, 21). But these metaphysical notions, they assure their readers, are nonsense. In fact, "The state provides the service of 'protection' and punishment, and through these it manipulates the level of order" (1979, 7). Thus, "Denying that governments are the agencies of public interest, the new political economy has gone on to designate a typology of government that focuses on the state as a Leviathan or predatory state, or as factional, or as bureaucratic" (Meier 1990, 185). The implication is, of course, that if the state fails to provide adequate "protection" or perhaps overcharges for its services, one may legitimately seek to avoid paying tax. The public has the right, indeed the duty, to be vigilant in its dealings with the state: the public needs to tie down the state and prevent it from pursuing its own "parochial" set of interests.

This is essentially the metalanguage of neo-Weberian state theory: it is the message of a "new contract" between rulers and ruled. But who then are the ruled? Who belongs to this new community? The "nation" (i.e. all those who reside in a defined territory)? Clearly the nation no longer defines the community because national unity is debunked as well. Once the mythical shared destiny of the "people" is shown to be a "myth," the correlated notion of mutual responsibility between individuals and classes located within the boundaries of the state is difficult to uphold. Thus, ambiguities about national boundaries raise serious questions about the nature of the unity of the people, and these questions, in turn, raise equally serious ones about the need for and indeed morality of the politics of co-responsibility that has defined the period of the nation-state. Worse, if sovereignty, that most sacred symbolic aspect of the people, can become a commercial instrument, the most hallowed aspect of the nation is destroyed.

The commercialization of sovereignty no doubt punches a hole precisely in this most sacred aspect of the conception of community: because it suggests that if the nation-state's sovereignty over its territory is not an expression of the unity of the people, but rather a commodity that can be packed up and sold to the highest bidder then there is no spiritual unity to defend. As the nation is denied the most visible mark of its unity, the sacred union of the people and the state cannot help but be questioned. As a result the nation is divorced from its political arm, the state, and the state then begins to be viewed in a different light altogether. The connection among those who share in citizens' rights is shown to be spurious; a mere historical accident.

National unity is represented as a class compromise: the unity of purpose and choice in which employee and employers come together in order to compete with other similar national alliances (Vogler 1985). This is the space into which Michael Porter could interject his notion of the "competitive advantage of nations" (1990). This is no longer the horizontal transnational alliance of classes but vertical alliances of classes facing one another over loosely defined territorial fences.

The link between offshore and global constitutionalism now becomes clearer. The practice as well as the imagery of offshore help cement a utilitarian view of the world no longer anchored in the theory and practice based on the spiritual unity of the nation. The nation-state is undermined simultaneously from below, as the very concept of a higher unity of the people is replaced by a more individualistic, utilitarian concept of "society" whose role is to guarantee the "freedoms" of the "consumer-voters"; and from above, as claims for globalization and the need for "global governance" deprive the state of its traditional role. Offshore and the commercialization of sovereignty accelerate as much as serve as affirmation of these trends.

# CHAPTER SEVEN

# Numerical Organizations, Nomadic Spaces, and Modern Capitalism

Throughout this book I have insisted that offshore is not a territorial space but a juridical innovation, an economy that is serving to destabilize established concepts of place, territory, and identity. But offshore not only undermines traditional concepts of sovereignty and state; it also presents in a more profound way the spectacle of a fundamental discontinuity in the world economy, between the realms of state, power, and production, and a putative but strange dislocated "nomadic" world of virtual territories inhabited by virtual corporations (Davidow and Malone 1992), digital money (Kurtzman 1993), commodified sovereignty, and fictional juridical locales. This world undermines not only the nation-state, but also the traditional familiar world of *stato*, *status*, the "state system,"[1] the world of territorial units, borders, and national production facilities, in which power is viewed as capability and is firmly anchored to a conception of "strong states." Offshore is a world of flow rather than of place, of fluxes in place of *stato*. Business theorists have long proclaimed "the abstraction of industrial work" (Zuboff 1988) and the death of industrial society.

There is, indeed, a pervasive sense that social life is becoming somehow more "fictional" or "virtual." Some people talk of the increasing abstraction of modern capitalism, others speak of "virtualism," others again of "hyperrealism." Cultural texts of the late twentieth century replay "various versions of the fraught relationship between (sexed) human bodies and machines of awesome power. . . . The strange yet increasingly familiar spectacle of diverse couplings between bodies and technology . . ." (Botting 1999, 1). The question must therefore be asked: Is the offshore economy not a symptom of, or has it not managed unwittingly to unleash, deeper processes which are dissolving the prior solidity of the political-juridical territorial spaces?

### ABSTRACTION, DISEMBEDDEDNESS, AND OFFSHORE

Paradoxically, an inquiry into the relationship between offshore and modern spatiality requires us to downplay precisely what may appear as the most revolutionary aspect of offshore, its virtual or disembedding tendencies. There is some evidence to support the proposition that capitalism is becoming increasingly "disembedded," in the sense that territorial spaces are no longer as dominant as they used to be. But the trouble with this reading is that the presentation of a general trend towards the abstraction and disembedding of capitalism (and of offshore as symptomatic of that) is predicated on an unwarranted assumption that the state system somehow was less abstracted during some unidentified period in the past. Hence, the story goes, we are moving precariously from an ordered, stable system to a non-ordered and unstable system. Such nostalgic yearning for an idealized past fails to comprehend that social relationships are mediated through what today we would call constructed "truths" (or contingent realities). The appearance of "increasing abstractness" or "disembeddedness" cannot be taken at face value as depicting a historical trend from grounded social relationships to groundless or, at least, less grounded ones—a conservative-romantic view of history as that of "fallen man" (Levy 1993). There is no such movement here, but rather, as Deleuze and Guattari (1987) would put it, a change in the nature of "flow."

But even that is only half of the story: If we accept the proposition that "truth" is discursive and contingent, then "conventional" perceptions of social phenomena, including the discourses in which such perceptions are embedded and the method by which they are understood, cannot be reduced to an error of judgment or false consciousness. Rather, they must be treated as concepts rich in meaning, telling us something important about the nature of the society where they occur. While capitalism is clearly not less embedded today, the changes that a great number of social theorists have identified cannot be dismissed for lack of authenticity, but must be interrogated in their own realm, that of representation.

Following in this line of thought, the supposed abstracting tendencies engendered in capitalism, and expressed so vividly in offshore, can be interpreted in two ways. Ideologically, the perception of abstracted capitalism and in particular of the financial system, and the popular impression that it cannot operate efficiently under social control or that it has in fact evaded control, serves, as we saw in chapter 5, to reaffirm and strengthen neoliberal globalization. Thus, paradoxically, critiques of the modern financial system often unwittingly reaffirm the power of finance by confirming its abstract, cyber-spatial, amorphous, and hence inherently uncontrollable nature—in effect marshaling such ideas in support of the status quo. This powerfully neutralizing image of un-controllable finance, allegedly driven by technological advances, is pre-cisely what Susan Strange (1998) sought to challenge by pointing out the relations of force, including state policies, that have led to a shift in the balance between the goals of capital accumulation and societal goals, demonstrating that while goals may change, capitalism as such has not. One way of explaining, or explaining away, the abstraction of capital is therefore as an ideological ploy—the sort of vulgar ideology that Marx attributed to classical political economy. On this view off-shore has to be "unmasked" and shown to be onshore, located within the power of the state.

But it is not enough to point to the ideological implications of such theories. The apparent trend of capitalism toward "disembeddedness" may be taken as evidence, however opaque, of the successful commod-ification of previously uncommodified aspects of social life. Perhaps, then, offshore may be understood within the context of what Deleuze and Guattari (1987) call the "recomposition" of capital by even the "most artificial means." By this they mean that capitalism goes through phases of destruction and production: it is a dynamic system, and each stage of recovery and reorganization appears, at first, abstract and artificial. Thus, the "apparent" artificiality of offshore, including the commercialization of sovereignty and the appearance of postmod-ern subjectivities is no different in principle from the bemusement and sense of outrage that greeted the policies of the New Deal and the rise of Fordism in the 1930s. In fact each wave of this cycle of destruction and recomposition is initially viewed with suspicion as artificial and disembedded, and the latest phase is no different. At the same time, a pervasive sense of apparent artificiality may create spaces for progres-sive politics, because of the double-edged nature of myth-making.

The commodification of hitherto nonmarketed aspects of social life generates this odd sense of dematerialization as the fetished commod-ity loses something of its fetished value (Van Der Pijl 1998, chap. 1). We can identify similar effects in different realms. Thus, modern semiotics and aesthetics proceed by offering a critique of the commodified subject (à la Adorno and Horkheimer), and it does so precisely by celebrating it in the manner described by Sloterdijk (1988) as "Kynicism." The liberal ideal of "individuality," itself an after-effect of the commodity economy, is then celebrated as the subject is "individuated" through his or her consumption habits. The subject is encouraged to "construct" his or her "individuality" through his or her consumption habits; indeed, the subject is encouraged to purchase a gendered or (as the case may be) transgendered persona, as it reflexively constructs itself. But as the subject celebrates its own auto-subjectification, it also mobilizes cynicism against itself as a form of "kinetic auto-critique." The very act of "individuation" in which the subject "takes control" over his or her own subjectification is simultaneously celebrated and questioned.

### THE CONCEPT OF NUMERICAL OR NOMADIC CIVILIZATIONS

At the heart of the matter, therefore, is the shape of capitalist recomposition that is taking place nowadays. It is a process that, on the one hand, is path-dependent, stretching clearly into the past and drawing on institutions and practices whose origins lie sometimes in antiquity. But on the other hand, it is a process that forces into existence, through a recombination of factors and mutations, an entirely new political economy. Since offshore is at best only a component of a complex and multifaceted process, of necessity our study here emphasizes only aspects of a larger whole. Nonetheless, we cannot but note an interesting convergence between one of the most celebrated themes in the work of Deleuze and Guattari (1987), namely, their theory of numerical or nomadic social organizations, and the offshore economy. Deleuze and Guattari seem to celebrate nomadism, the rhizome, as an expression of openness and liberation. I doubt this normative aspect of nomadism, but I believe their theory can shed light on some of the more intriguing characteristics of the offshore economy. A brief introduction to the concept is in order.

It should be stated at the outset that there is nothing in Deleuze and Guattari's work to suggest that they think that modern capitalism is becoming increasingly nomadic—if anything, their view is the opposite. I am therefore drawing on their ideas in a way they may not have appreciated. In any case, in developing the concept of nomadism, Deleuze and Guattari draw on a concept of society as a system of signs, an idea first mooted in the late nineteenth century by anthropologists (and discussed at some length in the previous chapter). The basic idea is that unlike individuals and activities, social relations are invisible and intangible; they are an abstraction "established by inference" (Fortes 1969, 60). This is true for the observer as much as for the sub-

166The Offshore World

ject, for the subject operates (vaguely, no doubt) according to a cognitive map of the social relationships which he or she apprehends; the world, for the subject, is a world of signs. As Goodchild notes: "In each social formation, the mode of economic production, the mode of representation, and the mode of reproduction all derive from a single machine formation that gives its society its consistency. A society is therefore defined by the mode of representation that is given by its machine of expression or 'regime of signs' " (1996, 93). A regime of signs, in turn, assigns meaning to human action and invests it with value. Thus, for example, the expression of "wealth" as money and power is specific to the capitalist regime of signs. In contrast, in lineal (or filial) societies the basic principles of organization are "individualized," i.e., each society exhibits variants of a general theme of social organization, including rights, privileges, and obligations conferred and imposed upon members (Fortes 1969).

In their "Treatise on Nomadology—the War Machine," Deleuze and Guattari point to an important distinction among three major types of human organization (i.e., different "regimes of signs"): lineal, territorial, and numerical (1987, 351–423). Lineal societies maintain homeostasis, as the structural functionalists see it, by a system of naming or kinship. It is a particular regime of signs. These basic or "primitive" forms of human organization are founded on what anthropologists have described as "relations of actual interconnectedness" (kinship), which subsist between persons and are mediated through their customary behavior (Fortes 1969, 44). There is of course a political economy to these societies. It "operates through exchanges of different kinds: women, consumer goods, ritual objects, rights, prestige, and status" (Lévi-Strauss 1953). Indeed, such exchanges may themselves be regarded as communicative encoding: "a man is coded by his property, and his scars are his property" (Goodchild 1996, 92). The various operations of tattooing, excising, incising, carving, scarifying, mutilating, encircling, and initiating are the tangible effects of this political economy of inscription, generating an "alliance of meaning" created in "the non-affective form of a code or convention" (Goodchild 1996, 91). The particular "political economy" of such lineal societies is based on an economy of debt (Mauss 1968). In Wilden's words:

> The gift exchanges can be called symbols. But they do not stand for what they "represent" in some fixed relationship to an unconscious "meaning. . . ." They are the symbols of the act of exchange itself,

which is what ties the society together. Thus, they cease to be symbols in any important sense; it is the act of exchange, with its attendant *mana* or *hau*, which symbolizes the unconscious requirement of
exchange through displaced reciprocity as means of establishing and
maintaining relationships between the members of that society.
(Wilden 1972, 231)

These complex forms of what may be called "primitive discourses"
come under threat from three potential sources. First, the encoded
flows can escape social accumulation (which is how Deleuze and Guattari understand the characteristics of modern capitalism). Capitalism
therefore destroys the discursive unity of lineal societies. The second
threat is that of excessive accumulation of surplus value of code in the
person of the chief, leading to an autocratic imperial system based on
the principle of paranoia. The third source of imminent danger lies in
the potential stoppage of the social dynamics of circulation if alliances
are made within the filial system. This is traditionally counteracted by
the prohibition of incest (Lévi-Strauss 1953).

Filial societies therefore contain the seeds of their own destruction.
Of the potential three threats to such organization, the second, state societies based on the territorial principle, proved the most immediate.
Thus, according to Deleuze and Guattari "everything changes with
state societies: it is often said that the territorial principle becomes
dominant" (1987, 388). It is important, however, at this stage to dwell
briefly on their concept of territorialization.

Deleuze and Guattari reject a positivist rendering of the concept of
territory as natural, self-evident category. In fact, they argue, the natu-
ralizing of territory is the outcome of a complex socio-psychological
process. Indeed, "one could also speak of deterritorialization, since the
earth becomes an object, instead of being an active material element in
combination with lineage. Property is precisely the deterritorialized relation between the human being and the earth"(1987, 388). Robert Sack,
demonstrating that the "territorial principle" is a social mechanism of
power, expressed the same idea in different language: "Territoriality
neither dispenses with action by contact nor violates it. Rather it ex-
tends the particulars of action by contact to the point where a new principle relating space and action seems to emerge; and, which, in turn affects the details of action by contact" (1981, 55). Territoriality works by
enforcing control over the territory. It "makes the territory appear to be
filled with power, influence, authority, or sovereignty" (Sack 1981, 56).

In territorial systems the land loses those unique singular meanings it had within the systems of meaning of filial systems, and is treated as an abstraction: the land is "deterritorialized" and then "reterritorialized," endowed with certain communal "intersubjective" meanings.

Territorial organizations are power organizations—they mobilize the subject's capacity to work and innovate. Ronald Cohen (1981) contends that the state is distinguished from lineal organizations by what he calls its "nonfissionable" characteristics. The complexity and fragility of lineal organizations set limits on their physical size by their very nature. The political economy of inscription is necessarily immediate and visual and consequently, when a certain threshold is exceeded, lineal organizations split and a group wanders off. The territorial principle generated nonfissionable characteristics which allow the state to grow indefinitely in size (at least in principle), while maintaining the state's coherence as a social, political, and economic whole. The territoriality principle is a mechanism of power that produces a new density of population and which seeks, at later stages, to control the movement of labor and confine it territorially. As we saw in the previous chapter, European states sought to homogenize their territories either by expelling "foreign" elements, or by normalizing the population with the aid of national education. States or territorial organizations are able therefore to accommodate classes, races, and peoples, and are premised on, at the very least, rudimentary forms of stratification.

Territorial organizations do not simply replace lineal organizations but transcend them as much as they incorporate elements from them. For example, Stevens brilliantly shows that the rules of citizenship which are normally based on place of birth or parentage demonstrate the extent to which lineal principles are still deeply embedded in the modern state and the nation (Stevens 1999). Territorial organizations, however, do not only contain traces of the past, they also contain the future. The movement of deterritorialization and reterritorialization prepares the way, argue Deleuze and Guattari, for the ascendancy of numerical civilization, which they view as symptomatic of the nomadic principle of human organization.

For Deleuze and Guattari, numerical organization operates on numerical relationships. The paradigmatic type of numerical organization is the army: "An army is composed of units, companies, and divisions. The numbers may vary in function, in combination; they may enter into entirely different strategies; but there is always a connection between the number and the war machine. *It is not a question of quan-*

*tity but of organization and composition"* (1987, 387; my emphasis).
Relationships between different components in the army are expressed
on a numerical principle; soldiers are perhaps "fathers," "mothers"
"uncles" as in the lineal mode, or "Englishmen," "Yorkshiremen," or
"Frenchmen" as in the territorial mode, but in the context of the army
they are defined in their singularity, as numbers in a numerical organization. Bureaucratically, the army is organized on the numerical principle: there are so many soldiers in a unit, so many units in a brigade,
so many brigades in a division, and so on.

To explain the idea Deleuze and Guattari use the metaphor of the
games of chess and Go.

> Chess is a game of the state, or of the court. Chess pieces are coded;
> they have an internal nature and intrinsic properties from which their
> movements, situations, and confrontations derive. They have quali-
> ties; a knight remains a knight, a pawn a pawn . . . each is like a sub-
> ject of a statement endowed with a relative power, and their relative
> powers are combined in a subject of enunciation, that is, the chess
> player or the game's form of interiority. Go pieces, in contrast, are pel-
> lets, disks, arithmetic units, and have only an anonymous, collective,
> or third-person function: "it" makes a move. . . . Go pieces are ele-
> ments of a nonsubjectified machine assemblage with no intrinsic
> properties, only situational ones. (1987, 352)

Numerical organizations can move swiftly, as the Mongol troops did,
over vast tracts of land because they are not attached to the territorial
principle. In fact, nomadic or numerical civilizations operate through
qualitatively different types of spaces: state or territorial spaces are
"striated" or gridded. As Massumi explains, "movement in striated
spaces is confined as if by gravity to a horizontal plane, and limited by
the order of that plane to present paths between fixed and identifiable
points" (Massumi 1987, xiii). Numerical spaces, by contrast are
"smooth" and open-ended: the nomad moves from one place to another,
but unlike in territorial organization where "lines or trajectories tend
to be subordinated to points," numerical spaces do not privilege the
point. For the nomad "it is the opposite: the points are subordinated to
the trajectory" (Deleuze and Guattari 1987, 478). The nomad has a "territory"; "He follows customary paths; he goes from one point to another; he is not ignorant of points . . . but the question is what in
nomad life is a principle and what is only a consequence . . . although
the points determine paths, they are strictly subordinated to the paths

they determine. . . . the nomad goes from point to point only as a consequence and as a factual necessity" (Deleuze and Guattari, 1987, 380). The nomad may move from Damascus to Baghdad, but these are only nodes on an eternal journey; the nomad subordinates these points to the journey.[2] In striated space, in contrast, one goes from Paris to London and the journey is a dead time spent "in-between"; space is, therefore, a distance between different locales, but the locales, the points on the map, are the targets of movement. In numerical societies space is therefore undifferentiated or smooth as numbers form the paramount lines of divisions and aggregation. "The number becomes a subject. . . . The independence of the number in relation to space is a result not of abstraction but of the concrete nature of smooth space, which is occupied without itself being counted. The number is no longer a means of counting or measuring but of moving: it is the number itself that moves through smooth space" (Deleuze and Guattari 1987, 389).

### CYBERSPATIALITY

The type of smooth spatiality that Deleuze and Guattari identify as a distinct mode of social organization is now in evidence in, and is in fact characteristic of, the offshore economy. Indeed, if offshore inhabits, as much as facilitates, such smooth spaces of nomadic populations, then the Euromarket and the Internet are the paradigmatic cases of capitalist nomadism. The Euromarket is not a territorial space, although various nodes of the Euromarket are territorially embedded; the Euromarket, as we have seen, is invariably described as "stateless" or nonterritorial. It is an accounting device, created by maintaining separate sets of books; and hence it is a fictional space located everywhere and nowhere. In chapter 1 we struggled to explain how tax havens create a form of juridical bifurcation of state spaces, something that was more difficult to envisage than the territorial bifurcation enacted by export processing zones. But export-processing zones also generate an integrated "smooth" space for commodities and goods through territorial bifurcation. The "movement" of capital, which is in reality the frantic exchange of title rights recorded in various "centers," is the heart and soul of the market.

Deleuze and Guattari's description of nomadic spaces applies with surprising accuracy to the offshore foreign exchange market: here, too, money "follows customary paths," and like the nomad, "goes from one point to another" (London, Tokyo, Frankfurt, New York); but the traded currency or stock "moves" from one point to another only as a consequence and as a factual necessity—"although the points determine paths, they are strictly subordinated to the paths they determine." The trader in the financial market recognizes the paths and the points, but they are only points in the endless journey of money (or exchange of title rights) performed in the offshore foreign exchange market. This phenomenon has been described as the decoupling of financial markets from production. The traditional indicators of the "real" economy, such as employment, trade balances, and retail sales, are recognized, but the indicators are "important only in the way they affect the market" (Kurtzman 1993, 65).

Consequently, in offshore we see a trend whereby the number becomes a subject. The number is no longer a means of counting or measuring but of moving: rather, it represents movements in the offshore foreign exchange market. Like Go pieces, deterritorialized soldiers in the player's army, money is deterritorialized so that it no longer reflects a "store of value" but simply a relationship of exteriority. As Alliez notes, "Detaching money from its political condition of mediation, this activity mobilizes and expropriates wealth, monetarizes and dissolves ancient property"; in these conditions "interest is no more than the number of the movement of (monetary) growth following the desire for money that binds individuals to each other" (Alliez 1991, 10). This depiction is reminiscent of a financial system that has done away with the notion of "patient" capital. Joel Kurtzman, editor of the *Harvard Business Review*, points out that "No longer do institutions buy stocks to hold because they believe in the underlying value of the company. Instead, with the touch of the button and the aid of a few mathematical formulas, institutions increasingly trade in and out of stocks, keeping their holdings for decreasing periods of time" (1993, 39). Indeed, Kurtzman unwittingly employs Deleuze and Guattari's Go metaphor in his description of the modern financial system: "Money remains a naked symbol with no intrinsic value of its own and no direct linkage to anything specific. It is, as the French economists like to say, merely a 'token,' a simple game-board piece moved from one file to another in the world's vast computerized database" (1993, 77). So whereas in the traditional concept of financial market, money, depicting a "store of value," moves within a territorial grid, in the smooth, nomadic offshore spaces the movement of money is represented by numbers, and the number is no longer a means of counting or measuring. Minute rises and falls in the stock valuation of a company or of a currency do not count or measure any aspect of the company or the country possessing the currency, but what moves is the number itself. "Currency managers who trade dollars for marks and yen each day are looking for return on investment . . . so the cues they look at first are the purely financial ones: interest rates, the level of the stock, bond, and futures markets, as well as the level of overall debt. . . . *From their point of view the economy really can be summarized by these numbers*" (Kurtzman 1993, 65; my emphasis).

The literature of tax havens celebrates the virtues of the PTs, the nomadic tribe of "permanent tourists" that inhabits the offshore economy. Writing about what he calls "cyberspatial sovereignties," Bill Maurer recalls the Somali nomads who offer a "survival lesson" to all of us in the age of offshore, and points out:

> In a nutshell, the PT merely arranges his or her "paperwork" in such a way that all governments consider him a tourist—a person who is just "passing through." The advantage is that being thought of by government officials as a person who is merely "parked temporarily," a PT is not subject to taxes, military service, lawsuits, or persecution for taking part in innocent but forbidden pursuits or pleasures. . . . PT stands for many things: a PT can be a "prior taxpayer," "perpetual tourist," "practically transparent," "privacy trained," or "permanent traveler" . . . the individual who is a PT can stay in one place most of the time. Or all of the time. PT is a concept, a way of life, a way of perceiving the universe and your place in it. (Maurer 1998, 505)

PT is not only a reflection of the wealthy individual's preferred tax planning, it is an ideology and an aspiration of the modern "virtual corporation" whose idea is to "park temporarily" not only in space, but also in tasks. The *Economist* investigates the "Branson way" of doing business: the idea is to finance new ventures by contributing his brand (Virgin), while others put up the money, then sell the brand for a premium. "Although it takes slightly less than a year to create an Internet company," reports the *Economist*, "even that is too long in a world where entrepreneurs and their backers think that the first person to get a new venture up and running will scoop the pool" (1999). Money turns value into a flow that tends to escape the juridical frame of political territoriality. "Money aims to trace out its proper space as a private space, split off from the political" (Alliez 1991, 6). What we are beginning to sense is that such "private spaces" are not simply branching off from communal or public spaces, they are not simply the extension of "privatization" vis-à-vis the declining powers of the state; rather they are intrinsic modes of human organization that contain their own unique dynamics and spaces of power.

### THEORIES OF NOMADIC CAPITALISM

Many, of course, are fearful of the nomadic character of modern capitalism. Besides impressionistic accounts taken from the realm of business studies, is there more serious theoretical elaboration of the nature of nomadic capitalism? The relationship between capital and the state, the latter being the paradigmatic form of territorial organization, has always been ambiguous. Indeed, Braudel posits an overlap between the two; for him the relationship between state and capitalism is one of mutual "infiltration and superimposition, of conquest and accommodation" (Braudel 1979, 2:519). Yet at a fundamental level, the two are very different. There have always been complaints about the lack of state theory in Marx's *Capital*. But if we understand *Capital* as the study of pure capitalism, it is not surprising in the least that capital lacks a state theory. Indeed, the basic principle of capitalist society, its socialization principle, is exchange value. "The existence of money presupposes the objectification of the social bond" (Marx [1858] 1973, 159–60). In such a society, the principle of unity is not necessarily territorial. On the contrary, "The reciprocal and all-sided dependence of individuals who are indifferent to one another forms their social connection. This social bond is expressed in exchange value, by means of which alone each individual's own activity or his product becomes an activity and a product for him; he must produce a general product— exchange value" (Marx [1858] 1973, 165). Consequently, "the social character of activity, as well as the social form of the product, appear as something alien and objective" (Marx [1858] 1973, 270). For Marx, the central tendency of capitalism is expansion: "the goal-determining activity of capital can only be that of growing wealthier, i.e. of magnification, of increasing itself"([1858] 1973, 270). Marx went further, arguing that the very nature of capital is leading capitalism to "drive beyond its own barriers"([1858] 1973, 270).

The numerical principle was, therefore, always at the heart of capitalist society. Indeed, Marx's concept of society is not a spatio-temporal concept but a generic form. Marx's capitalist society consists of all those touched by capitalism. Members of this society may be ignorant of or indifferent to one another. Unlike the lineal-territorial organization of the nation-state which is based, as we saw, on the myth of coresponsibility, the numerical-territorial principles at the heart of neoliberal globalization are principles of indifference; it is a society that does not recognize itself as a society, but rather attaches itself to the notion of the individuated, rent-seeking, utility maximizing, consumer-voter.

In territorial organizations power is allocated in the division or distribution of space, in "smooth" spaces, such reterritorialized forms of power lose their saliency, and the principle of numerical allocation begins to dominate. As Jonathan Nitzan observes: "As capitalism grows in complexity, the earnings of any given business concern come to depend less on its own industrial undertakings and more on the *community's overall productivity*. In this sense, the value of capital represents a *distributional* claim. This claim is manifested partly through ownership, but more broadly through the *whole spectrum of social power*" (1998, 173; my emphasis). In modern capitalism "power" itself is expressed in the distribution of numbers, rather than the distribution of space. Moreover, continues Nitzan, "power [now expressed in numbers] is not only a means of accumulation, but also its most fundamental end. For the absentee owner, the purpose is not to 'maximize' profits but to 'beat the average.' The ultimate goal of business is not hedonic pleasure, but *differential* gain" (1998, 173). Companies are compared nowadays not in terms of gross turnover or employment—the traditional measures of power—but in terms of market capitalization. In fact, high turnover, a large workforce, and good products can if anything be a sign of weakness in the new economy. "The numbering number is no longer subordinated to metric determinations or geometrical dimension [size] but has only a dynamic relation with geographical directions ["beating the average" in Nitzan's terms]; it is a directional number, not a dimensional or metric one" (Deleuze and Guattari 1987, 390). The numbers, as Bichler and Nitzan (1996) argue, do not measure wealth— because wealth is no longer the aggregation of goods. The numbers that we take to represent stock evaluations, profits, and wealth no longer stand for "real" tangible goods, the numbers measure "power" as pure relations—they measure "dynamic relations" as Deleuze and Guattari put it, or "differential gains" in the words of Bichler and Nitzan.

In striated, territorial organizations power can be apprehended visually: "Here is my land, here is my slave/serf/worker, here is my shiny new machine: This is *my* power." In numerical civilizations, such tangibles lose their shine. As Bichler and Nitzan (1996) note, the tangible "stock" of capital may turn in a few years into useless junk. Peter Taylor once remarked that "there is nothing the City of London would like more than getting rid of its messy hinterland, Great Britain." Modern corporations demonstrate their power by getting rid of workers, by shutting down factories, by selling land.

When property becomes economic power, private property which escaped or was portioned off from communal property becomes its own master. "Private property no longer expresses the bond of personal dependence but the independence of a Subject that now constitutes the sole bond." When that happens, "the flows reach this capitalist threshold of decoding and deterritorialization (naked labor, independent capital), it *seems* that there is no longer a need for a State. . . . The economy constitutes a world-wide axiomatic, a universal cosmopolitan energy which overflows every restriction and bond, a mobile and convertible substance" (Deleuze and Guattari 1987, 453). Today, "we can depict an enormous, so-called stateless, monetary mass that circulates through foreign exchange and across borders, eluding control by the States, forming a multinational ecumenical organization, constituting a de facto supranational power untouched by governmental decisions" (Deleuze and Guattari 1987, 435).

This is the reason that Simon Clarke (1988) and Bichler and Nitzan (1996) wish to dissociate neoliberal globalization from "finance capital." For neoliberal globalization does not signal the power of finance over production, it signals something more fundamental and important: the progressive "freeing" of capital from its territorial shackles, as the very logic of deterritorialized capitalism begins to manifest itself. Capitalism is by its very nature a nomadic social organization: "the essence of capitalism," says Nitzan, is "like other forms of social power, the essence of accumulation is not material, but *symbolic*" (1998, 174). This is what Deleuze and Guattari term "flow of desire." The principal difference between capital and other forms of social power is in its level of abstraction and universality.

## COMMERCIALIZED SOVEREIGNTY REVISITED

Sedentary civilizations erect boundaries, employing the principle of territorial power as the basis of their social organization. In territorial organizations control is effectuated by division, allocation, distribution, and confinement of space. The traditional concepts of divine and popular sovereignty were configured according to this basic principle. As Mefford observes, "Control over physical space, and the people and things located in that space, is a defining attribute of sovereignty and statehood. Lawmaking requires some mechanism for law enforcement, which in turn depends on the ability to exercise physical control over, and to impose coercive sanctions on, law violations" (1997, 213). For Mefford, power, control, law, and territoriality are intimately linked; the absence of one destabilizes all. It is clearly the case, as we saw, that territoriality is an instrument of power. The concept of sovereignty originated in the filial theories of Roman times, to be given a territorial inflection by Jean Bodin in 1576 (Barret-Kriegel 1986, chaps. 1 and 2). As Cardinal Richelieu began his extraordinary administrative reforms that laid the foundations of the French absolutist state, his lawyers discovered the work of Bodin of fifty years before and used it to justify their actions. Thus, an originally filial conception took on a territorial dimension. Sovereignty, seen as the ultimate authority within a given territorial space, became the juridical expression of territorial power. Thus, the law, the expression of routinized power, which is traditionally territorial in nature, operates within the boundaries of the state as an expression of territorial power. In territorial organizations power is therefore associated with the one who controls the division, allocation, distribution, and confinement of space—hence the concept of sovereignty stands so clearly in our minds at the confluence of power and territory.

Sovereignty without effective territorial control is considered sovereignty in name only; lack of sovereignty implies the lack of control over territory. Mefford notes that "States wishing to impose law on or in cyberspace [our paradigmatic case of "smooth" nomadic space] will find that they simply do not have the physical control over the Net necessary for lawmaking authority" (1997, 213). Mefford describes what appears as a power vacuum from the perspective of territorial organizations, the inability to confine, divide, and allocate in the realms of cyberspace and the Euromarket. But just as filial ideas were incorporated with slight differences into territorial organizations, so territorial sovereignty is proving useful in an increasingly numerical age. The "smooth" space of the Euromarket and the Internet prevents territorial organizations from exercising their territorial power, but offshore jurisdictions like the Cayman Islands have learned to apply the principle of sovereign supremacy not in order to contain and control, but rather in order to affect the trajectory of movement in this "smooth" space. They use their sovereign rights, and the basic principle of the "fictional" location of the contract, which, as we saw in chapter 3, is essential to modern capitalism, as a source of revenue by turning themselves into attractive points on nomadic capitalism's eternal journey. Like the ancient fairs and merchant cities dotted along the nomads' itineraries, they have learned to harvest their own variant of customs and duties from nomadic trade by charging license fees. Essentially they have reversed the relationship between spatiality and temporality; rather than assume that sovereign revenues are linked to the spatial dimension of the territory, they assume that nomadic capitalism is ever on the move and therefore the critical source of revenue is linked to the time capital is "parked" in any one juridical or fiscal location. The capitalist nomads, therefore, have to be seduced first to use the "realm" of offshore jurisdictions, and second, to stay there as long as possible. Bank secrecy laws, low regulation, and low taxation are the vectors affecting the movement of capital in this smooth space; but once the game is understood, everything becomes a game. Offshore jurisdictions have been using these lax laws as bait; they have now branched out and have began to think about the nature of the bait itself.

Thus, once they have understood that sovereignty is not, or is no longer, merely an ability to control physical territorial space, but a gatekeeping capability, they have perfected this capability. This can mean, as Tuvalu has discovered, control over an Internet domain name (".tv" in the case of Tuvalu) which then can be parceled out and sold off; as Niue has learned, it can mean control over phone numbers which can be sold off; as the Cayman Islands have found out, it can mean selling the privilege of residency, as a fictional territorial location, for an annual fee. And it can also still mean, as it always has in the past, control over the distributive capabilities of the state, which is what modern politics is about.

This leads to a surprising conclusion: the relationship between offshore and lax regulation is conjunctural. We can already discern that at a more fundamental level, offshore is the use of exclusive sovereign rights as bait to affect the trajectory of movement of nomadic capitalism. Offshore jurisdictions may well be prepared to abandon many of the overt signs traditionally associated with offshore, but they will continue inventing new lures, facilitating the increasing importance of the numerical principle.

It would be a mistake to think that offshore jurisdictions see themselves as "centers" in the traditional (territorial) sense: Liberia and Panama are not "really" the giants of world shipping; the Cayman Islands are not "really" the home of 57,900 companies and 465 banks, nor are they "really" the world's fifth largest financial center; these places have become "centers" precisely by using their peripheral status creatively. But then, the concept of "center" and "periphery" is alien to the smooth space in which these jurisdictions operate. It is a territorial notion that links power with territory; here, territorial marginalization can be a source of power and revenue in the smooth space of nomadic capitalism.

Commercialized sovereignty can be seen now in a new light. Like offshore in general, commercialized sovereignty is sometimes regarded as an abuse of sovereignty. But this is the view from a territorial perspective. From a nonterritorial perspective, the corollary of numerical power relationships is numerical sovereignty. What is the point in having territorial sovereignty over nonterritorial exchange? Such territorial sovereignty is obviously eroding. But does that mean that the state is eroding as well, as many seem to believe? Not at all. States, as condensations of power as Poulantzas described them, are learning to branch themselves out and assert their power in the form of numerical sovereignty. Since the law assumes territorial organization (notwithstanding the *lex mercatoria*), the numerical principle of capitalism can use "fictional" territories as ways of bringing the law into its numerical spatiality.

### LET'S GO ALL THE WAY TO THE MOON

I do not want to claim that the principles of nomadism and numerical organization have now replaced the territorial principle. As Deleuze and Guattari note, the three modes of social organization, filial, territorial, and numerical, are ever present in each social formation. However, the relationships as well as the balance of force among them undergoes changes. I am arguing that the inherently nomadic principle of capitalism can express itself more fully in the offshore economy. Thus, offshore is strangely new and yet old. It appears preordained, and yet we cannot find the "grand engineer" who designed this outcome (Lipietz 1987). But in fact, offshore itself is under threat not so much from the territorial principle, but because offshore jurisdictions embody a territorial-numerical principle rather than a purely numerical one. Capital may desert them.

Nonterritorial spaces are now avidly discussed. We have seen already that the pirate radio stations took advantage of any maritime objects, including relics from the Second World War, to locate themselves offshore. Offshore experts debate seriously nowadays the proposition of setting up the moon as a new offshore center. "And why be restricted to the globe? Why not go off-planet?" asks Professor Ian Angell of the

London School of Economics, "A satellite can act as a depository for digital cash. Customers send not only their digital cash and other information capital, but also the digital safe that secures it; and they hold the only key. The term 'capital flight' will take on a whole new meaning."[3] This is a serious proposition, although it is not about to happen in the next few years. The attraction of the moon—and other heavenly bodies—is precisely that they are purely numerical, freed from the territorial principle. Incredibly, in prophetic words, Deleuze and Guattari appear to have anticipated such a move:

> The decoding of flows and the deterritorialization of the socius thus constitutes the most characteristic and the most important tendency of capitalism. It continually draws near to its limit, which is a genuinely schizophrenic limit. It tends, with all the strength at its command, to produce the schizo as the subject of the decoded flows on the body without organ. This tendency is being carried further and further, *to the point that capitalism with all its flows may dispatch itself straight to the moon: we really haven't seen anything yet.* (1984, 34; my emphasis)

In fact, Deleuze and Guattari appear to be referring to the Apollo program. Nonetheless, their theory of capitalism identifies the basic force of deterritorialization that is at work here. The problem with offshore "centers" thus far is that they are ultimately territorial organizations. The moon is free from all this. The moon will borrow the principle of "commons" from the law of the sea and shift it one step further, essentially using space as the new "commons." The state system has already recognized the possibility of "commons" in the name of some "public goods," and "human goods." Once the assumption of the liberal market is accepted, the next logical step is to replace the unhappy relationship between state and markets with a more secure realm which eliminates rent-seeking possibilities. Either the moon will levy charges to finance space adventures, or it will charge only for its own upkeep. In both cases, the state system will create in effect a global space of sovereignty. That is consistent with other developments, like the reemergence of the *lex mercatoria*. The moon can then serve as a metaphorical home, a fictional territory for a fictional market, setting capitalism free at last from its territorial shackles.

I began this chapter by raising the question of whether the offshore economy is symptomatic of deeper processes that are dissolving the prior solidity of political-juridical territorial spaces. I have ended, however, with a different answer altogether. The processes that we are witnessing are not one-dimensional and dichotomous. It is not a matter of a simple, straightforward shift from the territorial state to nonterritorial globalization. Rather, the very nature of space and the relationship between territory and power is undergoing profound transformation.

# Offshore as an Inherent Tendency in Capitalism

This book began with a puzzle: Why is it that just as the state system appears to have colonized the entire globe, the very space of sovereignty is bifurcating into offshore and onshore? We found part of the answer, curiously enough, not in contemporary society but rather by going back in time and examining processes of state formation and capitalist expansion in the nineteenth century. Far from contradicting the concept of the discrete socio-economic formation of the state possessing political and legal sovereignty, offshore was in fact collateral and immanent to the bounded state. As sovereign states began to develop stricter boundaries out of what were traditionally rather amorphous frontiers, they also, apparently unwittingly, created fairly well-defined juridical territories that can be considered in retrospect to have laid down the foundations of the offshore economy. In that sense, offshore was intrinsic to the rise of the nineteenth-century nation-state and was not, as many authors claim, a development that appeared in reaction to rising taxation and state regulation during the second half of the twentieth century.

Dating offshore to the late nineteenth and early twentieth centuries hinges on acceptance of the category of latent or embryonic forms of offshore. Deliberate use of offshore as state policy was something that began only from the 1920s and even then in very few countries. But the fact remains that it was between 1850 and 1920 that important juridical, political, and administrative facilities of the offshore type were first put in place. This is not to say that rising taxation and regulation, or more appropriately, Fordism, are not pertinent to our understanding of the phenomenon of offshore—of course they are. But dating the origins of the offshore economy to an earlier period places the offshore economy within the context of an entirely different set of dynamics, and that in turn, among other things, adds new insights to our understanding of the relationship between the offshore economy and Fordism.

Dating the origins of the offshore economy to an earlier period also makes clear the link between the offshore economy and continuing processes of state formation. The state is not disappearing or withering away; rather it is the nation-state—a particular historical formation that emerged in the early nineteenth century, that is in decline. A different ideal-type form of state, more adept at handling globalization and even capable of surviving the relative decline of the territorial principle, is replacing it. Moreover, by developing offshore, the new type of state responds to the rise of nomadic capitalism. These are momentous changes in the nature of the state and politics, and offshore should be seen as no more than a contributory factor to them. Nevertheless, seen in this light, offshore can no longer be treated as a haphazard policy response adopted by marginal and insignificant social formations, but rather as a response immanent to the changing nature of the state system.

Why, then, did offshore became an issue of public concern only towards the later years of the twentieth century? To approach an answer to this related puzzle, we broadened the scope of the inquiry and asked: To what extent can the establishment of states fully insulated in law and modeled on the image of the national economy—a process that resulted, as we have seen, in the original bifurcation of the sovereign space—be considered "structurally coupled" (Jessop 1997) to capital? Indeed, considering that a rapidly expanding offshore economy serves as a central plank of neoliberal-driven processes of globalization, it was important that we try to discover the extent to which the bifurcation of the sovereign realm and the emergence of the offshore economy can be traced to capital. In other words, what can the history of the offshore economy tell us about current and future development of the capitalist system?

The earlier dating of embryonic forms of offshore rules out any simple, instrumental analysis of class power. After all, "ruling classes" do not set up structures and institutions in anticipation of what may happen fifty years hence. Offshore techniques appear to have evolved largely as a result of chance discoveries, whose significance often eluded their immediate progenitors. A host of disparate policies, tactics, and state forms, apparently unrelated geographically or thematically, became locked together like pieces of a gigantic jigsaw puzzle, ending up in the later decades of the twentieth century as an integrated offshore economy. It is difficult, therefore, to advance an explicit instrumental class analysis without putting the cart before the horse. In

any case, there are good theoretical reasons to discount both instrumental and crude structural theories of capital. Nonetheless, offshore
was, is, and is likely to continue to be used almost exclusively as a very
powerful and effective instrument of power supporting capitalist accumulation—(often) against people's democratic aspirations. It beggars belief, therefore, that such a powerful instrument has been a mere fortuitous accident of history. The question throughout has been how to
conceptualize the relationship between offshore and capital?

Considering that the advent of offshore, from its embryonic origins
to today's offshore economy, is clearly reciprocally constituted by the
growth of the nation-state, the key to the relationship between offshore
and capital lies in the changing nature of the nation-state. My thesis
hinges, however, on a particular interpretation of the nature of the
nation-state and its relation to capital. If we think of capitalism as a discursive system, we can demonstrate in ways that have never been explored very systematically—although there is work on the subject that
enables us to get a fairly good picture—that there were strong causal
links between the development of capitalism in the nineteenth century
and the overwhelming rationale that has led to the insulation of the
state in law. Although the insulation of the state was partly to do with
changes that had their roots in the policies of the absolutist state, the
commodification of social relationships through the medium of the
market generated a form of abstracted relationship between the discrete
national space and its citizens. There is therefore a nondeterministic
and yet functional relationship between the extension of capitalist relationships and the insulation of the state in law.

In that sense, the relationships between offshore and capital are not
of an instrumental or directly structural nature, but of a secondary, indirect structural nature. After all, it was not capital that established
embryonic forms of offshore. Rather, it was generations of lawyers and
policymakers intent on finding pragmatic solutions to problems attendant upon jurisdictional ambiguities that were inherent to a transnational cultural and economic system based on the principles of national
sovereignty. But the jurisdictional ambiguities were, and are still, exploited to advance a particular political project. There is little doubt
that the pragmatism of lawyers and policymakers suited big business,
but their attitudes or class position do not account for the emergence of
the offshore economy. Rather, the contradictory nature of the nation-
state presented them with problems which they solved in ways that can
now be seen to have laid the foundation of offshore, and some of the

contradictions can be derived from the nature of capital in the nineteenth century.

It may be argued in fact that in a very real sense a discrete state system was anathema to capital. As Braudel puts it: "capital laughed at frontiers" (1979, 2:528). What is perhaps less understood is that what capital laughed at (by the nineteenth century, borders and no longer frontiers) it ultimately helped to create. But here we have to maintain a clear analytical distinction between capital and capitalists. The former is a systemic relationship between elements, a particular logic; the latter are the human agents who are involved in the production of history. The former is implicated in the establishment of the discrete nation-state: it was the latter who laughed at borders and "naturally navigated beyond the narrow boundaries of the nation" (Braudel 1979, 2: 554).

The successful evolution of market relationships, the contract, "free labor," and so on, combined with the historical conditions of the second phase of the Industrial Revolution from the 1860s onward, and the opening up of the American hinterland, contributed to the formation of new types of organizational structures well adapted to the system of penalties and rewards of nineteenth-century capitalism. Crucially, governments sought to sustain the growth of new corporations and encourage them to internationalize. They first lent their support by promulgating "municipal" laws; then they began to erect systems of bilateral and multilateral treaties in support of trade; they then extended the same principles to deal with the problems of "double taxation" and property rights when the multinational enterprises began to expand.

The discrete nation-state system that was created in the nineteenth century was supported by and supportive of a discrete "positivist" concept of sovereignty and national independence based on the principles of "national self-determination." That system, sustained by the major advanced countries, gave apparent recognition and extension of the same "rights" to a host of secondary, apparently independent formations. In reality, these were not at all independent either economically or politically, and certainly not militarily. They were able, however, to experiment to some extent with laws and regulations (particularly if they appeared to merely emulate their larger brethren) that gave them some competitive advantage. A second phase in the development of the offshore economy began in the early 1920s and continued until the collapse of the Bretton Woods system in the early 1970s. During this phase, offshore techniques began to be used deliberately as instruments of state policy as a number of states and cities begin to take advantage of circumstances that were beyond their control.

Not many states adopted such "parasitic" policies, for three reasons. First, prior to decolonization the number of small, politically stable formations that could take advantage of such policies was limited. Second, the development of communication and transportation technologies did not yet permit the full extension of a viable offshore economy. Third, during the heyday of Fordism and the Bretton Woods system, advanced industrial countries were seriously committed to the principles of national regulation, particularly of finance (Palan 1998c). Consequently, only a small number of states, including Switzerland, the Bahamas, Uruguay, Lebanon, Tangiers, Panama, Liberia, and Puerto Rico, comprised the bulk of the offshore economy during this period. The offshore world emerged, therefore, at the very margins of the fledgling global economy; it was not hidden but was simply assumed to be relatively unimportant in the grand scheme of things.

But during this second phase, the foundations were also laid for the mushrooming of offshore from the late 1970s onward. Offshore techniques were innovated in piecemeal fashion—invariably, and contrary to popular perception, in the advanced industrial countries or at the least with their connivance. The British unwittingly invented "fictional" company residence and the Euromarket. The United States, more deliberately, invented competitive deregulation of incorporation rules, special economic zones, and international banking facilities, and was strongly implicated in the development of the export processing zones. The United States also played a critical role in the innovation of flags of convenience. The Swiss invented the numbered bank account and the strong version of bank secrecy laws.

Lawyers, businessmen, and criminals drawn, as a general rule, from the capitalist core spread these offshore techniques. In particular, they "taught" ruling groups of many apparently sovereign and independent Third World countries how to develop offshore facilities

Advanced industrial countries maintained throughout ambiguous relationships to the spread of offshore. Different administrative units of the same governments took diverging views of the phenomenon. Customs and treasury officials, generally speaking, took a dim view of offshore, but there is some evidence to suggest that financial interests used their political power to encourage governments to protect the fledgling offshore economy (Hampton 1996; Hudson 1999).

In this second phase (1920–70), too, the growth in taxation and regulation was not the main impetus for the extension of offshore. The lower taxation and regulation regimes offered by offshore became more attractive due to the crisis of profitability (or crisis of Fordism) that was felt toward the end of the 1960s. In that sense, it may be argued that a new phase in the evolution of offshore, beginning from the early 1970s, was caused by the decline in profit and exacerbated by taxation and regulation. In fact, the offshore economy can be considered to be an important contributory factor to the collapse of Fordism. Faced by labor unrest, rising taxation at home, but, most crucially, a declining rate of profit, multinational corporations began to shift operations toward the European peripheral zones and a number of Third World countries in Asia and Latin America. The Euromarket and tax havens in combination provided footloose companies with financial and administrative instruments that enabled them to move with much greater ease. The "push" factor from the center was complemented by a "pull" factor in the periphery, provided by the spectacular proliferation of export processing zones in the 1970s. Wealthy individuals and multinational enterprises were not only able to escape regulation and taxation via the services of the Euromarket, tax havens, and export processing zones, but perhaps more significantly, these facilities acted as deterrents to governments intent on holding the line. By the 1980s, the governments had lost out, particularly following the disastrous attempt of the Mitterrand government in the early 1980s to buck the trend by raising taxation and nationalizing privately owned banks. For the next twenty years OECD governments accepted, whether enthusiastically or reluctantly, the principle of reduction in personal and corporate taxes. During that period these taxes have declined, to be replaced to some extent by indirect or consumption taxes (Palan 1998b). However, the advent of the Internet and e-commerce may frustrate this tax strategy. In addition, Swiss numbered accounts gave Third World capitalists leverage against nationalizing or socialist governments (whose leaders were themselves, of course, hoarding their baksheesh in Switzerland). Only following the adoption of "liberal" policies by the mid-1990s, did money begin flowing back into Latin America and some Asian countries, now logged as "foreign direct investment."

The offshore economy effectively punched a hole, as Gary Burn argues, in the national system of Fordist regulation. Whether the offshore economy was the principal or the main contributory factor in the collapse of Fordism is something that is worth a detailed investigation.

Clearly, the entire Fordist social compromise was already under great stress, but the fledgling offshore economy certainly accelerated the tendencies toward disintegration, if not ensured that they would win. Here, relative sovereignty over offshore jurisdictions was used as an effective weapon against the absolute sovereignty that national Fordism was predicated upon. Again we are left asking: To what extent was offshore a mere accidental contributory factor to the rise of neoliberalism? On the one hand offshore was a mere accident of history. At the same time, however, the extent to which the growing offshore economy proved to support the neoliberal program is uncanny. My view is that this is where the overt, instrumental concept of class power comes into play. A myriad juridical and social solutions are lying dormant, so to speak, waiting to be put into effect; but the critical questions are which of these instruments is eventually used and by whom. As Braudel notes, "the chief privilege of capitalism, today as in the past, remains the ability to choose—a privilege resulting at once from its dominant social position, from the weight of its capital resources, [and] its borrowing capacity" (1979, 2: 622).

The important thing is that faced by corporatist compromises that demanded fairly heavy levels of taxation and regulation, capital was given a way out. Consequently, the advent of tax havens, the Euromarket, and export processing zones not only undermined national forms of regulation; more significantly, they undermined the belief in the ability of the state to advance policies voted for by its citizens. The sovereignty of the state, or rather the powers of governments, onshore became contingent on off-shore: states that strayed off the line and failed to comply with the demands of capital would simply see their sovereignty mysteriously melt away as business shifted operations offshore. The "fictional" or "juridical" nature of offshore ensured that the costs of "relocation" from onshore to offshore remained low. Offshore then became the whip with which capital ensured that onshore did not stray off the beaten track.

Not surprisingly, the offshore economy itself has grown spectacularly and, as a result, today plays a very different role in the world economy. At this point, the offshore economy constitutes a significant portion of the world economy, to the extent that a number of so-called hyper-globalizers appear to confuse offshore with globalization. The rise of the "competition" ideology forced smaller jurisdictions to adopt offshore legislation to finance themselves and hence indirectly gave an additional boost and support to the offshore economy. In reality there is no separate off-shore economy, for an integrated global economy is constituted through a myriad of jurisdictional arrangements. But there is massive political and ideological capital invested in offshore.

Is offshore, then, an inherent tendency in capitalism? My answer is that offshore is an inherent tendency in a transnational economy operating within the context of a particularistic political system. The offshore economy, however, has played different roles in different periods. My second conclusion is that far from the offshore economy reaching its zenith, its effects are likely to be felt more forcefully in the future.

This argument is founded on a simple proposition, namely, that once a particular solution or set of solutions is favored, their social, economic, and political impact is probably irreversible, although the effects are unlikely to evolve in simple linear trajectory from the past to the future. I have tried, therefore, to explore the possible effects of the offshore economy on state and society by adopting a nonlinear concept of social change. The commercialization of state sovereignty affects not only the state, but to an even greater extent what I have described as the politics of co-responsibility of the nation-state. In the collective psyche, the commercialization of sovereignty and the emergence of alternative spaces presented as "offshore" serve as material evidence for the decline of the nation-state and its attendant concepts of identity founded on the ideal of "the people." Here we see again how the offshore economy adds a strong contributory factor to profound changes in the discourse of politics and the state, supporting the new ideology of global constitutionalism centered on the sovereign investor/consumer.

The fascination with offshore goes deep in the (post) modern psyche: in many ways offshore is a parable and a metaphor for the relationships that subjects have to their communities; relationships based on material and spiritual needs mediated through unbridgeable distances. There is no such thing as society, declared Margaret Thatcher; in a way we are all castaways in offshore land. We are no longer assured of terra firma, the striated world of the nation-state, but we are not yet citizens of the world of flux. We recognize in this absurd and impossible tale of offshore the deep sense of displacement, of being stuck between two worlds, of living a transitory life, on the edge.

We therefore need to cast our eyes beyond global constitutionalism and offshore, and ask where capitalism is heading? What types of social relationship can be sustained in the era of such mobility of capital? Why has the "fictional" and "constructed" nature of social relationships become such a topical issue, not simply among the marginalized "critical" thinkers, but also among mainstream thinkers? What is the "material" reality reflected, however skewed the language may be, in these observations? This has led me to possibly the most speculative, and potentially the most profound, disturbing, or exhilarating (depending on one's point of view) conclusion about the effect of the offshore economy: that the very nature of mobility, of the spatiality of mobility, and the pertinence of territoriality, is changing. Capitalism is increasingly adopting the principles of numerical civilization, overlaying but not replacing the principle of territorial organization. The deeply confusing "nonterritorial," "fictional," "virtual" expressions of modern capitalism, the profound irrationality of modern accumulation appear to contain their own "nonterritorial rationality." Offshore is not an alternative territory, and certainly not a temporary ruse. It is, to use the economists' vocabulary (now taken in an entirely new meaning) an "anti-friction" device, the harbinger of a different, nonterritorial social space.

So as capitalism "recomposes" itself (reterritorializes) in front of our stunned eyes, by the most artificial means—i.e. through offshore and commercialized sovereignty and the numerical principle, we, the subjects, are in the position of both sovereign consumers/investors driving the new order and yet at the same time helpless observers, mere spectators of capitalism's grand journey. Capital represents itself, therefore, as paradoxically omnipotent, unchallenged, and perhaps unchangeable, and yet strangely intangible, neurotic, and sick. The offshore economy is not the cause of these monumental changes, but its unique form of nonterritorial spatiality is helping facilitate the expansion of the numerical principle.

I have not discussed in this book at great length the forces resisting the expansion of offshore. A lot has been written about the offshore economy: the United States, the OECD, and in particular the European Union appear to take the phenomenon very seriously and are beginning to enact laws to combat money laundering, drug trafficking, and harmful tax competition. These laws are certainly to be welcomed. But the debated solutions are precisely part of the problem: the focus on money laundering, drug trafficking, and financial stability ensures that the discussion remains firmly locked within the confines of a reformist agenda. Consequently, in mainstream debates the offshore economy is accepted as a legitimate, indeed, at times it is presented as a desirable element of the world economy. Offshore financial centers are asked politely to cooperate with their larger brethren; to "self-regulate" better, to provide information about possible criminal activities. They are not asked to desist from offering nonregulated, nontaxed, secretive juridical spaces.

The problem has partly to do with issues of selectivity. Whose interests are represented in these multilateral forums? What chances are there that the U.S. government, the European Union, or the OECD will contemplate policies deemed harmful to the profits not of this or that company or this or that wealthy individual, but of the entire financial and productive sector? Frankly, not much. There is no doubt an element of agenda control being exercised here. But then the problem goes deeper. Contrary to the common but mistaken belief that offshore is somehow a pathetic development at the margins of the world economy, the offshore economy is a by-product of the most basic institutional arrangements upon which the entire capitalist system is based. It is a system that advances what appears to be profoundly conflicting principles: the liberal principles of open markets and capital mobility, as against a particularistic political system based on the principles of sovereignty and national self-determination. Contrary to the false impression generated by the sterile state versus globalization debate, the system of sovereignty is not incompatible with globalization but in fact enables it. Sovereignty helps to compartmentalize global capitalism so that those who remain onshore, national political systems with their democratic aspirations, cannot touch offshore, even though both realms are clearly under the same rubric of sovereignty. The very term "offshore" is ideologically loaded, for it provides governments with the opportunity to support unfettered capitalism while denouncing it: to bemoan their loss of power and sovereignty, while contributing to that very loss. Offshore is the perfect foil for conservative social democrats like Tony Blair: it can be used as a dose of "refreshing reality" to deaden the qualms of old-line socialists.

The problem, however, is that irrespective of the ideological and political capital invested in offshore, as long as this very basic but contradictory institutional arrangement is in place, whereby governments are able to make laws in ways that are beneficial to them and harmful to others, the elimination of offshore is out of the question. To bring it about would require such a degree of agreement about principles of law enactment, such strong discipline and surveillance exercised by some multilateral body over so many countries, as effectively to eliminate sovereignty as we know it today. Such agreement will be the harbinger of a "global state," and I would urge progressive thinkers to think twice before subscribing to such a program. Offshore can end only when either the state system has ended its long half-millennial journey or capitalism itself has been replaced by another system.

# Notes

Introduction

1 On the Lysenko affair and other events leading up to the rejection of systems approach in the Soviet Union, see Day 1981.

2 A U.K. Inland Revenue document states: "These [tax havens] are sometimes referred to as designer rate regimes, as they enable companies to pay just the right amount of tax needed in any given situation to sidestep Controlled Foreign Companies rules." U.K. Inland Revenue 1999.

3 The figure of 27 million includes those employed in the Chinese Special Zones. Excluding these, there are approximately 750 EPZs employing between them about 4.5 million workers, about 90 percent of whom are female. Cling and Letilly (2001).

4 The *lex mercatoria* or merchant law is a private customary law that evolved from around the twelfth century among merchants to regulate trade. From around the sixteenth century many of its principles were incorporated into European national laws. The law merchant is experiencing, however, a renaissance in its private form. It should not be confused with offshore, but it is particularly suitable for offshore transactions. See Cutler 1997, Medwig 1992, and Teubner 1997.

5 Captive insurance companies are subsidiaries set up by large companies for the purpose of self-insurance.

6 "How could a city of just 7 million attract $64 billion in foreign direct investment in 2000?" asks an article in the *Financial Times*. "Nearly two thirds of the 'foreign' investment into Hong Kong in 1998, the most recent year for which detailed data is available, came from China, Bermuda and the Virgin Islands. The last two might seem unlikely sources of FDI, but they are offshore banking centers where Hong Kong companies have traditionally kept a sizeable share of their money." *Financial Times*, 30 March 2001, 12.

7 According to reports in the *New York Times*, Enron possessed 881 subsidiaries in tax havens, including 692 in the Cayman Islands, 119 in the Turks and Caicos, 43 in Mauritius, and 8 in Bermuda. *New York Times*, 18 January 2002).

8 Economists, they declare, "have already branded the next one hundred years as the 'Century of Offshore Investment'" (1998, 1). Unfortunately, they do not tell us who exactly these economists might be.

9 National capitalism took form in a rather haphazard manner in the competition between what Van Der Pijl (1998) calls, a growing "Lockean heartland," where a form of liberal state based on Locke's principles predominated, and the "Hobbesian states." There was no historical necessity for the victory of the Lockean heartland over Hobbesian contenders, nor was there some deep functional affinity between Lockean states and capitalism as such; rather, the form of state which proved successful over time shaped the nature of modern capitalism. Thus, in Van Der Pijl's view, there is no political-economic infrastructure that determines the political and legal superstructure; instead, the two are historically interrelated to produce a nonteleological, historically contingent outcome.

10 Throughout this book I make a distinction between the concepts "state" and "nation-state." States and state systems existed in different parts of the world for at least five millennia; the nation-state is a specific form of state that emerged in the early nineteenth century in Europe. What many take to be the demise of the state is in fact the demise of the nation-state. I take the concept of the nation-state from Braudel who argues: "The national market. This is the term used to denote the economic coherence achieved within a given political unit—a unit that is of a certain size, essentially corresponding to what I have called 'the territorial state' or, as it might also be called, 'the nation-state'" (1979, 3:177). Unfortunately, the relationship between the formation of the nineteenth-century nation-state and the nineteenth-century political economy has attracted relatively little interest. Poulantzas's (1978) last book provides an excellent and succinct—perhaps too succinct—analysis of the complex relationship uniting the territorial state, new spaces, and competitive capitalism. But considering the vastness of the subject, I am able in this book to provide only a brief sketch of these momentous historical developments.

11 In an earlier book written with Jason Abbott (Palan and Abbott 1996) we demonstrate how the contemporary state system provides the legal and political infrastructure for globalization. In our analysis this has come about through uncoordinated attempts by a variety of states to improve their competitive positions in the world economy.

Chapter 1. The Offshore Economy in Its Contemporary Settings
1 In recent publications, however, the IMF and BIS have expanded their concept of offshore to include the Euromarket and the IBFs, which at least indirectly includes such onshore-offshore centers as London (Errico and Musalem 1999).
2 The lack of clarity in the use of the term "offshore" is evidenced also by the growing number of journals dedicated to the subject. *Offshore Finance Canada*, for instance, publishes articles on tax havens and tax issues. In contrast, *Offshore Outlook*, an on-line journal published in the

United States, lists the following items as offshore: international private and family trusts, multicurrency dealings, global custody, unit trusts, pension funds, export processing, ship registration, and aircraft leasing.

3 But there may be "strictly-for-export" laws that are not offshore, i.e., that do not operate through sovereign bifurcation. Conrad refers to the incorporation laws of Delaware and New Jersey, which, as we will see in chapter 3, do not fall in into the category of offshore.

4 "The first known reference to 'offshore' in the sense of an unregulated financial center was published in a periodical called *The Banker* in November 1971. It referred not to some sun-drenched island, or even to the Channel Isles, but to our very own City of London" (Atkinson 1999, 18).

5 Miroslava Filipovic explains the causes of the confusion: "Financial markets are usually classified according to the type of participants, foreigners and national residents, and according to the existence or non-existence of a specific jurisdiction over it. Strictly speaking, classification of banking activities can be done according to three main criteria: a) currency of denomination; b) the residence of the bank customer; and c) the geographical location of the bank office where the business is carried out" (1997, 6). The classification of financial markets according to participants does not always accord with that of the existence or nonexistence of specific jurisdictions. To complicate matters, the three additional classificatory criteria are not necessarily consistent, and indeed this classificatory scheme is not always adhered to.

6 "The Euromarket is not an entirely new phenomenon." (*Bank of England Quarterly Bulletin* 1964:17). But as Schenk (1998, 2) notes: "The Bank of England initially interpreted the emergence of the Eurodollar deposits in the late 1950s as merely a return to a practice of the 1920s market." The bank later changed its mind. Schenk, however, accepts the bank's original view and therefore dates the origins of the modern Euromarket to 1955.

7 The Bank of England used arguments drawn from English common law to claim that it could not extend regulation over the new market. Unlike continental law, which assumes practice is prohibited unless stated otherwise, in common law prohibited practices must be clearly specified. Consequently the government never knows whether a new practice is legal or not. The government sometimes takes financial operators to court when they devise new practices, as test cases to clarify the law. For discussion see Burn 2000.

8 The Interest Equalization Tax Act, signed by President Johnson on 2 September 1964, was made retroactive to 18 July 1963. It did not apply to bank loans generally but was extended in 1965 to cover such transactions. In 1966 the Congress enacted the Foreign Investors Tax Act which allowed certain important tax benefits to foreigners making portfolio investments in the United States.

9 The Euromarket is now subject to a minimal degree of self-regulation (Kapstein 1994; White 1996). The Bank for International Settlements notes a shift "towards a greater market orientation of regulation, which is evident in the shift from an approach based on mechanical rules to reliance on market discipline. This was illustrated by the recent amendments to the Basel Capital Accord to permit the use of internal models for market risk, as well as the ongoing discussions on possible alternatives (including the pre-commitment approach, which would allow a self-determined ex ante allocation of capital, accompanied by ex post penalties if losses exceed the pre-committed amount)" (BIS 1998, 161).

10 The Bank for International Settlements used to keep separate statistics on the Euromarket, but by the early 1990s it no longer did so. The bank provided separate listings for Euronotes up to 1995, but due to their spectacular growth rate, averaging around 50 percent a year in the early 1990s, it gave this up too. As far as the bank is concerned, the distinction between the Euromarket and international market is no longer tenable.

11 This subject has been covered well elsewhere and hence I will not discuss it further in this book. See OECD 1997.

12 Some argue that Luxembourg, for instance, is not a tax haven. Luxembourg is heavily regulated and has distinguished itself by having no withholding tax (Hornsby 1997).

13 There are a number of quantitative definitions. For example, the U.K. Inland Revenue's Controlled Foreign companies rules "regard a company as being in a tax haven or preferential regime if it is subject to a level of taxation less than 75% of what it could have paid if it had been resident in the UK" (U.K. Inland Revenue 1999).

14 However, to Blum (1984) there are one hundred tax havens throughout the world.

15 Tax avoidance has to be distinguished from tax evasion. Tax evasion is done fraudulently to escape legal obligations. Tax avoidance uses legal means to reduce the tax burden. Tax avoidance is legally accepted; tax evasion is not. In practice the complexities of the modern financial world do not easily correspond to the niceties of this theoretical distinction, and the borderline between avoidance and evasion is a very fine one.

16 Leading in some cases to chronic labor and housing shortages (Reuters, in *OffshoreWeek* 2, no. 83 (24–30 August 2001).

17 Noel Reilly (tax lawyer working in the Cayman Islands and Hong Kong), private communication.

18 Of these, 7,965 were international companies and 293 were offshore trusts (Panafrican News Agency 2001).

19 The Bahrain Monetary Agency reports that assets of offshore banking units (OBUs) operating there rose to $91.04 billion by the end of March

2000, ahead of the previous year's first quarter total of $82.49 billion (*OffshoreWeek*, 20 May 2000).

20 It is difficult to distinguish between EPZs and many other similar arrangements such as free ports or free trade zones. Strictly speaking, free ports and free trade zones are commercial zones only; their functions involve warehousing and transshipment of goods with no change in the nature of the goods themselves (Dicken 1992, 183). The Chinese special economic zones, by contrast, are very much like the traditional EPZs. In addition, special trade deals such as the one negotiated between Germany and the Czech Republic may count as offshore arrangements according to the definition used in this book. The German-Czech deal, negotiated through the EC, permits inputs to be sent from Germany to Czech firms to be processed by cheap labor, and returned to Germany tariff-free. The arrangement is crafted on the model of the U.S. tariff provisions that gave birth to the EPZs in Mexico, and an estimated 70 percent of bilateral trade is carried on under its terms. I am indebted to the late Professor Susan Strange and to an anonymous referee for Cornell University Press for pointing this out to me.

21 The ILO (1998) identifies Shannon as the first modern EPZ, but acknowledges that special zones go back to medieval times.

22 A maquiladora is a Mexican corporation that operates under a maquila program approved by the Mexican Secretariat of Commerce and Industrial Development. The maquila program allows up to 100 percent foreign investment participation in the capital and in company management without any special authorization. It also entitles the company to special customs treatment, allowing duty-free importing of machinery, equipment, parts and materials, and administrative equipment such as computers and communications devices—subject only to a guarantee that such goods will be in Mexico only temporarily. The maquiladoras tend to be assembly lines and the vast majority of the products are exported (Baz 2002).

23 This figure includes over two hundred U.S. free trade zones, which are different from EPZs in that they are primarily import-oriented, as well as the Chinese special processing zones and the European enterprise zones.

24 Electronic commerce is defined as "the use of computer networks to facilitate transactions involving the production, distribution, and sale and delivery of goods and services in the marketplace" (McLure 1997, 731).

25 Dutyfreezone.com, a company based in Curaçao, is planning to ship duty-free liquor and cigarettes to anyone in the United States. The *Financial Times* reports that "Reynald Katz, the man behind dutyfreezone.com, says he has discussed his business with U.S. customs authorities and is assured that he is breaking no rules" (10 September 1999).

26 The Dominion of Melchizedek (DOM) evolved throughout the 1990s from the acquisition of several islands in the vicinity of Fiji and the Marshall islands. DOM offers, as its official Website (http://www.melchizedek.com) boasts, "tax-free, minimal banking legislation and maximum banking secrecy laws, Melchizedek is fast becoming known as the Switzerland of the Pacific" (Dominion of Melchizedek, 2002).

27 The U.S. Securities and Exchange Commission has charged a New York lawyer and his firm with defrauding investors in the United States and Dominica of $1.2 million in a scheme promoted by Credit Bank International Co., which is purportedly chartered in Melchizedek. The securities regulator alleged that Credit Bank is not a bank and Melchizedek is not a country (reported in *Offshore Week*, January 2000). Melchizedek is one of a dozen "jurisdictions" whose legality is in question. For discussion of Melchizedek and similar "jurisdictions," see Diamond and Diamond 1998, 1–15.

28 Conrad insists on the difference between tax havens and the "exportation of liberality within the United States [which] depends on a principle of conflict of laws, according to which the law governing the internal affairs of a corporation is the law of the state of incorporation" (1973, 634).

29 "Treaty shopping means that a taxpayer 'shops' into the benefits of a treaty which normally are not available to him. To this end he generally interposes a corporation in a country that has an advantageous tax treaty" (Becker and Wurm 1998, 1).

30 A U.S. State Department report alleges that the Dominica government sold three hundred citizenships to Russians, thereby increasing the suspicion of money laundering on the island. In response, Julius Timothy, Dominica's minister of finance, has stated that the government no longer grants passports to Russians. Nonetheless, in defending the island's economic citizenship program, Timothy said that the government got the idea for the program from wealthy countries (*National Post* 1999). Many countries grant citizenship to anyone willing to invest sufficient money in them—$500,000 in the case of the United States. There is a market in citizenship. Susan Strange calls this the "commodification of civic rights" (personal communication).

Chapter 2. State, Capital, and the Production of Offshore

1 Carlson and Hufbauer argue that "formula apportionment interferes with the disciplinary mechanism of Tiebout-type" (1981, 47).

2 The concept of co-evolution is drawn from research into the structural evolution of industries, in particular recent changes in electronic and computer technologies. For an overview of co-evolutionary theories in business and geography, see Phillips (1999).

Chapter 3. The Emergence of Embryonic Forms of Offshore

1 Throughout this book I distinguish between the modern offshore economy and its predecessors. Tax havens, or rather asset havens—jurisdictions where wealthy individuals placed their savings for protection—existed since Roman times (Doggart 1997). Special economic zones existed in Europe since the Middle Ages (ILO 1998). Variants of flags of convenience can be found in the nineteenth century (Carlisle 1961). But as these authors acknowledge, the modern offshore economy is different: it is a premeditated state policy which aims to attract business or bring revenues to offshore states.

   As we saw in the previous chapter, the two basic jurisdictional standards for assertion of business income liability are source and residence. In the source standard, countries assert tax jurisdiction over income earned within their geographic area. The source standard does not distinguish between resident and nonresident income. The residence standard, on the other hand, taxes on the principle of residence rather than source income. Residency had become the standard principle of worldwide taxation of corporations, but the residence approach raises the danger of double taxation—that companies will be taxed in their host country and then again in their home country. Many governments signed bilateral agreements to avoid double taxing their residents. Unfortunately, companies have learned to take advantage of this system by playing one jurisdiction against the other. Furthermore, the veil of secrecy that surrounds operations in tax havens, combined with the practice of "transfer pricing" has made the calculation of their residency income complex. To resolve this problem, a number of tax experts have been advocating the use of an apportionment formula according to which a portion of a corporation's total taxable income is assigned to a particular jurisdiction based on the relationship between the corporation's activities in that jurisdiction and its total activities. This is a radical formula which will require, among other things, an international body to manage and administer the complex calculations required for the apportionment of tax. Notwithstanding this complexity, apportionment tax may prove a useful weapon in the fight against tax competition. Not surprisingly, we find that the Tiebout efficiency argument is harnessed against the principle of apportionment.

2 To complicate matters, this is not the case with export processing zones. The nature of the tasks performed in EPZs necessitates real as opposed to purely virtual relocation. It is often the case, however, that companies relocating to EPZs have little interest in the host countries' economies, but merely in the bundle of regulations that is offered to them. As mentioned in chapter 1, there is a debate over whether EPZs can be considered offshore. I believe they can and should be so considered, but the difference between EPZs and other offshore sectors must be acknowledged.

3 Sovereign exclusivity does not mean much without a concomitant recognition of sovereign equality, understood in time in terms of the right of national self-determination. The history of one is bound up with the other. But as Rigo Suerda (1973) notes, national self-determination is an even more recent development, essentially something that we have witnessed only since the early years of the twentieth century.

4 It is often said that the modern concept of sovereignty, as formulated by Jean Bodin ([1576] 1986), asserts the primacy of the prince in devising the laws, but this view can be misleading. True, the Church's power was in decline and Westphalia was an important symptom of the changing balance of power. But the emergence of modern *territorial* sovereignty took a while to evolve.

5 "Society, in the thought of the Middle Ages, was a body composed, like all living organisms of non-homogeneous parts, that is, of a hierarchy of functions" (Richardson 1998, 80).

6 Martin maintains that Montesquieu was the first to speak of "the international competition of armaments as 'the new malady' which 'has spread itself over Europe; it has infected our Princes and induces them to keep up an exorbitant number of troops'" (1929, 263).

7 Murty (1978) traces the origin of the distinction to Ratzel. I return to the subject at greater length in chapter 6.

8 Positive international law can be traced back to Wolff and Vattel in the middle of the eighteenth century, but its principles became generally accepted only in the nineteenth century. For discussion see Neff 1990.

9 "A soul, a spiritual principle." My translation.

10 T. S. Murty comments that "Very few boundaries of states prior to the nineteenth century were either formalized or determined" (1978, 32), although he concedes that many European frontiers trace their origins to the medieval period.

11 Not until 1930 did an international conference held at The Hague universalize this as part of the law of the sea.

12 Lindholm argues, however, that "the provision of legal regimes to be enjoyed in other jurisdictions is a uniquely American phenomena. It should not be confused with the 'tax haven' game" (1944, 634).

13 Bureau of Corporations, *Taxation of Corporations*, pt. 2: *Middle Atlantic States* (1910), 82, quoted in Lindholm 1944, 160.

14 Crucially, however, the IBFs do not have bank secrecy arrangements.

15 In particular, there is international disagreement over the scope of U.S. state taxation of multinational enterprises, as a number of states—in particular California—use the worldwide combined reporting standard for calculating local taxable income of multinational enterprises. Devgun 1995.

Chapter 4. The Growth of an Offshore Economy
1 For a different view see Peillon and Montebourg 2000.
2 I am omitting the Vatican City which, however, does in fact many ways act as a tax haven. See Naylor 1987.
3 Casinos migrated first from France, where they were outlawed, to the German spas and then set up shop in places like Monaco and lately in other tax havens.
4 *Http://www.sigma.net/fafhrd/andorra/intro.htm.*
5 Aggregate assets of the big three Swiss banks reached $8 billion by 1918, a huge sum for that time. Fehrenbach 1966, 51.
6 The following draws on Carlisle 1961.
7 W. Comyn, an officer of Pacific Freighters, in an interview in the *New York Herald* cited in Carlisle 1961, 11.

Chapter 5. Offshore and the Internationalization of the State
1 Not to be confused with its sister organization, the Financial Action Task Force on Money Laundering (FATF), which has been very active since 11 September 2001. The FATF has published detailed country-by-country accounts of anti-money laundering legislation and international cooperation. The FATF also publishes a list of noncooperative jurisdictions and updates the list every few months. See FATF 2001 and 2002.

Chapter 6. Offshore and the Demise of the Nation-State
1 "The original usage of the term 'social sciences' dates from the early years of the French Revolution, and is closely related to the rationalist concern for an ordered and prosperous society of free and happy citizens." Head 1985, 110.
2 See above, chapter 3.

Chapter 7. Numerical Organizations, Nomadic Spaces, and Modern Capitalism
1 There is a fascinating debate on the etymological origins of the word *state* from *status*. Stevens reports on the widely held view of the Latin origins of the word that "implies a condition of stability" (1999, 58).
2 "One can rise up at any point and move to any other. Its mode of distribution is the *nomos*: arraying oneself in an open space, as opposed to the *logos* of entrenching oneself in a closed space" (Massumi 1987, xiii).
3 He continues: "The worldwide government conspiracy over the issuing of money will finally be smashed. Then, like in William Gibson's science fiction novels, governments will try to ban money. The 'control freaks' of government will have finally lost the plot" (Angell 1997).

# References

Abbott, Jason. 2000. "Isolated Enclaves or Strategy for Economic Development? Export Processing Zones in the Developing World." Unpublished.

Acton, John Emerich Edward Dalberg, 1st Baron. 1948. *Essays on Freedom and Power*. Glencoe, Ill.: The Free Press.

Aglietta, Michel. 1979. *A Theory of Capitalist Regulation: The U.S. Experience*. London: Verso.

Alesina, Alberto, and Geoffrey Carliner, eds. 1991. *Politics and Economics in the Eighties*. Chicago: University of Chicago Press.

Aliber, Robert Z. 1976. *The International Money Game*. London: Macmillan.

Allen, Roy E. 1994. *Financial Crises and Recession in the Global Economy*. London: Edward Elgar.

Alliez, E. 1991. *Capital Times*. Minneapolis: University of Minnesota Press.

Althusser, Louis. 1969. *For Marx*. London: NLB.

Anderson, Benedict. 1981. *Imagined Communities: Reflections on the Origin and Spread of Nationalism*. London: Verso.

Angell, Ian, O. 1997. "The Future of Money," *Financial Times*, December 22.

Ardant, Gabriel. 1975. "Financial Policy and Economic Infrastructure of Modern State and Nations." In *The Formation of National States in Western Europe,* edited by Charles Tilly. Princeton, N.J.: Princeton University Press.

Aris, Reinhold. 1965. *History of Political Thought in Germany from 1789 to 1815*. London: Frank Cass.

Arrighi, Giovanni. 1994. *The Long Twentieth Century*. London: Verso.

Atkinson, Dan. "Laundered in Britain." *The Guardian*, 3 September 1999.

Atman, Oscar L. 1969. "Eurodollars." In *Readings in the Euro-Dollar*, edited by Eric B. Chalmers. London: W. P. Griffith.

Aubrey, Henry G. 1966. "The Political Economy of International Monetary Reform." *Social Research* 33:218–54.

Auster, Richard D., and Morris Silver. 1979. *The State as a Firm: Economic Forces in Political Development*. Boston: Martinus Nijhoff.

Badie, Bertrand. 1999. *Un Monde sans souveraineté: Les états entre ruse et responsabilité*. Paris: Fayard.

Badie, Bertrand, and Pierre Birnbaum. 1994. "Sociology of the State Revisited." *International Social Sciences Journal* 140:153–68.

Bank of England. 1964. "UK Banks' External Liabilities and Claims in For-
  · eign Currencies." *Bank of England Quarterly Bulletin.* June.
Banoff, Sheldon I., and Burton W. Kanter. 1994. "States Compete to Save
  Taxes Owed to Other States." *Journal of Taxation* 80:382–84.
Barret-Kriegel, Blandine. 1986. *Les Chemins de l'état.* Paris: Calmann-Lévy.
Bauman, Zygmunt. 1992. *Intimations of Postmodernity.* London: Routledge.
Baz, Aureliano Gonzalez, 2002. *What is a maquiladora?* Fuente:
  http://www.bancomext-mtl.com/invest/vox128.htm
Beaune, Colette. 1985. *Naissance de la Nation France.* Paris: Gallimard.
Becker, Helmut, and Felix J. Wurm, eds. 1998. *Treaty Shopping: An Emerg-
  ing Tax Issue and Its Present Status in Various Countries.* Dordrecht:
  Kluwer Law and Taxation.
Bichler, Shimshon, and Jonathan Nitzan. 1996. "Putting the State in Its Place:
  U.S. Foreign Policy and Differential Capital Accumulation in Middle East
  Energy Conflicts." *Review of International Political Economy* 3:608–61.
BIS. 1995. *BIS Statistics on International Banking and Financial Market
  Activity.* Bank for International Settlements Monetary and Economic
  Department, August. Basle: Bank for International Settlements.
———. 1996. *The Supervision of Cross-Border Banking.* Basle: Bank for In-
  ternational Settlements.
———. 1997. *Bank for International Settlements Annual Report.* Basle:
  Bank for International Settlements. June 9.
——— . 1998. *Bank for International Settlements Annual Report.* Basle:
  Bank for International Settlements. June 7.
———. 2002. *The 2001 Triennial Central Bank Survey of Foreign Exchange
  and Derivatives Market Activity.* Basle: Bank for International Settle-
  ments. 18 March.
Blum, Richard H. 1984. *Offshore Havens, Banks, Trusts, and Companies:
  The Business of Crime in the Euromarket.* New York: Praeger.
Blum, Richard H., and John Kaplan. 1979. "Offshore Banking Issues with
  Respect to Criminal Use." Paper prepared for the Ford Foundation, No-
  vember.
Bodin, Jean. 1986 [1576]. *Les Six livres de la république.* Paris: Fayard.
Boland, Vincent. 1999. "Survey—Guernsey: Spotlight Goes on 'Offshore.'"
  *Financial Times,* 21 October.
Booth, Garry. 2000. "Bermuda: Despite Their Diminished Returns,
  Offshore-Based Companies Are Better Equipped than Most to Ride Out
  the Storm." *Financial Times,* 4 September.
Born, Gary B. 1992. "A Reappraisal of Extraterritorial Reach of U.S. Law."
  *Law and Policy in International Business* 24:1–100.
Botting, F. 1999. *Sex, Machines and Navels: Fiction, Fantasy and History
  in the Future Present.* Manchester: Manchester University Press.
Boughton, James M. 2000. *The IMF and the Silent Revolution: Global Fi-
  nance and Development in the 1980s.* Pamphlet.http://www.imf.org/ex-
  ternal/pubs/ft/silent/index.htm#pref. April 6.

Bounds, Andrew. 2001. "Blacklist Difficulties Overcome: Mutual Funds." *Financial Times*, 16 July.

Braithwaite, John, and Peter Drahos. 2000. *Global Business Regulation*. Cambridge: Cambridge University Press.

Branscomb, A. W. 1994. *Who Owns Information? From Privacy to Public Access*. New York: Basic Books.

Braudel, Fernand. 1979. *Civilization and Capitalism 15th–18th Century*. New York: Harper & Row.

Budd, Leslie. 1999. "Globalization and the Crisis of Territorial Embeddedness of International Financial Markets." In *Money and the Space Economy*, edited by Ron Martin. Chichester: John Wiley.

Burn, Gary. 1999. "The State, the City and the Euromarkets." *Review of International Political Economy* 6:225–60.

———. 2000. "The Role of the British State in the Reemergence of Global Capital." Ph.D. thesis. Sussex University, Brighton, U.K.

Bush, Paul D. 1988. "The Theory of Institutional Change." In *Evolutionary Economics*, vol. 1: *Foundations of Institutional Thought, edited by* Marc R. Tool. Armonk, N. Y: Sharpe.

Calleo, David. 1982. *The Imperious Economy*. Cambridge: Harvard University Press.

Cameron, Angus, and Ronen Palan. 1999. "The Imagined Economy: Mapping Transformations in the Contemporary State." *Millennium* 28:267–89.

*Cana*. 2000. "Cayman Offshore Sector Booming Despite Blacklist." 26 October.

Caribbean News Agency. 2000. "Bahamas Looks to E-commerce." 7 April.

Carlisle, Rodney. 1961. *Sovereignty for Sale: The Origins and Evolution of the Panamanian and Liberian Flags of Convenience*. Annapolis, Md.: Naval Institute Press.

Carlson, George N., and Gary C. Hufbauer. 1981. "Tax Frontiers and National Frontiers." In *Business Taxation, Finance, and Firm Behavior*, edited by George N. Carlson, and Gary C. Hufbauer. New York: Almqvist and Wiksell International.

Cassard, Marcel. 1994. *The Role of Offshore Centers in International Financial Intermediation*. IMF Working Paper WP/94/107. Washington, D.C.: IMF.

Cerny, Philip G. 1990. *The Changing Architecture of Politics: Structure, Agency and the Future of the State*. London: Sage.

———. 2000. "Structuring the Political Arena: Public Goods, States and Governance in a Globalizing World." In *Global Political Economy: Contemporary Theories*, edited by Ronen Palan. London: Routledge.

Chandler, Alfred D. 1977. *The Visible Hand: The Managerial Revolution in American Business*. Cambridge, Mass.: The Belknap Press of Harvard University Press.

———. 1990. *Scale and Scope: The Dynamics of Industrial Capitalism.* Cambridge, Mass.: Belknap Press.

Chapman, Brian. 1970. *Police State.* London: Pall Mall.

Chavagneux, Christian, and Ronen Palan. 1999. "Qui a besoin des paradis fiscaux?" *L'Economie Politique* 4:14–44.

Chesher, Richard. 2000. "Vanuatu Sets Out Its Stall for Offshore E-commerce." *E-business Incorporated,* 24 May.

Clark, Steven, and Flip de Kam. 1998. "OECD Taxes Revisited." *The OECD Observer,* no. 214, October/November.

Clarke, S. 1988. *Keynesianism, Monetarism and the Crisis of the State.* London: Edward Elgar.

Cling, Jean-Pierre, and Gaëlle Letilly. 2001. "Export Processing Zones : A Threatened Instrument for Global Economy Insertion?" Document de travail DIAL/Unité de Recherche CIPRE (Paris).

Cohen, Ronald. 1981. "Evolution, Fission, and the Early State." In *The Study of the State,* edited by Henri J. M. Claessen and Peter Skalnik. The Hague: Mouton Publishers.

Cole, Kenneth C. 1948. "The Theory of the State as a Sovereign Juristic Person." *American Political Science Review* 42:16–31.

Colebrook, Claire. 1997. *New Literary Histories: New Historicism and Contemporary Criticism.* Manchester: Manchester University Press.

Commons, John. 1959 [1924]. *The Legal Foundations of Capitalism.* Madison: University of Wisconsin Press.

Conrad, Alfred F. 1973. "An Overview of the Laws of Corporations." *Michigan Law Review* 4:623–90.

Cooper, Richard N. 1974. "Implications of the Euro-Dollar for Monetary Policy and the U.S. Balance-of-Payments Deficit." In *National Monetary Policies and the International Financial System,* edited by Robert Z. Aliber. Chicago: University of Chicago Press.

Craton, Michael. 1962. *A History of the Bahamas,* London: Collins.

Cutler, Claire A. 1997. "Artifice, Ideology, and Paradox: The Public/Private Distinction in International Law." *Review of International Political Economy* 4:261–85.

*Daily Herald* (Anguilla). 2000. "More Companies Registering in Anguilla." 3 August.

Davidow, William H., and Michael S. Malone. 1992. *The Virtual Corporation: Structuring and Revitalizing the Corporation for the 21st Century.* New York: HarperBusiness.

Day, Richard B. 1981. *The "Crisis" and the "Crash": Soviet Studies of the West, 1917–1939.* London: NLB.

Debray, Regis. 1981. *Critique of Political Reason.* London: Verso.

Deleuze, Gilles, and Félix Guattari. 1984. *Anti-Oedipus: Capitalism and Schizophrenia.* London: Athlone Press.

————. 1987. *A Thousand Plateaus: Capitalism and Schizophrenia*. Min-neapolis: University of Minnesota Press.

Devgun, Derek. 1995. International Fiscal Wars for the Twenty-first Cen-tury: An Assessment of Tax-Based Trade Retaliation. *Law and Policy in International Business* 27:353–422.

De Wilde, Jaap. *1991*. *Saved from Oblivion: Interdependence Theory in the First Half of the 20th Century*. Aldershot, U.K.: Dartmouth.

Diamond, Walter, and Dorothy Diamond. 1998. *Tax Havens of the World*. New York: Matthew Bender Books.

Dicken, Peter. 1992. *Global Shift: The Internationalization of Economic Activity*. 2d ed. London: Paul Chapman Publishing.

Dixon, Liz. 2001. "Financial Flows via Offshore Financial Centers." *Finan-cial Stability Review* 10:104–15.

Doggart, Caroline. 1997. "Tax Havens and Their Uses." London: EIU.

Dominion of Melchizedek. 2002. Overview. Http://www.mechizedek.com/profile.htm.

Donzelot, Jacques. 1984. *L'Invention du social: Essai sur le Declin des pas-sions politiques*. Paris: Fayard.

Douglas, Ian. 2000. "Globalization and the Retreat of the State." In *Glob-alization and the Politics of Resistance*, edited by Barry Gills. London: Macmillan.

Dow, Sheila C. 1999. "The Stages of Banking Development and the Spatial Evolution of Financial Systems." In *Money and the Space Economy*, ed-ited by Ron Martin. Chichester: John Wiley.

Dowling, Donald, Jr. 1995. "Forum Shopping and Other Reflections on Lit-igation Involving U.S. and European Business." In *Introduction to Transnational Legal Transactions*, edited by Marylin J. Raische and Roberta I. Shaffer. New York: Oceana Publications.

Drucker, Peter F. 1990. *The New Realities*. London: Mandarin.

Dufey, Gunter, and Ian H. Giddy. 1987. *50 Cases in International Finance*. London: Addison-Wesley.

Duménil, Gérard, and Dominique Lévy. 2001. "Costs and Benefits of Neo-liberalism: A Class Analysis." *Review of International Political Econ-omy* 8:578–607.

Duggan, Patrice. 1991. "The Mouse That Wants to Roar." *Forbes*, 4 March.

*Economist*. 1993. "Sun, Sea and Policies." 10 July.

————. 1994. "Survey of World Taxation (8): Islands in the Sun: Offshore Centers." 20 May.

————. 1996. "Any Old Port in a Storm." 16 December.

————. 1997. "Cybersex: An Adult Affair." 4 January.

————. 1998. "Comment and Analysis: Winds of Change on Treasure Is-lands: As Countries Relax Bureaucratic Controls, the Offshore Centre's Role Is Being Eroded." 4 January.

————. 1999. "The Branson Way." 31 December.

Emadi-Coffin, Barbara. 1996. "Towards a New Theory of International Organization: The Multinational Corporation, the State, and International Regulation in the Establishment of Enterprise Zones and Export Processing Zones." Ph.D. diss. University of Sussex, Brighton, U.K.

Emerson, Rupert. 1928. *State and Sovereignty in Modern Germany*. New Haven, Conn.: Yale University Press.

Ernst, Dieter, and David O'Connor. 1989. *Technology and Global Competition: The Challenge for Newly Industrializing Economies*. Paris: Organization for Economic Co-Operation and Development.

Errico, Luca, and Alberto Musalem. 1999. *Offshore Banking: An Analysis of Micro- and Macro-Prudential Issues*. IMF Working Paper WP/99/5. Washington, D.C.: International Monetary Fund.

*Euromoney*. 1989. *Treasure Islands: A Supplement to Euromoney*. May.

———. 1996. "Switzerland, a Euromoney Survey—A Special Report Prepared by Bank J. Vontobel." March.

———. 1998. "Luxembourg: The Slow Demise of a Capital Market." May.

Evans, John. 1994. "Currency Trading Hits New Heights." *The European*.

Fabri, D., and Godfrey Baldacchino. 1999. "The Malta Financial Services Center: A Study in Microstate Dependency Management?" In *Offshore Finance Centers and Tax Havens*, edited by Mark Hampton and Jason Abbott. London: Macmillan.

Faith, Nicholas. 1982. *Safety in Numbers· the Mysterious World of Swiss Banking*. New York: Viking Press.

FATF, 2001. *The Forty Recommendations*. Financial Action Task Force on Money Laundering. http://www1.oecd.org/fatf/pdf/40Rec_en.pdf.

———. 2002. *Non-Cooperative Countries and Territories*. Financial Action Task Force on Money Laundering. http://www1.oecd.org/fatf/NCCT_en.htm.

Fedou, René. 1971. *L'Etat au Moyen Age*. Paris: PUF.

Fehrenbach, Theodore R. 1966. *The Gnomes of Zurich*. London: Leslie Frewin.

Ferro, Marc. 1997. *Colonization: A Global History*. London: Routledge.

Fichte, J. G. [1808] 1981. *Discours à la nation allemande*. Paris: Aubier.

Filipovic, Miroslava. 1997. *Governments, Banks and Global Capital: Securities Markets in Global Politics*. Aldershot: Ashgate.

*Financial Post*. Canada, 2000. "Online Gambling Confronts National Laws." 19 March.

Financial Stability Forum. 2000. Report of the Working Group on Offshore Centers. Available at www.fsformum.org/Reports/RepOFC.pdf. Accessed April 16.

*Financial Times*. 2000a."UK Targets Offshore Tax Evasion." 20 March.

———. 2000b. "U.S. Slams Brussels Plan for Internet Tax." 9 June.

———. 2001. "Flow of Hot Money Dries Up, Bahamas." *Financial Times Survey*. 19 December.

Fisher, Herbert. 1989. *The Medieval Empire*. London: Macmillan.

Fitzgerald, P. 1979. *Offshore*. London: Collins.

Ford, Robert. 1990. "The Cost of Subsiding Industry." *OECD Observer* 166 (October/November).

Fortes, Meyer. 1969. *Kinship and the Social Order: The Legacy of Lewis Henry Morgan*. London: RKP.

Foucault, Michel. 1977. *Discipline and Punish*. London: Allen Lane.

———. 1979. "Governability." *Ideology & Consciousness* 6:5–21.

Friedman, Jonathan. 1993. "Order and Disorder in Global Systems: A Sketch," *Social Research* 60:205–34 Friedmann, W. 1964. *The Changing Structure of International Law*. London: Stevens.

Fröbel, Folker, Jürgen Heinrichs, and Otto Kreye. 1980. *The New International Division of Labor*. Cambridge: Cambridge University Press.

Fry, Richard, ed. 1970. *A Banker's World: The Revival of the City 1957–1970: Speeches and Writings of Sir George Bolton*. London: Hutchinson.

Fulton, T. W. 1911. *The Sovereignty of the Sea*. Edinburgh: William Blackwood and Sons.

Garlin, Thomas. 1990. "Where There's a Drug Deal, There's a Way to Launder." *CQ* 48:1717–19.

Garrett, Geoffrey. 1998. *Partisan Politics in the Global Economy*, Cambridge: Cambridge University Press.

Gettell, Raymond G. 1924. *History of Political Thought*. London: George Allen and Unwin.

Gill, Stephen. 1995. "Globalization, Market Civilization, and Disciplinary Neoliberalism." *Millennium: Journal of International Studies* 24:399–422.

———. 1998. "New Constitutionalism, Democratization and Global Political Economy." *Pacific Review* 10:23–38.

Gilmore, William C., ed. 1992. *International Efforts to Combat Money Laundering*. Cambridge: Grotius Publications.

Ginsburg, Anthony S. 1991. *Tax Havens*. New York: New York Institute of Finance.

*Globe and Mail* (Canada). 1999. "Lotus CEO Comments on The On-Line Industry." 28 October.

Goenenc, Rayf. 1990. "From Subsidies to Structural Adjustment" *OECD Observer* 166 (October/November).

Goldman, Ian. 2001. "The Relationship between Corporate Power and State Structural Power: The Role of Offshore Financial Centers." Prepared for the British International Studies Association Conference, Edinburgh, December 17–19.

Goodchild, Philip. 1996. *Deleuze and Guattari: An Introduction to the Politics of Desire*. London: Sage.

Goodman, John B., and Louis Pauly. 1993. "The Obsolescence of Capital Controls? Economic Management in an Age of Global Markets." *World Politics* 46:50–82.

Gordon, R. 1981. *Tax Havens and Their Use by United States Taxpayers—An Overview*. Washington D.C.: U.S. Department of the Treasury.

Grande, Carlos. 1999. "US to Retain Global Lead in Internet Business." *Financial Times*, 22 December.

Grant, A. T. K. 1967. *The Machinery of Finance and the Management of Sterling*. London: Macmillan.

Graveson, Ronald Harry. 1977. *Comparative Conflict of Laws: Selected Essays*. Vol.1. Amsterdam: North-Holland.

Grundy, Milton. 1987. *Grundy's Tax Havens: A World Survey*. London: Sweet and Maxwell.

Hadari, Yitzhak. 1973. "The Structure of the Private Multinational Enterprise." *Michigan Law Review* 4:731–802.

Halperin, Sandra. 1997. *In the Mirror of the Third World: Capitalist Development in Modern Europe*. Ithaca: Cornell University Press.

Hampton, Mark. 1996. *The Offshore Interface: Tax Havens in the Global Economy*. Basingstoke: Macmillan.

Hampton, Mark, and Jason Abbott, eds. 1999. *Offshore Finance Centers and Tax Havens: The Rise of Global Capital*. Basingstoke: Macmillan.

Hankiss, Elemér. 2001. *Fears and Symbols: An Introduction to the Study of Western Civilization*. Budapest: CEU Press.

Hanzawa, Masamitsu. 1991. "The Tokyo Offshore Market." In *Japan's Financial Markets*. Tokyo: Foundation for Advanced Information and Research.

Harrington, Richard. 1992. "Financial Innovation and International Banking." In *Financial Innovation*, edited by Henry Cavana. London: Routledge.

Head, B. W. 1985. *Ideology and Social Science: Destutt de Tracy and French Liberalism*. Dordrecht: Martinus Nijhoff.

Hegel, Georg Wilhelm Friedrich. 1975. *Lectures on the Philosophy of World History: Introduction*. Cambridge: Cambridge University Press.

Heidegger, Martin. 1993. "Modern Science, Metaphysics and Mathematics." In *Basic Writings*, edited and translated by D. F Krell. London: Routledge.

Helleiner, Eric. 1994. *States and the Reemergence of Global Finance: From Bretton Woods to the 1990s*. Ithaca: Cornell University Press.

Hewson, J. R. 1982. "Offshore Banking in Australia: Consultant's Report." In *Australian Financial System Inquiry: Commissioned Studies and Selected Studies*, pt. 2: *Macroeconomic Policy: External Policy*. Canberra: Australian Government Publishing Services.

Higonnet, René P. 1985. "Eurobanks, Eurodollars and International Debt." In *Eurodollars and International Banking*, edited by Paolo Savona and George Sutija. London: Macmillan.

Hines, James R., and Eric M. Rice. 1994. "Fiscal Paradise: Foreign Tax Havens and American Business." *Quarterly Journal of Economics* 109:149–82.

Hirschman, A. O. 1970. *Exit, Voice and Loyalty : Responses to Decline in Firms, Organizations, and States*. Cambridge, Mass.: Harvard University Press.

Hirst, P., and G. Thompson. 1996. *Globalization in Question,* London: Polity.

Hobbes, Thomas. [1651] 1951. *Leviathan.* Harmondsworth: Penguin.

Hobsbawm, E. J. 1975. *The Age of Capital, 1848–1875.* London: Weidenfeld and Nicolson.

Hodjera, Zoran. 1978. "The Asian Currency Market: Singapore as a Regional Financial Center." *International Monetary Fund Staff Papers* 25:221–53.

Holloway, John, and Sol Picciotto, eds. 1978, *State and Capital: A Marxist Debate.* London: Edward Arnold.

Hornsby, Julie. 1997. "Luxembourg as a Tax Haven: Fact or Fiction?" *Tax Notes International,* 2051–52.

Hudson, Alan C. 1998. "Reshaping the Regulatory Landscape: Border Skirmishes around the Bahamas and Cayman Offshore Financial Centers." *Review of International Political Economy* 5:534–64.

———. 1999. "Offshores Onshore: New Regulatory Spaces and Real Historical Places in the Landscape of Global Money." In *Money and the Space Economy,* edited by R. Martin. London: Wiley.

Hufbauer, Gary. 1992. *U.S. Taxation of International Income: Blueprint for Reform.* Washington, D.C.: Institute for International Economics.

Hussein, Bernadette. 1997. "Sex on the Line." *Pacific Islands Monthly,* 38–39.

ILO. 1998. *Export Processing Zones: The Cutting Edge of Globalization.* Geneva: International Labor Organization.

IMF. 2000. *Offshore Financial Centers.* Background Paper prepared by the Monetary and Exchange Affairs Department. http://www.imf.org/external/np/mae/oshore/2000/eng/back.htm 23 June.

ITF. The International Transport Workers Federations Mission Statement. http://www.itf.org.uk

Jenks, Wilfred C. 1958. *The Common Law of Mankind.* London: Stevens and Sons.

Jessop, Bob. 1997. "Capitalism and Its Future: Remarks on Regulation, Government and Governance." *Review of International Political Economy* 4:561–81.

Jeune, Philip. 1999. "Jersey Hits Back over Tax Haven Allegations." *Financial Times,* 25 September.

Johansson, H. 1994. "The Economics of Export Processing Zones Revisited." *Development Policy Review* 12:387–402.

Johns, Richard A. 1983. *Tax Havens and Offshore Finance: A Study of Transnational Economic Development.* New York: St. Martin's Press.

Johns, Richard A., and C. M. Le Marchant. 1993. *Finance Centers: British Isles Offshore Development since 1979.* London: Pinter.

Johnston, David Cay. 2002. "I.R.S. Says Offshore Tax Evasion Is Widespread." *New York Times,* March 26.

Kane, Daniel R. 1983. *The Eurodollar Market and the Years of Crisis.* London: Helm.

Kapstein, Ethan B. 1994. *Governing the Global Economy: International Finance and the State.* Cambridge, Mass.: Harvard University Press.

Kerber, L. L. H. von, ed. 1996. *Stalin's Aviation Gulag: A Memoir of Andrei Tupolev and the Purge Era*. Washington, D.C.: Smithsonian Institution Press, 1996.

Khoury, J. Sarkis. 1990. *The Deregulation of the World Financial Markets*, London: Pinter.

Kish, John. 1973. *The Law of International Spaces*. Leiden: A. W. Sijthoff.

Knudsen, Olav. 1973. *The Politics of International Shipping: Conflict and Interaction in a Transnational Issue-Area 1946–1968*. Lexington, Mass.: Lexington Books.

Kohn, Hans. 1944. *The Idea of Nationalism*. New York: Macmillan.

Kolko, Joyce, and Gabriel Kolko. 1972. *The Limits of Power: The World and United States Foreign Policy, 1945–1954*. New York: Harper and Row.

Kristof, Ladis K. D. 1969. "The Nature of Frontiers and Boundaries." In *The Structure of Political Geography*, edited by Roger Kasperson and Julian Minghi. Chicago: Aldison Publishing Co.

Kurtzman, Joel. 1993. *The Death of Money: How the Electronic Economy Has Destabilized the World's Markets and Created Financial Chaos*. Boston: Little, Brown.

Lapper, Richard. 2000. "Cayman Islands: Survey—Caribbean and Atlantic Financial Centers." *Financial Times*, 22 February.

Larcom, Russell Carpenter. 1937. *The Delaware Corporation*. Baltimore: Johns Hopkins University Press.

Leben, Charles. 1980. "Une Tentative de perception globale; Le Recourse a la nationalité des Sociéteé." In *L'Entreprise multinationale: Face au droit*, edited by B. Goldman and Ph. Francescakis. Paris: Librairies Techniques.

Le Breton, Ian. 2000. "Offshore Banking in the New Millennium," Offshore today.com, http://www.offshoretoday.com/index.shtml. 8 November.

*Lectric Law Library Lawcopedia*. 2002. http://www.lectlaw.com/ttax.htm

Lévi-Strauss, Claude. 1953. "Social Structure." In *Anthropology Today: An Encyclopedic Inventory*, edited by A. L. Kroeber. Chicago: University of Chicago Press.

Levy, David J. 1993. *The Measure of Man: Incursions in Philosophical and Political Anthropology*. London: Claridge Press.

Lewis, Mervyn K. 1999. "International Banking and Offshore Finance: London and the Major Centers." In *Offshore Finance Centers and Tax Havens: The Rise of Global Capital*, edited by Mark Hampton and Jason Abbott. London: Macmillan.

Lindholm, Richard W. 1944. *The Corporate Franchise as a Basis of Taxation*. Austin: University of Texas Press.

Lipietz, Alain. 1987. *Mirages and Miracles: The Crisis of Global Fordism*. London: Verso.

Liu, Shih Shun. 1925. *Extra-Territoriality: Its Rise and Decline*. New York: Columbia University Press.

Liverani, Mario. 1990. *Prestige and Interest: International Relations in the Near East ca. 1600–1100 B.C. Padua: Sargon Sri*.

Lukauskas, Arvid. 1999. "Managing Mobile Capital: Recent Scholarship on the Political Economy of International Finance." *Review of International Political Economy* 6:262–86.

Mairet, Gérard. 1997. *Le Principe de souveraineté: Histoires et fondements du pouvoir moderne*. Paris: Gallimard.

Mann, Michael. 1984. "The Autonomous Power of the State: Its Origins, Mechanisms and Results." *Archives Européens de Sociologie* 25:185–213.

Maraval, Jose Antonio. 1995. "The Origins of the Modern State." *Journal of World History* 6:28–41.

Maritain, Jacques. 1950. "The Concept of Sovereignty." *American Political Science Review 44*: 343–57

Marshall, Don D. 1996. "Understanding Late Twentieth-Century Capitalism." *Government and Opposition* 31:193–214.

Martin, Kingsley. 1929. *French Liberal Thought in the Eighteenth Century: A Study of Political Ideas from Bayle to Condorcet*. London: Ernest Benn.

Marx, Karl. [1858] 1973. *Grundrisse*. London: Penguin.

Mason, Terry B. 1987. "Deregulation of the World Capital Markets." In *The Handbook of International Investing*, edited by Carl Beidleman. Chicago: Probus.

Massumi, Brian. 1987. "Translator's Foreword: Pleasure of Philosophy." In Deleuze and Guattari 1987.

Maurer, Bill. 1998. "Cyberspatial Sovereignties: Offshore Finance, Digital Cash, and the Limits of Liberalism." *Indiana Journal of Global Legal Studies* 5:493–519.

Mauss, Marcel. 1968. *Oeuvres: Représentations collectives et diversité des civilizations*. Paris: Minuit.

Mayne, A. 1961. *Designing and Administering a Regional Economic Development Plan, with Special Reference to Puerto Rico*. Paris: OECD.

McClam, Warren D. 1974. "Monetary Growth and the Euro-Currency Market." In *National Monetary Policies and the International Financial System*, edited by Robert Z. Aliber. Chicago: University of Chicago Press.

McDougal, Myres, and William T. Burke. 1962. *The Public Order of the Oceans: A Contemporary International Law of the Sea*. New Haven, Conn.: Yale University Press.

McLure, Charles Jr. 1997. "Electronic Commerce, State Sales Taxation, and Intergovernmental Fiscal Relations." *National Tax Journal* l:731–49.

Medwig, Michael, T. 1992. "The New Law Merchant: Legal Rhetoric and Commercial Reality." *Law and Policy in International Business* 24:589–616.

Mefford, Aron. 1997. "Lex Informatica: Foundations of Law on the Internet." *Indiana Journal of Global Legal Studies* 5:211–37.

Meier, Gerald. M. 1990. "Trade Policy, Development, and the New Political Economy." In *The Political Economy of International Trade: Essays in*

*Honor of Robert E. Baldwin*, edited by R. W. Jones, and Anne O. Krueger. Oxford: Basil Blackwell.

Michalet, Charles-Albert. 1976. *Le Capitalisme mondial.* Paris: Presses Universitaires de France.

Moran, Michael. 1986. *The Politics of Banking.* 2d ed. London: Macmillan.

Morris, J. 1996. " 'Flags of Convenience' Give Owners a Paper Refuge: Banners Don't Always Represent a Nation—and They Can Mean a Way around Shipping Regulations." *Houston Chronicle.* 21 August 1996.

Murty, Tadepalli Satyanarayana. 1978. *Frontiers: A Changing Concept.* New Delhi: Palit and Palit.

*National Post* (Dominica). 1999. "Washington Blasts Economic Citizenship." 16 November.

Naylor, R. T. 1987. *Hot Money and the Politics of Debt.* London: Unwin Hyman.

Neale, Allan D., and Michael L. Stephens. 1988. *International Business and National Jurisdiction.* Oxford: Clarendon Press.

Neff, Stephen C. 1990. *Friends but No Allies: Economic Liberalism and the Law of Nations.* New York: Columbia University Press.

*New York Times.* 2000. "In Offshore Bunker, Computer Rebels Proclaim a Regulation Haven." 5 June.

Nitzan, Jonathan. 1998. "Differential Accumulation: Towards a New Political Economy of Capital." *Review of International Political Economy* 5: 169–216

Nussbaum, Arthur. 1961. *A Concise History of the Law of Nations.* New York: Macmillan.

Oakley, Francis. 1991. "Christian Obedience and Authority, 1520–1550." In *The Cambridge History of Political Thought 1450–1700*, edited by J. H. Burns. Cambridge: Cambridge University Press.

OECD. 1987. *International Tax Avoidance and Evasion: Four Related Studies.* Committee on Fiscal Affairs, Issues in International Taxation, no.1. Paris: OECD.

———. 1995. *The Changing Role of Telecommunications in the Economy: Globalization and Its Impact on National Telecommunication Policy.* Paris: OECD.

———. 1998. *Harmful Tax Competition: An Emerging Global Issue.* Paris: OECD.

*Offshore Echo Magazine.* 2002. Http://www.guernseyweb.co.uk/offshore.html. Accessed 28 February.

Oppenheimer, Peter M. 1985. "Comment on Robert Z. Aliber, 'Eurodollars: An Economic Analysis.' " In *Eurodollars and International Banking*, edited by Paolo Savona and George Sutija. Basingstoke: Macmillan.

Oxfam. 2000. *Tax Havens: Releasing the Hidden Billions for Poverty Eradication.* Oxfam Policy Papers. Http://www.oxfam.org.uk/policy/papers/taxhvn/tax.htm

Palan, Ronen. 1998a. "Trying to Have Your Cake and Eating It: How and Why the State System Has Created Offshore." *International Studies Quarterly* 42:625–44.

———. 1998b. "Luring Buffaloes and the Game of Industrial Subsidies: A Critique of National Competitive Policies in the Era of the Competition State." *Global Society* 12:323–41.

———. 1998c. "The Emergence of an Offshore Economy." *Futures—Journal of Forecasting.* 30:63–75.

———. 2002. "Offshore and the Institutional Environment of Globalization." In *New Spaces in International Theory*, edited by R. J. Barry Jones and Yale Ferguson. Albany, N.Y.: SUNY Press.

Palan, Ronen, and Brook Blair. 1993. "On the Idealist Origins of the Realist Theory of International Relations." *Review of International Studies* 19: 385–99.

Palan, Ronen, and Jason Abbott, with Phil Deane. 1996. *State Strategies in the Global Political Economy*. London: Pinter.

Panafrican News Agency. 2001. "Mauritius Registers 14,000 Offshore Companies." Http://allafrica.com/stories/200011050002.html.

Park, Y. S. 1982. "The Economics of Offshore Financial Centers." *Columbia Journal of World Business* 17 (4):31–35.

Pashukanis, Evgeni B. 1983. *Law and Marxism*. London: Pluto Press.

Peillon, Vincent, and Arnaud Montebourg. *Rapport d'information de MM. Vincent Peillon et Arnaud Montebourg, déposé en application de l'article 145 du Règlement par la mission d'information commune sur les obstacles au contrôle et à la répression de la délinquance financière et du blanchiment des capitaux en Europe.* No. 2311, 30 March 2000. Tome I: *Monographies.*http://www.assemblee-nationale.fr/documents/index-information.asp
The following volumes are cited.

———. 2000a. Vol. 1: *La Principauté du Liechtenstein.* March.

———. 2000b. Vol. 2: *La Principauté de Monaco.* June.

———. 2001a. Vol. 3: *La Suisse.* February.

———. 2001b. Vol. 4: *Grande-Bretagne, Gibraltar et les dépendances de la Couronne.* October.

———. 2002. Vol. 5: *Le Grand Duché du Luxembourg.* January.

Phillips, Richard. 1999. "The Problem of Organizational Representation under Alliance Capitalism: Industrial Organization and a Design Approach to the Political Economy of Complexity," Paper delivered at the EAPEA Annual Convention, Prague.

Picciotto, Sol. 1992. *International Business Taxation.* London: Weidenfeld and Nicolson.

———. 1999. "Offshore: the State as Legal Fiction." In *Offshore Finance Centers and Tax Havens: The Rise of Global Capital*, edited by Mark Hampton and Jason Abbott, Basingstoke: Macmillan.

Poggi, Gianfranco. 1978. *The Development of the Modern State: A Socio-logical Introduction*. Stanford, Calif.: Stanford University Press.

Pollard, Sidney. 1981. *Peaceful Conquest: The Industrialization of Europe 1760–1970*. Oxford: Oxford University Press.

Porter, Michael. 1990. *The Competitive Advantage of Nations*. New York: Free Press.

Poulantzas, N. 1973. *Political Power and Social Classes*. London: Verso.

———. 1978. *State, Power, Socialism*. London: Verso.

Prescott, J. R. V. 1965. *The Geography of Frontiers and Boundaries*. London: Hutchinson.

———. 1975. *The Political Geography of the Oceans*. New York: John Wiley.

Ranke, Leopold von. 1840. *The Ecclesiastical and Political History of the Popes in Rome during the Sixteenth and Seventeenth Centuries*. 3 vols. London: John Murray.

Raton, Pierre. 1970. *Liechtenstein: History and Institutions of the Principality*. Vaduz: Liechtenstein-Verlag.

Renan, Ernest. 1996. *"Qu'est-ce qu'une Nation" et autres écrits politiques*. Collection dirigée par Georges Duby. Paris.

Reuters. 2000. "Bahrain's Offshore Banking Q1 Assets at $91.04 Billion." *Offshore Week*. 20 May.

Richardson, M., ed. 1998. *Georges Bataille—Essential Writings. Theory, Culture and Society*. London: Sage.

Rigo Sureda, A. 1973. *The Evolution of the Right of Self-Determination: A Study of United Nations Practice*. Leiden: A. W. Sijthoff.

Robbie, K. J. H. 1975–76. "Socialist Banks and the Origins of the Euro-Currency Markets." *Moscow Narodny Bank Quarterly Review*. Winter: 21–36.

Robé, Jean-Philippe. 1997. "Multinational Enterprises: The Constitution of a Pluralist Legal Order." In *Global Law without a State*, edited by Gunther Teubner. Aldershot: Dartmouth.

Roberts, Susan. 1994. "Fictitious Capital, Fictitious Spaces: The Geography of Offshore Financial Flows." In *Money, Power, and Space*, edited by Stuart Corbridge, Ron Martin, and Nigel Thrift, 91–115. Oxford: Blackwell.

Robinson, Jeffrey. 1995. *The Laundrymen: Inside the World's Third Largest Business*. London: Pocket Books.

Rodrik, Dani. 1997. *Has Globalization Gone Too Far?* Washington, D.C.: Washington Institute for International Economics.

Rose, Harold. 1995. "Mastering Management—Part 5 Euromarkets: Their Uses and Worth." *Financial Times*. 24 November.

*Royal Gazette* (Bermuda). 2000. "Bermuda Debuts E-commerce Code of Conduct." 4 May.

Rubin, Isaac Ilyich. [1928] 1989. *A History of Economic Thought*. London: Pluto Press.

Ruehl, Sonja, and Janice Hughes. 1986. "Tokyo 2000: The World's Third International Financial Center?" *The Economist Advisory Group Report*, no. 1055. London: The Economist.

Ruggie, J. G. 1982. "International Regimes, Transactions and Change: Embedded Liberalism in the Postwar Economic Order." *International Organization* 36: 397–415.

Sabin, George H., and Walter J. Shephard. 1922. "Translator's Introduction." In Herman Krabbe, *The Modern Idea of the State*, pp. x–xxxii. London: Appleton and Co.

Sack, Robert D. 1981. "Territorial Base of Power." In *Political Studies from Spatial Perspectives*, edited by Alan D. Burnett and Peter J. Taylor. London: John Wiley and Sons.

Sassen, Saskia. 1991. *The Global City: New York, London, Tokyo*. Princeton, N.J.: Princeton University Press.

Sayer, Andrew. 1992. *Method in Social Science: A Realist Approach*. London: Routledge.

Schenk, Catherine R. 1998. " The Origins of the Eurodollar Market in London 1955–63." *Explorations in Economic History* 2:1–19.

Schmitthoff, Clive M. 1954. *The English Conflict of Laws*. London: Stevens and Sons.

Schnapper, Dominique. 1998. *Community of Citizens: On the Modern Idea of Nationality*. New Brunswick, N.J.: Transaction Publishers.

Schonfield, Hugh J. 1970, *The Politics of Gods*. London: Hutchinson.

Schwarz, Jonathan. 1994. "Survey of World Taxation (9): Corporate Dilemmas." *Financial Times*. 20 May.

Sengupta, J. 1988. "Internationalization of Banking and the Relationship between Foreign and Domestic Banking in the Development Countries." *International Journal of Development Banking*, 6, no. 1. 139–198.

Serres, Michel. 2001. *Hominescence*. Paris: Le Pommier.

Shapiro, M. J. 1997. *Violent Cartographies*. Minneapolis: Minnesota University Press.

Siegfried, André, 1950. *Switzerland: A Democratic Way of Life*. London: Jonathan Cape.

Sinclair, Timothy. 1994. "Passing Judgement: Credit Rating Processes as Regulatory Mechanisms of Governance in the Emerging World Order." *Review of International Political Economy* 1:133–159.

Sloterdijk, P. 1988. *Critique of Cynical Reason*. London: Verso.

Smith, Adolph. 1912. *Monaco and Monte Carlo*. London: Grant Richard.

Smith, Anthony D. 1986. *The Ethnic Origins of Nations*. Oxford: Basil Blackwell

Sneddon Little, J. 1985. "Comment." In P.G.S. Savona, *Eurodollars and International Banking*. Basingstoke: Macmillan.

Starchild, Adam. 1993. *Tax Havens for International Business*. Basingstoke: Macmillan.

Stead, W. H. 1958. *Fomento : The Economic Development of Puerto Rico*, National Planning Association. Washington, D.C.

Stevens, Jacqueline. 1999. *Reproducing the State*. Princeton, N.J.: Princeton University Press.

Strange, Susan. 1986. *Casino Capitalism*. Oxford: Basil Blackwell.

———. 1987. "The Persistent Myth of 'Lost' Hegemony." *International Organization*. 41:551–74.

———. 1998. *Mad Money.* Manchester: Manchester University Press.

Swary, Itzhak, and Barry Topf. 1992. *Global Financial Deregulation: Commercial Banking at the Crossroads*. Oxford: Blackwell.

Stewart, Jules. 1996. "Cleaning Up Offshore." *Euromoney*, April.

Stopford, John, and Susan Strange, with John S. Henley. 1991. *Rival States, Rival Firms: Competition for World Market Shares*. Cambridge: Cambridge University Press.

Stuart, Sue. 1990. "Survey of The Channel Islands (2): Emphasis on Quality Banking." *Financial Times*, 19 December.

Summers, Larry. 2000. http://www.tax-news.com/html/oldnews/st_Xsummers_11_07_00.html

Swedberg, Richard. 1994. "Markets as Social Structures." In *The Handbook of Economic Sociology*, edited by Neil J. Smelser and Richard Swedberg. Princeton, N.J.: Princeton University Press.

Terrell, Henry S., and Rodney H. Mills Jr. 1985. "International Banking Facilities and the Eurodollar Market." In *Eurodollars and International Banking*, edited by Paolo Savona and George Sutija. London: Macmillan.

Tesner, Sandrine. 2000. *The United Nations and Business: A Partnership Recovered*, Basingstoke: Macmillan.

Teubner, Gunther, ed. 1997. *Global Law without a State*. Aldershot: Dartmouth.

TheStandard.com. 2000. "Internet Tax Panel Agrees to Disagree." 27 March.

Thrift, Nigel. 1998. "Virtual Capitalism: The Globalization of Reflexive Business Knowledge." In *Virtualism: A New Political Economy*, edited by J. Carrier and D. Miller. Oxford: Berg.

Tiebout, Charles M. 1956. "A Pure Theory of Local Expenditure." *Journal of Political Economy*, 416–24.

Tigar, Michael E. 1977. *Law and the Rise of Capitalism*. New York: Monthly Review Press.

Tirschwell, Peter M. 1995. "APL Heads Toward Full Foreign-Flag Registry." *Journal of Commerce*. Http://www.joc.com.

Tugendhat, Christopher. 1971. *The Multinationals*. London: Eyre.

Turin Group, The. 2002. "Eurodollar." *The Turin Group – Financial Services.* Http://www.toerien.com/neg_financial_instruments/eurodollar.htm# The Nature of the Eurodollar. Accessed 5/2.

UNCTAD and UNCTC. 1991. "The Impact of Trade-Related Investment Measures on Trade and Development: Theory, Evidence and Policy Implications." New York: UNCTC and UNCTAD.

U.K. Inland Revenue. 1999. "Controlled Foreign Companies (CFCs)—Designer Rate and Similar Regimes." Inland Revenue Press Release 165/99, 6 October.

U.S. Treasury. 2001. "Treasury Secretary O'Neill Statement on OECD Tax Havens. From The Office Of Public Affairs." PO-366, May 10. http://www.ustreas.gov/press/releases/po366.htm

Van Asbeck, Frederik M. 1976. *International Society in Search of a Transnational Legal Order*. Leyden: A. W. Sijthoff.

Van Der Pijl, Kees. 1984. *The Making of an Atlantic Ruling Class*. London: Verso.

———. 1998. *Transnational Classes and International Relations*. London: Routledge.

Van Fossen, Anthony B. 1992. *The International Political Economy of Pacific Islands Flags of Convenience*. Griffith University, Center for the Study of Australia-Asia Relations.

Veblen, Thorstein. [1889] 1994. *The Theory of the Leisure Class*. London: Dover.

Versluyen, Eugene L. 1981. *The Political Economy of International Finance*. London: Gower.

Vogler, C. M. 1985. *The Nation State: The Neglected Dimension of Class*. London: Gower.

Waldmeir, Patti. 1999. "Global E-commerce Law Comes under the Spotlight: International Business Is Clashing with Local and National Law in the Borderless New World. *Financial Times*, 23 December.

*Wall Street Journal*. 2000. "House Approves Internet Tax Moratorium." 11 May.

Webb, Michael. 2002. "Defining the Boundaries of Legitimate Practice: Norms, Transnational Actors and the OECD's Project on Harmful Tax Competition." Paper presented at the International Studies Association Annual Conference, New Orleans, March 24–27.

White, William R. 1996. "International Agreements in the Area of Banking and Finance: Accomplishments and Outstanding Issues." Basle: Bank for International Settlements.

Wilden, Anthony. 1972. *System and Structure: Essays in Communication and Exchange*. London: Tavistock.

Wilber, Ken. 1982. "New Perspective on Reality: The Special Updated Issue of The Brain/Mind Bulletin." In *The Holographic Paradigm and Other Paradoxes*, edited by Ken Wilber. London: New Science Library.

Winston, Brian. 1998. *Media, Technology and Society: A History, from the Telegraph to the Internet*. London: Routledge.

Zuboff, Shoshana. 1988. *In the Age of the Smart Machine: The Future of Work and Power*. London: Basic Books.

# Index

Abacha, General Sonny, 5
abstraction, 163, 165
Aglietta, Michael, 64
American Revolution, 101
Amin Dada, Idi, 5
Anderson, Benedict, 149
Andorra, 40, 112, 114
Anguilla, 68
   and e-commerce, 55
Antigua, flags of convenience, 53
Argentina, 128
Australia, government of, 18
Austria, 12, 104, 105
   and competition between tax
      havens, 137

Badie, Bertrand, 88
Bahamas, 41, 47, 103, 110, 120–23,
      147, 185
   and e-commerce, 57
Bahrain, 47, 51
   and competition state, 142
Bank of England, 28–29
Bank for International Settlements,
      18, 39, 44, 132, 145
Barbados, 17
Bartolous, 24
Belgium, 101
Bermuda, 45, 83, 103, 110
   and competition between tax
      havens, 137
   and e-commerce, 55, 57
Bodin, Jean, 176
Braudel, Fernand, 173, 184, 187
Brazil, 128

Bretton Woods, 124–27, 130, 133,
      184, 185
British government, 49
   and beginnings of offshore, 102–3
   and competitiveness, 49
   and financial deregulation, 132–
      35
   and re-regulation of currency
      markets, 33
   and role in emergence of
      Euromarket, 28–30
   support for internationalization of
      business, 99
   support for London as financial
      center, 27
British Virgin Islands, 47, 49
broadcasting, 21–23, 55, 178
Bundesbank, 29

captive insurance companies, 43,
      137
Catholic Church, 88, 94, 95
Cayman Islands, 3–4, 43, 44, 47, 49,
      60, 83, 101, 103, 120–23, 147,
      176, 177
   and competition between tax
      havens, 137
   and competition state, 142
   criticism of, 143
Central Intelligence Agency, 126
Channel Islands, 49, 101, 112
   and competition between tax
      havens, 137
   and offshore casinos, 59, 60
China, status of Hong Kong, 33

class-based theories of offshore,
    71–72, 182, 187
  limitations of, 73
  transnational classes, 70, 78
Clinton, Hilary, 144
Cobden Treaty, 84, 99, 109, 110
Colombia, export processing zones,
    120
competition state, 140–42
contracts, and sovereignty, 86
Coopers & Lybrand, 49
corporate taxation, 88
Costa Rica, e-commerce, 57
cumulative causation, theories of,
    80–82
cyberspatiality, 170–73

decolonization, 185
Delaware Corporation, 100–102
Deleuze, Gilles, 163, 164, 165, 167,
    168, 169, 170, 171, 174, 175,
    178, 179
disembeddedness, 163–65
Dominican Republic, 123
Dutch Antilles, 60
  and telecommunication services,
    58–59

East India companies, 98
e-commerce, 54–57. *See also*
    Internet
Elf Aquitane, 107
England, origins of nation, 154
Enlightenment, 90
Enron, 5
Eurobond markets, 29
Eurocurrency markets, 74
Eurodollar market, 71
  and Indo-China war, 34
Euromarket, 2, 12–13, 18, 21, 26–27,
    71, 72, 83, 123, 127, 129, 185,
    186, 187
  and cyberspatiality, 170, 176
  and Eurodollar market, 27–31, 74
  and financial deregulation, 132–35
  rise of, 28–31
European Union, 189, 190

export processing zones, 2, 4, 13, 18,
    19, 20, 51–52, 66, 70, 187
  Puerto Rico as example of, 119–20
  and theories of structural coupling,
    73
  and trade patterns, 130–32

feudalism, 89
Fichte, Johann Gottlieb, 150, 154
*Financial Times*, 41
flags of convenience, 52–54, 66, 70,
    71, 83, 96
  and globalization, 127
  Panama as example of, 117–19
Fordism, 10, 12, 64, 111, 112, 123, 124,
    126, 130, 164, 181, 185, 186, 187
France, 101, 115, 151
  Fronde movement in, 93
  origins of nation, 154
French Revolution, 154, 155

gambling, 57–59, 113
  *See also* offshore casinos
General Agreement on Tariffs and
    Trade (GATT), 124
Germany, 12, 103, 115
  and support for
    internationalization of business,
    99
Gibraltar, 44, 48–49, 60, 112, 118
  and competition between tax
    havens, 137
globalization, 8
  and export processing zones, 51
Greece, 128
  and flags of convenience, 118–19
Grotius, Hugo, 91
Guatemala, flags of convenience, 117
Guattari, Felix, 163, 164, 165, 167,
    168, 169, 170, 171, 174, 175,
    178, 179
Guernsey. *See* Channel Islands
Guyana, telecommunication services,
    58

Hegel, Georg Wilhelm Frederick, 152,
    153

Heidegger, Martin, 90
holism, 78
Honduras, flags of convenience, 52,
    117
Hong Kong, 128
    and export processing zones, 52,
    121
    as spontaneous off-shore center,
    33
Horkheimer, Max, 164

IBM, 107
India, 52
Industrial Revolution, 84, 184
international banking facilities,
    33–35, 134, 185
international business corporations,
    43–44
International Labor Organization, 51,
    73
international law, 77
International Monetary Fund, 18, 26,
    46, 125, 133, 140, 143
    and criticism of tax havens, 145
international tax planning, 84, 108
International Telecommunications
    Union, 58
International Transport Workers
    Federation, 52, 60
Internet, 54–57, 147, 176, 185
    See also e-commerce
Ireland
    and competition between tax
    havens, 137
    and export processing zones, 120,
    121

Jamaica, 123
Japan, 134
juridical bifurcation, 20

Kynicism, 164

Lebanon, 103, 185
Liberia, 147, 185
    and flags of convenience 53, 122,
    177

Liechtenstein, 101, 103, 110, 112, 114
    criticism of, 143
London, City of, 49, 174–75
    and competition between tax
    havens, 137
    criticism of, 143
    and global currency markets,
    27–33
    as spontaneous off-shore center,
    33, 35
Luxembourg, 44, 48, 60, 101, 112
    and broadcasting, 21–23
    and competition between tax
    havens, 137
    criticism of, 143

Marcos, Ferdinand, 5
market, origins of, 85
Marshall Islands
    and flags of convenience, 53, 122
    and passport sales, 59
Marx, 164
    and state theory, 74–75, 173
Mauritius, 47
    and competition state, 142
Melechizedek, 60
Mexico, 123, 128
    and maquiladora, 52
Monaco, 40, 101, 112–14, 123
    criticism of, 143
money laundering, 48–49, 66, 71
multinational corporations, and tax
    avoidance, 42

Nassau, 49
nationalism, 78–79
NATO, 124
Nauru, 68
neoliberalism, rise of, 12
Netherlands, The, and competition
    between tax havens, 139
New Deal, 112, 124, 164
New York, 49
    as onshore-offshore center, 33–35
New Zealand, telecommunication
    services, 58;
Nicaragua, flags of convenience, 117

Niue, telecommunication services,
    58, 177
nomadism
    nomadic capitalism, 173–75, 182
    nomadic civilizations, 165–70
    *See also* numerical civilization
numerical civilization, 165–70,
    174
    *See also* nomadism

off-planet, offshore as, 178–80
offshore banking licenses, 42
offshore casinos, 57–59
    *See also* gambling
O'Neill, Paul (U.S. Treasury
    Secretary), 68, 69, 143
on-line sex, 57–59
    *See also* pornography
onshore-offshore centers. *See*
    international banking facilities
Organization for Economic
    Cooperation and Development,
    18, 39, 73, 131, 185, 186, 189,
    190
    and competition state, 141
    and tax competition, campaign
        against, 143–46
Oxfam, 48

Panama, 51, 101, 185
    and e-commerce, 55, 57
    and flags of convenience, 52–53,
        117–19, 177
passports, 98
    sale of, 59
patent laws, 98
Pax Americana, 124, 126, 127
permanent tourist, concept of, 172
pornography, 57–59
    *See also* on-line sex
Portugal, 128
postglobalization, 16
power
    nature of, 76
    political, 71–72
    of the state, 76–77
private banking, 43, 46, 147

property rights, and global
    constitutionalism, 13
public choice theory, 68–70
Puerto Rico, 51–52, 185
    as example of export processing
        zone, 119–20
Pufendorf, 91

Radio Caroline. *See* broadcasting
Radio Luxembourg. *See* broadcasting
Ratzel, Friedrich, 156
regulatory competition, 68–70
Renaissance, 85–86, 90
Renan, Ernest, 95, 153
Roman Empire, 89, 94, 96

segregated accounts companies, 45
semiotics, 164
Seychelles, 17
Singapore, 51
    and export processing zones, 52,
        119, 122
    as onshore-offshore center, 33–35
South Korea, 128
sovereignty
    bifurcation of, 8, 182
    commercialization of, 21, 59–62,
        148–49, 157–61, 164, 175–78,
        188, 189
    and cyberspatiality, 172
    economic sovereignty, 85–87
    and epistemology, 90–91
    and Euromarkets, 32
    and the law of the sea, 23–26
    nationalization of, 92–95
    origins of, 88
    and sovereign exclusivity, 87–91
    Veblen on, 93–94
    and the Von Kármán line, 25, 97
Soviet Union, 1, 3, 126
Spain, 104, 128
special economic zones. *See* export
    processing zones
special purpose vehicles, 44–45
stagflation, 111
Standard Oil, and flags of
    convenience, 52–53

sterling crisis, 27–28
structural coupling, theory of, 72–74
subjectivism, 78
Summers, Larry (U.S. Treasury
    Secretary), 56
Switzerland, 101, 110, 112, 123, 147,
    182
    private banking in, 46
    and money laundering, 48
    and commercialization of
        sovereignty, 60–61
    and modern banking law, 103–4
    as tax haven, 114–17
    and competition between tax
        havens, 137
    criticism of, 143

Taiwan, 52, 128
    and export processing zones, 122
tax avoidance, 67, 77
    and the Internet, 57, 186
    techniques for, 41–45
tax havens, 36–40, 66, 67, 83, 101,
    186, 187
    and commercialization of
        sovereignty, 60–61
    competition between, 136–40
    and "real" financial activity, 43
    and regulatory powers of states,
        46–49
    Switzerland as example of, 114–
        17
    and tax avoidance, 42
    use of by individuals, 45
Taylor, Elizabeth, and Swiss
    government, 61, 159
Taylorism, 10, 112
telecommunications, 57–59
Thailand, as onshore-offshore center,
    33–35
Thatcher, Margaret, 188
Tiebout, Charles, efficiency
    postulate, 69, 159

Tokyo, 49
    as onshore-offshore center, 33–35
Toyota, 107
trade unions, and rise of EPZs, 73
Tuvalu, telecommunication services,
    58, 177
Tyco, 5

UNCTAD, 120
    and flags of convenience, 122
United Kingdom, 139
United Nations, Charter of, 124
United States
    Bush administration, 53
    and e-commerce, 55
    and export processing zones,
        119–20, 185
    and financial deregulation, 132–35,
        185
    and flags of convenience, 52–53,
        117–19, 185
    government policies and rise of
        Euromarket, 30–31
    origins of nation, 154
    post-war social consensus of, 64
    promotion of international
        banking facilities, 34, 185
    and support for
        internationalization of business,
        99
    and tax enclaves, 6–7, 64
    Treasury, 49
Uruguay, 185

Vanuato
    and e-commerce, 55
    and flags of convenience, 53
Veblen, Thorsten, 81, 93–94, 149, 158
Venezuela, 123, 128

World Bank, 18, 125

Yugoslavia, 128